CHANGE OF PACE

CHANGE OF PACE

SOUTH AFRICA'S ECONOMIC REVIVAL

CEES BRUGGEMANS

FOREWORD BY F. VAN ZYL SLABBERT

WITS UNIVERSITY PRESS

Wits University Press
1 Jan Smuts Avenue
2001 Johannesburg
South Africa
http://www.witspress.wits.ac.za

http://www.fnb.co.za/economics

The views expressed in this book are those of the author and do not reflect in any way those of FirstRand Bank Limited.

ISBN 1-86814-384-8

Cover and design by STE Publishers, Johannesburg
Printed and bound by Creda Communications, Cape Town

And all the innumerable persons who took part in the war acted similarly, in accordance with their personal peculiarities, habits, circumstances, and aims. They were all impelled by fear or vanity, enjoyment, indignation, or rational consideration, supposing that they knew what they were about and that they were acting independently, while they were all the involuntary tools of history and were working out a result concealed from themselves but comprehensible to us. Such is the invariable fate of all practical leaders . . .

(Leo Tolstoy, *War & Peace*, 1877: 739).

Dr Cees Bruggemans has been a passionate observer of the South African political and economic scene for many years. For much of that time he has held the position of Chief Economist of First National Bank where his insightful observations about the local and international scene have contributed significantly to risk and policy debates. His ability to interpret economic data and critically analyse the political framework in which economic decisions are made, have played a large role in making him one of the most widely read economists in the South African market. In addition, the whimsical turn of phrase which he uses to elaborate matters of profound economic substance, have endeared him to many readers of both in-house economic bulletins and the popular media.

The views expressed in this publication are those of Dr Bruggemans, but First National Bank associates itself with the thoughtful analysis provided and recommends the book to all those serious about understanding the background to South Africa's socio-economic standing.

V.W. Bartlett
Deputy Chief Executive Officer
FirstRand Bank Limited
May 2003

Contents

Preface xiii

Foreword by F. Van Zyl Slabbert xiv

Acknowledgements xvi

Introduction 1

1: The Legacy 15
A Modernising Economy 16
Discriminating Policies and Laws 18
The Economic Struggle Decades, 1970–1993 21
An Inheritance of Inequality 25
Confidence in South Africa 27
Contrasting Black and White Consumer Confidence 30
Convergence of Black and White Confidence Post-1997 33

2: Political Pre-Conditions for Change 35
The Many Crucibles of South African Nationalism 36
The Inheritance at Democracy, 1994 44
The Challenges Facing Democracy 45
Summarising South Africa's Historic Condition 49

3: A Planned Economic Revival 55
The Origins of Gear 57
The Main Policy Objectives of Gear 60
Examining Gear 62
Policy Choices Going Forward 71
Criticism of Government Policy 78
'Gradualism' and the Future 79
The Cost of 'Gradualism' 80

4: Progress with Financial Restructuring 83
Policy Stances Prevailing in the Mid-1990s 85
Exchange Controls 88
Early Reforms 89
Interest Rate Policy 91

Inflation 93
Exchange Control Liberalisation 95
The 'Impossible Trinity' 100
A 'Genuine Floating' of the Rand since October 1998 102
The Rand Crisis of Late 2001 104
Inflation Targeting 108
A Less Disruptive Monetary Policy 113
Low Foreign Reserves and Savings Rate 116
Privatisation 118
Looking Ahead 123

5: Progress with Micro-Economic Restructuring **125**
Changes in Employment Levels 126
Labour and Employment Rationalisation 127
Formal versus Informal Employment 131
Improved Labour Surveys 135
Future Projections for Unemployment 141
Absorbing Change: A Productivity Revolution 143
Expected Changes in Employment 146
Real Wage Growth Going Forward 147
Deregulation 149
A Competitively Organised Economy 152

6: A Social Transformation **157**
Demographic Interruption 158
Demographic Changes before HIV/Aids 160
The Standard Worst-Case of HIV/Aids 164
The Wider Impact of HIV/Aids 167
The Adventuresome Worst-Case of HIV/Aids 170
The Potential Impact of HIV Medication in the Absence of Behaviourial Change 171
The Potential Impact of Medication and Effecting Behavioural Change 172

7: Progress with Social Delivery **175**
Physical and Social Services Delivery 177
Improving Services Delivery 179
Social Limits to Growth 180

8: A Technology Revolution **185**
New Technology as a Source of Growth 186
A New Technology Wave 187
The New Economy 190
The Global 'Tech-Wreck': A Temporary Interruption 198
The New Technology in South Africa 201

9: Future Prospects **203**
Economic Reforms and their Resulting Achievements 204
Our Growth Story Going Forward 211
Changing Sources of Growth in the Regions 216
Growth Drivers for the Future 218
The Prospects for Skilled Labour 219
Revolving Doors: Migration and Aids 229
The Aids Pandemic and the Skills Drain 230
A Generation of Newcomers 233
Changing Income Distribution 235
The Population Distribution by Income Category 237
The Income Distribution by Population Group 239
The Latin American Option in Perspective 242

10: Conclusion **247**
The Role of Economic Policy 248
Exogenous Surprises: Technology and Demographics 250
Main Risks and Development Constraints 252
Survivors' Inheritance 255
Profiling the Next 30 Years 256
Transitional Mistakes and Costs 259
Strategic Imperatives Going Forward 263
Policy Advice for 2003–2050 264

Epilogue **267**
Why Pragmatic Confidence is Warranted about South Africa 268
The Bigger Civilisational Dimension 273

Select Bibliography **279**

Index **289**

List of Tables

Table 1: The Unwinding of Economic Growth, 1960–2002 22
Table 2: Composition of Income Quintiles by Race, 1990 26
Table 3: Economic Policy: With and Without Gear, 1996–2000 59
Table 4: Expected Outcomes: With and Without Gear, 1996–2000 61
Table 5: Gear Objectives: Prior, Targeted and Actual, 1996–2000 63
Table 6: Changing Composition of South Africa's Exports, 1995–2001 129
Table 7: Labour Growth and Composition in South Africa 134
Table 8: Changes in Formal 'Core' Employment, 1990–2000 135
Table 9: Composition of the Labour Force, 1996–1999 140
Table 10: Business Ranking of Main Constraints, Fourth Quarter 2000 220
Table 11: Education Profile and Skilled Labour, 1970–1999 222
Table 12: Estimated Changes in the Composition of Skilled Labour, 1970–1995 225
Table 13: Age Distribution of Those Holding a Matric as Highest Level of Education 228
Table 14: Share of Total Income per Population Group 236
Table 15: Racial Composition of Income Categories, 1975 238
Table 16: Racial Composition of Income Categories, 1991 238
Table 17: Racial Composition of Income Categories, 1996 239
Table 18: The Composition of Income Quintiles by Race 240

List of Graphs

Graph 1: RMB/BER Business Confidence Index 28
Graph 2: FNB/BER Consumer Confidence Index 29
Graph 3: FNB/BER Consumer Confidence: White versus Black 32
Graph 4: Government Budget Deficit, 1993–2006 87
Graph 5: Investment-to-GDP: Private Sector, 1960–2002 206
Graph 6: Investment-to-GDP: Public Sector, 1960–2002 207

Preface

At lunch following the Bureau for Economic Research's (BER) annual end-of-year conference in November 1999, it first struck me that South Africa was experiencing not one but many 'revolutions'—political, social, technical and economic—simultaneously. Furthermore, these fundamental breaks with the past all pointed to a better economic performance to come.

By Easter 2001, policy reform was steadily firming up, yet many in my business and professional audiences could only think of Zimbabwe, a fast depreciating rand and emigration. In contrast, the reforms were steadily pointing towards an outcome that warranted a far more cheerful interpretation.

The result is this book which aims to describe the main economic and social changes driving our economic performance, and what gave rise to them. It does not aspire to tell the political story: how regimes changed, the role of business (if any), how governance issues were handled or the aims of redistribution.

Instead, we leave the bridge and descend into the country's engine room, encountering reforms aimed at re-establishing macro-economic stability and achieving an improvement in the allocation of resources, both in time leading to a better economic performance. In the process, we encounter other forces as well, especially technological and demographic changes that will have a major bearing on the ultimate outcome.

Change of Pace examines key policy reforms, including the stumbles that were made in the process. It considers the historic context, and explores the likely future consequences. As such, it concentrates on results/outcomes, including relative shifts that may already have come about or which may be impending. It notes initial underperformance, but seeks to understand any future pay-off, and the distance already travelled as the country attempts to rejoin the global mainstream. The book's tone is a positive one, for a very simple reason: there is much to be positive about, as an examination of the facts will show.

C. Bruggemans
April 2003

Foreword

The problem with many economic overviews—not only of South Africa—is that they suffer from a self-fulfilling dilemma: all the teasing, interesting problems are suspended by a kind of 'if-then' logic, and the resulting predictions become true by definition. For example, does it make sense to do a comparative analysis of economies as diverse as Zimbabwe, Hungary, the United Kingdom, Australia, Taiwan, and so on, without taking into account fundamental differences in social and political life?

A simple correlation between democracy and growth conjures up four hypothetical possibilities which can be illustrated empirically: no democracy and growth (Chile post-1973, Singapore); democracy and growth (Australia, the United States of America); no democracy, no growth (Sudan, Democratic Republic of the Congo, Somalia); and democracy and no growth (Argentina and Chile pre-1973). Each example contains social and political dynamics which obviously must impact on economic performance.

It is one of the distinctive virtues of Cees Bruggemans' comprehensive and compelling economic analysis that he avoids this trap. From the outset of *Change of Pace* he engages the reader by the manner in which he produces a dynamic model of economic development over the last three to four decades in South Africa. He deliberately focuses on the interactive relationship between political, social, economic and technological variables in trying to 'guess' the future of South Africa's economy. In addition, he contextualises this country's development in a global setting. Globalisation is seen as the greater flexibility and transferability of capital, information, technology and skills. This is what Bruggemans calls the 'global gorilla', in the sense that particular countries do not ask it where it wants to sit, but react to what it does as best they can.

Bruggemans does not write as a partisan, but certainly as an involved and committed South African. He constantly talks about 'our problems, policies, responses', and what 'we' should do to overcome obstacles. Implicit in this is the acceptance of the reality and viability of the South African nation state. There are commentators who talk prematurely of the end of the nation state (for example, Kenichi Ohmae), because of the impact of globalisation. By contrast, Bruggemans finds himself in the company of Stiglitz, Sen and Soros, who argue that the nation state increases in importance precisely because of globalisation. How can we even begin to think of the future of South Africa, if we do not take as our point of departure the nation state, and the instruments at its disposal to respond to and set policy directions in the face of economic, social and political trends as well as international shifts and changes?

This is precisely where the substance of Bruggemans' analysis lies. The government, state and Reserve Bank are constantly in focus as he tries to anticipate the factors that could affect political stability, economic discipline and social delivery. What comes through often and clearly is the continual trade-off between the imperatives of a market economy and the promises, and temptations, of a liberal democracy. Given where our country has come from (pre-1990), Bruggemans is justifiably impressed with the South African performance.

Although he does not ignore the mistakes and shortcomings of policy, he is essentially optimistic about the future. However, it is not a Pollyanna brand of optimism, but a realistically and pragmatically argued one. Of course, there are 'if-then' assumptions, particularly with regard to the effectiveness of broadening the skills base through public and private sector education, as well as the impact of HIV/Aids, and the big 'if' of unpredictable international events. But these assumptions do not suspend reality; rather, they come through as challenges which can be responded to given the resources at our disposal.

Change of Pace is not bedside reading and in places the arguments are dense and technical. However, generally speaking, Bruggemans succeeds in keeping the analysis at the level of provocation that engages and invites argument. Above all, he persuades the reader that South Africa has a future worth struggling for and working towards, because it is achievable. In the current mood of fashionable pessimism this viewpoint is extremely refreshing.

F. Van Zyl Slabbert
May 2003

Acknowledgements

I would like to say 'thank you' for the encouragement and inspiring guidance I found along the way once embarked upon writing from Viv Bartlett, Peet Strydom, Sue Kell, Andrea Nattrass, Ben Smit, Jack Heyns, Wolfgang Thomas, Johan Snyman, Freddie Marais, George Mulcaire, Jac Laubscher, Johan Lamprecht, Sandra Mulcaire and Wanda Buhrmann. You were all an inspiration to me to see this through. A special word of thanks to Dion Rasodi for always helping out with a smile. Also my deep appreciation to friends in public service, who over the years in friendly banter taught me much about public institutions. And I cannot forget the many foreign friends who forever have a way of holding up mirrors in which we can see ourselves so much more clearly than is usually the case in our everyday preoccupations.

INTRODUCTION

For a long time South Africa's political, social and economic history has been a clear example of government failure, captured memorably in the words of De Kiewiet (1941): 'South Africa advances through political disasters and economic windfalls' (89).

When political change came in 1994, it was specifically aimed at breaking this mould. A discriminatory, exclusive political system was replaced by an all-embracing, inclusive democracy capable of effecting the will of the majority of people.

A similar positive change happened to the management of the economy. An economic system rife with controls and dirigiste guidance, aiming to sustain political exclusivity, was to be recast along market principles.

For many years, though, this final outcome had hung in the balance and had been a source of much concern—especially for White South Africans and foreign investors—as the majority of South Africa's population appeared far more in favour of increasing governmental control by nationalising the 'commanding heights' of the economy.

This explosive phrase was originally Lenin's. He used it for the first time in his penultimate public appearance at the Fourth Congress of the Communist International in St Petersburg (then called Petrograd), in November 1922, when he declared that the state would control the 'commanding heights'—the most important elements of the economy (Yergin and Stanislaw 2002, xii; Carr 1966).

Some 30 years later this revolutionary sentiment was reflected in the Freedom Charter, representing the African National Congress's (ANC) basic political philosophy: 'the mineral wealth beneath the soil, the banks and monopoly industry shall be transferred to the ownership of the people as a whole' (Mandela 1994, 163).

Instead, common sense prevailed, with the deciding events and the drama of the early 1990s captured vividly by Sampson (1999), as modernity won through. In the modern democratic South Africa, the proven allocation efficiency of markets would be allowed to assert itself more fully instead of the country opting for the uncompromising rigidity of a centrally commanded economy.

South Africa thus accepted a total (rather than a partial) transformation of principle. Democracy after all is nothing more than a political 'market place', in which information gets disseminated and acted upon, within a robust framework of constitutional checks and balances. Similarly, the larger economy was to become more fully market-based as well.

This decision was not, however, as clear-cut in favour of unfettered neoliberal market capitalism as made out by the ANC government's modern-day critics, for the new political dispensation would require the adherence to important checks and balances. This was in line with international experience favouring 'mixed' economic systems, for in the process of attempting to achieve an efficient allocation of resources, private markets are at times known to fail. For any country to achieve the best economic performance, market failure should be prevented as much as government failure.

Examples of market failure are the inclination of markets to under- and overshoot during financial panics and bubbles as sentiment overreacts to events. Markets also fail to provide certain types of public goods adequately in instances where a large part of the long-term benefits accrue to society rather than to the private investors incurring the costs (such as common protection, mass education, basic health care). The resulting impairment of financial returns prevents such investments from being undertaken privately.

Government can play an important role in correcting such market failures. Through institutional regulation it can secure financial market stability. Similarly, government is far better equipped to provide key public goods such as security, education and health care, which can yield to society important long-term benefits it would otherwise have to forgo if left to private markets. This is, of course, provided that government acquires the capacity to deliver such services effectively.

Thus there is a role for both markets and government to enhance economic and social returns in modern society. The subtle ideal of not overstating either role is a fine one.

The essence of the modern policymaker's dilemma is captured by De Hen (2002) when he says: 'The real art lies in taming the cruelty of the (capitalistic) system without undoing its efficiency. That is statesmanship' (10).

In today's South Africa, government policy remains firmly engaged in shaping economic performance, mostly for the good as mistakes from the past are gradually rectified (though not without a stumble or two). The main economic breakthrough, on a par with politically progressing to inclusive democracy, is to give private agents (markets) considerable more leeway (freedom) than they were allowed in the past to drive economic activity efficiently. Going by international experience, in this resides our greatest performance promise for the future, compared to a rightly discredited past. This may finally lay to rest De Kiewiet's age-old truth about the nature of South Africa's progress. The aim, in short, is to progress less through 'political disasters and economic windfalls' (De Kiewiet 1941, 89), and more through wise political choices, sound social and economic policies and sheer hard work.

Our politics have been transformed, thereby breaking a logjam of centuries. This, in turn, has opened the way for economic policy to be greatly reformed:

- fiscal finances have been restored;
- trade competition has been unshackled;
- a better allocation of highly—skilled and lower—skilled labour has been largely achieved;
- the economy has become more productive and flexible. This has assisted in making a start with transforming the balance of payments constraint of the past; similarly much progress has been made with taming inflation, which has structurally become more contained; and
- monetary policy has become less disruptive (now rolling with the external punches, letting the rand take the pressure rather than trying to absorb such shocks by way of growth sacrifice through interest rate shocks of its own).

The result in coming years should be less interruption of the business cycle, longer growth runs, and greater government support for growth through higher capital spending. As a consequence, we should see a steady rise in resource utilisation throughout the economy. It is this that should prompt a gradual change for the better in business expectations, and a consequent greater willingness to commit to increased private fixed investment spending (and therefore to the training and productive absorption of more labour). This is the way to faster sustainable economic growth, with the preparation phase now lying mostly behind us. As a consequence, we are well on our way to achieving a better all-round growth and social delivery performance in coming decades.

However, it is not as if our transition back towards a better overall economic performance has been without pitfalls. The 'struggle' decades of the previous political regime were marked by self-defeating economic policies, destroying our financial health in the process, but we did not entirely cease stumbling once past the 1994 political watershed. Significant policy mistakes—whose after-effects are still with us—have continued to be made over the past decade regarding:

- reform sequencing, preferring an early beginning with exchange control relaxation rather than with privatisation;

- monetary policy which stuck with defending the currency for too long, incurring expensive interest rate shocks that also succeeded in unnecessarily breaking the economic growth momentum;
- labour reform which contributed to a high-labour-cost environment at the expense of broad-based employment, creating additional incentive for labour shedding and boosting unemployment; and
- the still-limited capacity to deliver quality public services (such as security, education and health care—see Chapter 7) in support of faster economic growth.

The lessons of some of these post-1994 mistakes have only relatively recently been fully learned and their effects wholly or partially reversed. As Chapters 3 and 4 will show, monetary policy changed direction from late 1998, forswearing high interest rate defences in favour of a more flexible currency regime. This pivotal change alone will contribute significantly to the gradual rebuilding of the country's growth momentum that was nearly lost again in the course of the late 1990s. Exchange control liberalisation went temporarily on hold as of early 2001, with a shift in emphasis towards favouring privatisation as the main attempt at strengthening the national finances and contributing to stability and economic growth (both discussed in Chapter 4). Unfortunately, international events in late 2001 and for much of 2002 have led to a further delay in the privatisation process, but in principle its benefits continue to inspire policy, despite stiff resistance from the ranks of organised labour. Labour policy has softened, apparently in appreciation of some of the costs being levied on the less-skilled unemployed, but more will need to be done (by way of labour policy, education, training, as well as faster economic growth) to achieve a fuller development and employment of available labour.

A sceptic might scoff at such favourable sentiment, even to the point of considering it misplaced and unrealistic. There remain many who are disillusioned by the low growth of recent years, the extensive loss of formal sector jobs, the high unemployment, the pervasive crime and the limited social delivery to date. Many of these dissidents have never agreed with the policy paradigm in place for the past seven years. They do not see evidence of structural progress that will herald faster economic growth and a much more generous social bonanza soon, and are generally fatigued by the insistence on orthodox economic policies in which markets figure centrally. In the presence of such a large contingent of would-be interventionists ready to change the direction of the policy rudder at a moment's notice, if only they could, there are sound reasons for keeping an eye on the odds that the reform agenda as presently constituted will proceed uninterrupted without unwelcome detours.

Foreign investors tend to exhibit a healthy scepticism, too, and this is far more serious. The Chinese, as has been their modern wont (as Marxists), would point to 'contradictions' in our collective message—the contradiction of claiming to need White skills to develop the economy and applying market principles to do so, only to simultaneously emphasise the need for political activism in achieving clear social goals, pertaining to social delivery, employment practices, corporate ownership and the land question. This is what Strydom (2000) calls 'sailing a socialist ship with a free-market flag' (9).

These two approaches can sit uneasily together. This is not necessarily so for large multinational companies, which tend to buy into local cultures relatively easily, but whose investment policies are nonetheless still mostly swayed by economic growth and financial returns in the host country. Global fund managers, though, have less direct operational contact with the host country and tend to focus more closely on financial returns and what inhibits them. It is this moneyed global audience, never mind a local one, which seeks improved economic and financial performance. These investors will focus on any aspect of the government's policy message that appears at variance with enhanced performance, be it fiscal stances, monetary practices, trade interference, privatisation delays, labour market inefficiencies, poor corporate governance, public corruption or any other public policies that interfere with a better performance of the economy (see, for instance, the critical analysis by Vulliez 2002).

The ANC government's incorporation of competing world views in its policy mix, in which it attempts to give rein to market processes while also pursuing political activism, made a confusing impression on many in its local and global audiences. This confusion about eventual outcomes was deepened further by the gradual manner in which key reforms were implemented (see Chapter 3). This is partly as a result of the government's need to gain clarity in its own mind about ways and means of implementing reform and also reflected the government's reckoning as to what the political rank and file would accept. While a gradual approach to reform may have prevented revolt, from the left as much as from the right, the government had to accept a trade-off in the manner that outsiders were more inclined to take a wait-and-see approach, just when we needed them to engage most whole-heartedly.

According to Yergin and Stanislaw (2002), it was this kind of concern that had encouraged Polish reformers in 1989 to be far more decisive in their reform approach. Leszek Balcerowicz, the Polish 'Ludwig Erhard' of the late 1980s, after closely investigating Korean and Taiwan growth dynamics and the real Ludwig Erhard's reforms of 1948, was convinced that reform 'gradualism' was doomed to failure. Unless enough changes were combined and applied rapidly, the necessary 'critical mass' (of reform) would not be reached. Instead, confusion (cognitive dissonance) would prevail, holding back progress. Balcerowicz (1995) formulates the significance of critical mass for economic reform: 'People are more likely to change their attitudes and their behaviour if they are faced with radical changes in their environment, which they consider irreversible, than if those changes are only gradual' (341–342).

Thus, Latin American 'shock therapy' came to Eastern Europe, though Balcerowicz prefers to call it simply 'market revolution'. In contrast, many South Africans appeared to think the political election of April 1994 was enough shock therapy, preferring thereafter to use kid gloves with the economic reforms that followed. The price paid was ambiguity in the policy message, and the economy's response in subsequent years was shaped accordingly.

Greater equity in our society would clearly yield considerable benefits, by way of a broader middle class and increased political stability. This would be welcomed in all quarters. It is the manner in which it is to be achieved, though, that remains an issue, as some approaches could be damaging to our general condition in the long-term. In particular, political activism aimed at directly promoting redistribution may do less good compared to strengthening the main policy levers (for example, fiscal discipline) and providing wide access to key social goods (for example, quality public education) that decide participation in the economy. Both faster economic growth and a better-trained labour force are the most powerful engines for creating more skilled employment, in turn the main redistributive agent over time.

As it is, with few illusions, too many participants look for safe havens and easy options, alternatives away from the main action still in progress. Too many South Africans, Whites especially, find themselves at a crossroads that is reminiscent of Europe a century ago. Roberts (1996) writes:

> By 1914, universal adult male suffrage existed in France, Germany and several European countries; Great Britain and Italy had electorates big enough to come near to meeting this criterion. Many among the better-off feared, in consequence, that despoliation and social revolution lay ahead. The gains already made by liberalism and democracy were ominous; further and more radically threatening advances might (lie ahead) (474).

Such concerns at watersheds like ours are understandable as political, social and economic arrangements are changed beyond recognition. But it could equally be a mistake to fear the worst for the simple reason that things did not quite work out north of the border. Do we evaluate Singapore by the company it keeps in the form of Indonesia, whose travails due to its proximity will always be a concern to Singaporeans? The old West Germany the same way as the old East Germany? There are many more such examples where proximity, and even a shared history, is no firm predictor of what happened next.

If anything, modern history is replete with non-performing countries having to adjust to high-performing neighbours, and not the other way round. The old Eastern Europe and Russia clearly lost the race against Western Europe and the United States, and finally started to reform. China and Vietnam, too, eventually adopted market capitalism (though not as yet, if ever, Western democracy). And Mexico ultimately decided to model itself on the United States.

Just because we happen to reside in Africa, a continent with a very poor modernising record, it does not mean that we are necessarily going to be the exceptional continent (and country) on this score forever, a neighbourhood by definition presumed to be doomed and lost to the global community.

One way of evaluating Africa's track record of modernisation is to examine the extent to which its roots have taken hold. The shallower such roots, the less chance the modernising force has of thriving. This is not meant as a reflection on the ability of Africans to modernise, but rather refers to the obvious importance of technical competence, experience and commitment in managing modernisation—apparently a matter of having robust institutions, the rule of law and a large cadre of well-educated, skilled, competent people. Without such a well-established human infrastructure, little may be achieved. The *Economist* (May 2000) observes that:

> The most damaging impact of imperial rule on Africa was neither economic nor even political. It was psychological. In most places, effective European rule lasted a couple of generations or less: just long enough to undermine African societies, institutions and values, but not long enough to replace them with new ways of life or establish new systems of government (24).

By these yardsticks, South Africa should be the one African country to have the greatest potential for successfully modernising itself further, given our 'longish' history, the 'critical mass' in nearly every dimension, and the confidence of tackling 'our' reforms, meeting the *Economist*'s preconditions where other countries have failed miserably. And this despite the real damage of apartheid in social and economic terms as well as the large-scale emigration of recent years.

Such sentiment is borne out by the many reforms (mainly economic, that is, fiscal, monetary, trade, productivity) currently underway, as well other rapid, even dramatic changes (for example, technological and demographic events taking place).

Once these broad reforms have reached full term, we are likely to be surprised by the economic and social potential that this could unlock in our country, and in the region. When this eventually happens, we are likely to experience a second 'change of pace', not unlike the first time this happened in our modernising economy following the discovery of diamonds and gold over a century ago. The gold rush that followed then gave South Africa in a matter of decades a modern underpinning that the country had lacked completely up to that time, and which it had little hope of achieving quickly from the underdeveloped agricultural base that was then supporting most of our still-rudimentary society.

The present change of pace will follow on from two decades of stagnation (1970–1990) and one of restructuring (the 1990s), in which growth at first dwindled and then idled, before gradually resuming. When our economic engine eventually goes back to full throttle, though, it will probably in time be shown that we went from no growth momentum in the late 1980s and early 1990s back towards 4% plus growth annually in the early decades of the twenty-first century. This may still be slower than what was achieved in the 1960s, but certainly in per capita terms there is likely to be more significant growth than the fastest pace we have ever achieved, short of those dream decades in the closing years of the nineteenth century when mining development took us into its firm grip and pushed us into modernity.

What areas qualify at present as sites of revolutionary change in South Africa? The defining break is our own 'glorious' political revolution (in the tradition of Britain's 1688, America's 1786, France's 1789, Russia's 1917, China's 1949 and Central Europe's 1989), for the first time embracing freedom collectively under one national roof. In addition, there are our fundamental economic, demographic and technological breaks with the past. Of these, the macro-economic financial restructuring and the micro-economic trade and labour restructuring are well advanced. These will shortly start yielding benefits by way of a growth revival that many among us no longer thought was possible. The last remaining reforms (privatisation of public assets and abolition of exchange control), though already begun, are yet to be successfully completed. These are necessary reforms (though not sufficient in their own right) in order to complete our financial restructuring and benefit from its supporting higher economic growth over longer periods of time. This, in turn, will provide the main encouragement to both foreign capital inflow and faster capital formation.

Probably the two most startling discontinuities are the social and technological ones, of which the latter has impacted strongly on recorded productivity.

Technology appears globally to be in the grip of one of those periodic breaks with the past, when the pace of change and innovation appears to speed up and which during the Industrial Revolution yielded steam power, electricity, railways, the motor car, chemicals and electronics, amongst other things. Today, it is information technology (IT), telecommunication, computing and biotech that are the leading sectors driving innovative change. As South Africa tends to be an efficient adapter of new technology, with the evidence of its spreading everywhere, such improved capability probably plays an important role in enhancing our productivity growth, although its role is difficult to isolate.

Even more important regarding technical change may be the supply-side innovations of recent years. Deregulation, privatisation, labour rationalisation, exchange control relaxation, tax reform and trade liberalisation are all a vigorous part of the organisational changes impacting on our institutions, the efficiency of our markets, and the behaviour of our labour. All this contributes in poorly understood ways to higher productivity, which is real nonetheless, and has to be acknowledged as a fundamental break with the past in light of its apparent magnitude (and its virtual absence in earlier decades).

Probably the most unsettling break with the past concerns the social environment. There are various powerful demographic cross-currents (HIV/Aids, migration and the cultural values they impact upon) colliding with economic and technological trends, potentially creating fundamental changes in the demand and supply of labour, especially for skilled labour. In the process, it may be changing our values fundamentally in the coming generation, while yet another overlay of imported cultures (mostly African) may thicken the cosmopolitan brew already present.

What is missing from such breaks with the past is an education revolution. Such an effort will clearly be needed in the medium-term if the promises of the other changes are to come to full fruition in the longer-term, allowing us to sustain the higher economic growth rate now coming within reach, or even to go beyond it.

The government is tackling its task from many sides simultaneously. It talks of transformation and of empowerment. But at the heart of its general policy approach there is a global 'best-practice', market-driven forcefulness that too many seem to underestimate. As Van Zyl Slabbert (2000) puts it: '. . . the official policy of the government is that of a strong, competitive market economy . . .' (114).

If political reform gave us freedom of association, its impact stretches far further than just politics. It is our newly gained social freedoms, and economic freedoms, freer from interfering regulations than ever before, which are setting the pace in our society and economy today. It is this freedom of action, rather than only political activism, that is likely to be the primary force in shaping our performance in coming years, provided we retain and nurture these newly gained freedoms.

The aim, in short, is to achieve a better allocation of capital, labour and talent in our economy ensuring higher economic returns. This change is very much in evidence already, stimulated by trade and labour reform and pervasive deregulation already begun in the late 1980s. The aim is also to make fiscal policy less burdensome, an objective that has already been largely achieved in the way the budget deficit and tax rates have been reduced, though the crowning reform here awaits in the form of privatisation proceeds. The idea is to privatise key public assets, raising funds to strengthen both the external and internal finances.

Taken together, these changes will make the country financially more robust, and less exposed to balance of payments interruption from the outside, while creating scope on the budget for greater social delivery, by lowering the interest burden and making those freed funds available for more productive usage over time. The aim, moreover, is to have a less disruptive monetary policy, by more genuinely 'floating' the rand while anchoring policy by targeting inflation. This would reduce the exposure to both currency and interest rate shocks while capitalising on the economic restructuring to get inflation down, and to gradually liberalise exchange controls.

Government thus has accepted the important principle that efficiency needs to precede equity, that we can build a better national house only once we start to generate the resources that will make this possible. That its main policy vehicle, Growth, Employment and Redistribution (Gear), did not deliver on its promises was partly due to the mistakes that were made. But as already hinted at, and discussed at greater length in Chapters 3 and 4, course corrections have been made. The current policy mix is more than ever geared for delivering a stronger economic performance in future years. The stumble of the late 1990s is specifically not a reason to change the direction of the policy rudder at this crucial juncture in favour of more interventionist policies, as these would certainly jeopardise our future performance.

As things stand, our economic framework is in the full flux of modernisation. While completion has still some way to go, the scaffolding in place promises enough reform to stun the most critical observer, once we are fully operational. The biggest and most promising surprises may therefore still lie ahead, and in the not too distant future.

As Huntington (1998), in an even broader sweep of our strengths and attractions, puts it:

> South Africa's peaceful and negotiated transition from apartheid, its industrial strength, its higher level of economic development compared to other African countries, its military capability, its natural resources, and its sophisticated black and white political leadership all mark South Africa as clearly the leader of southern Africa, probably the leader of English Africa, and possibly the leader of sub-Saharan Africa (136).

To many this must sound dubious, indeed glibly optimistic and as unwarranted as such optimism has been on many historic occasions, surrounded as we are every day by the crime, corruption and bedlam that is our modern life. Yet generally improved economic performance will go a long way to providing the means to address such visible evidence of social decay. The cleanup has to start somewhere. Having achieved a political breakthrough, a better-performing economy would be a natural platform from which to address our remaining ills, as it would generate more employment and greater means for wider social delivery and the reduction of poverty. Only by addressing these imbalances successfully do we ultimately have any hope of alleviating the social strains still overburdening our changing society.

As a society we are not riddled with religious strife, despite harbouring many diverse religions. We do not suffer from the debilitating class distinctions of much older societies, despite our still extremely unequal distribution of income and wealth. And though race has marked us out historically for conflict, other societies have a history of much deeper enmity that South Africans claim to be foreign to them, and rightly so; something outsiders consider a challenge understanding fully, for it nearly always comes as a complete surprise to them.

So our biggest problem of the moment, relatively speaking, is a matter of money. And the money problem is the easiest of all human problems to fix, given adherence to a few simple rules of thumb figured out over many centuries. Together with political stability, it provides a more stable springboard from which other things can be fixed. Crime is in essence a matter of economic deprivation, and only secondly a social deviation. If we successfully address the former, the latter should become more amenable to correction, too. Though it should be borne in mind that much of our present anarchy had its origin as much in social and economic inequalities as it did in politically inspired consumer boycotts in the 1980s, and the non-payment for services in the 1990s. In this respect an important change is long overdue. Instead of practising so-called peaceful resistance as befitted a liberalisation movement, social behaviour should again become disciplined as becomes a sovereign power.

All great transitions tend to be marked by upheaval. On a global historical scale ours has been relatively uneventful. Still, we do not only need to get our performance back in order, but restore the social peace, too, if life is to be worth living. The one will not come without, or before, the other.

1 THE LEGACY

Inequality in the distribution of income and wealth prevails to some degree in all countries. This is reflective of natural ability, inheritance and social and economic circumstances pertaining to the country in question. However, when placed alongside world standards, the distribution of income and wealth in South Africa is very unequal. A very small number of households receives a large proportion of the national income, compared to a very large number of households receiving a very small share. This primarily reflects a history of uneven economic development. Over a period of time, a small minority (mainly Whites) developed a modern economy, relying to an important degree on Black, Coloured and Indian labour, while leaving intact a large subsistence economy (mainly Black). Political ideology ensured that Whites were the main beneficiaries from economic development, with a much slower, less viable development path accorded to the majority of Blacks, Indians and Coloureds.

This political, social and economic legacy of inequality was closely tied up with how South Africa as a mostly agricultural, pre-modern society revolutionised itself and launched into modernity. In this process, imbalances of an economic, social and political nature were acquired that would ultimately prove to be a development cul-de-sac. By the end of the twentieth century, these imbalances in all their complexity needed to be unwound *before* the country could again proceed with modernising development. Breakthroughs were required in political organisation, economic behaviour and social delivery in order to escape the dead-end that three centuries of tumultuous engagement had created. This Gordian Knot is our legacy, and untying it is the task facing our generation. The rewards of succeeding are likely to prove startlingly generous, especially to succeeding generations.

A Modernising Economy

The South African economy had a humble agricultural beginning. By the 1850s, the country's economic potential as a largely semi-arid area, with non-navigable rivers and few natural harbours appeared very limited. For centuries farming had been a matter of pastoral subsistence. Nomadic trekboers, stockfarmers and hunters were independent frontiersmen who scraped out an existence that was largely non-specialised, non-market and non-urban in nature. For both Black and White, the age was preindustrial, with little inkling of an imminent economic take-off.

Starting with the diamond discovery of 1867 and followed by gold in fabulous quantities from 1886, South Africa experienced an abrupt change of pace in its economic, social and political development in the closing decades of the nineteenth century. Mining drew in capital and many fortune seekers, and created a shortcut for a quick dash to economic modernity (see, for example, Crisp 1974).

Despite the interruption of the Anglo-Boer War during 1899–1902, mining activity in the interior expanded at a rapid rate. As its output was nearly entirely exported, it provided a growing stream of foreign exchange. This funded the appetite for imported goods, primarily machinery and stores used in mining, but also consumer goods of all kinds which were in short supply locally. This condition lasted until the onset of the First World War. From then on, the isolation of the war period as well as growing economic activity, income and demand for goods and services, stimulated the rudimentary presence of industrial activity. From 1925, a more formal industrialisation policy evolved when import tariffs were raised with the purpose of encouraging local production. The process of import replacement was to create a rudimentary industrial base, which could be steadily expanded as local demand increased, thereby acquiring more substantial economics of scale and production ability. This was further enhanced by the isolation of the Second World War.

For half a century, mining had given stimulus to modern economic development, providing the main impetus for large inflows of foreign capital and fixed investment. From the 1920s, industrial expansion by way of import replacement would provide another great push to modernity for a further 50 years. But whereas the initial mining phase had offered a rambunctious beginning to accelerated economic development along free market lines, making the 'Randlords' (in)famous for their skulduggery and fabulous overnight fortunes, the drive to industrial maturity was to be marked by discriminating practices and laws that protected and deepened the privileged positions of Whites at the expense of other population groups. A major political, social and economic detour lay ahead, even as the 'easy' century of industrial development leveraged off a rich gold endowment was ending.

Not only the unacceptable features of the political dispensation would need to be undone. There were also inefficiencies in the economic dispensation, which were to greatly deepen in the course of the political clash. Together over time, these factors would undermine economic performance. These inefficiencies would also need to be undone before a much better performance would again be possible, the fruits of which would now be able to be more fairly shared by way of wider social delivery in a more just political dispensation.

Discriminating Policies and Laws

The notorious pass laws were responsible for particular hardship among Blacks. These were originally introduced in Southern Africa by the Dutch East India Company 350 years ago and were specifically intended to restrict freedom of movement, preventing people from moving in search of employment opportunities. Thus, the market mechanism for labour was inhibited from operating freely from an early stage in Southern Africa's modern development.

According to Benson (1966), one of the earliest protests against this form of discrimination occurred in 1906, when the Transvaal Natives' Congress sent a petition to the Imperial government, 'respectfully' reminding the House of Commons of their loyalty and claiming, as British subjects, their right to liberty, freedom and equality. They said that the pass laws in the Transvaal were 'repugnant, unnecessary, undesirable and un-British' (19). During the apartheid years in the second half of the twentieth century, the pernicious effects of the pass laws were greatly reinforced by the promulgation of the Physical Planning Act, intended to narrowly limit the employment of Blacks in the manufacturing industry. This measure was further bolstered by influx control regulation, which prevented Blacks from residing in the metropolitan areas where most employment opportunities existed. Restrictions on geographical location and commercial activity were similarly imposed on Indians (see, for example, Lipton 1985).

As formulated in Hiemstra (1972), a further discriminatory measure was job reservation. This was intended to protect the existing racial pattern in industrial labour and thereby to ensure industrial peace. Job reservation was introduced as a policy in 1926, but considerably tightened up in 1957, as a concomitant of energetic industrial growth. The need for job reservation allegedly arose from an increasing threat to more highly paid racial groups by those who were used to a lower standard of life and prepared to do the same work at a lower wage. This had first arisen during the industrial advance immediately after the First World War. In the gold mines a policy of replacing skilled and semi-skilled Whites with lower-paid Blacks led to the greatest industrial upheaval that South Africa has ever seen—the miners' strike of 1922. In response to these disturbances, the Mines and Works Act of 1911 was amended by Act 25 of 1926 so that certificates of proficiency for particular kinds of work could be withheld from Black workers. This position was entrenched in 1937 when the Chamber of Mines entered into a 'closed shop' agreement with labour unions, according to which only members of these unions could be employed. Even before this step was taken in the gold mines, the Hertzog government had introduced its 'civilised labour policy' in state enterprises, notably the railways and harbours. The purpose was to relieve unemployment among unskilled and semi-skilled Whites. This was done by reserving jobs in favour of Whites, even in unskilled tasks. In industry generally the same end was achieved without discriminating overtly, by prescribing a 'rate for the job', the 'logic' being that the employer would prefer the White or Coloured workers if he in any event would have to pay the same wage to Blacks.

The first direct job reservation on the basis of colour was the Native Building Workers Act of 1951. It made provision for the training of Blacks, but limited them to building work for Blacks only, thereby protecting White and Coloured artisans from Black competition. Such direct job reservation was extended in general by the Industrial Conciliation Act of 1957. Further refinement of these measures was enforced through Act 41 of 1959. In time, the shortage of skilled labour caused increasing pressure in trade and industry for the easing of restrictions, especially in favour of Coloureds. Workers in several industries accordingly became exempt from the job reservation provisions, especially in building and construction, the clothing industry, the meat industry, trade and the iron and steel, engineering and metallurgical industries. It would only be in the 1980s that general abolition of these practices took place (Hiemstra 1972, 210–211).

The pass laws, the Physical Planning Act and job reservation were all features that served to bring into being and sustain a growing inequality in terms of skills, income and wealth distribution between the various population groups in South Africa. This inequality was further sharpened by discriminatory practices in education and property ownership, and regulations governing all forms of commercial activity, including trading, farming, share cropping and manufacturing (see, for example, Van Onselen 1997).

Land ownership by Blacks was prohibited, except for reserved areas (the so-called native reserves that later became the bantustans). This was formalised through the land acts, in particular the Natives' Land Act of 1913, one of the most important and far-reaching pieces of legislation in South African history and a cornerstone of the apartheid state (see Plaatje 1987; Benson 1966; and Willan 1996). The original Act was reinforced by further legislation in subsequent amendments. It prohibited farming amongst Blacks outside the reserves and resulted in the dumping of people in economically non-viable, so-called Black homelands. These rural areas would eventually become the poverty traps of the late twentieth century.

Central to South Africa's skill deficit was its skewed allocation of public resources in favour of Whites, at the expense of other population groups. From the earliest days, Whites were favoured in the provision of education. Other population groups did benefit from growing missionary activity during the nineteenth century, but these efforts were not equal to the task of providing for a large and explosively growing population, and ultimately the government took over these missionary activities in order to enforce its own educational system. In the second half of the twentieth century this was marked by huge discrepancies, such as up to seven times more expenditure on White compared to Black children, and generally poor facilities being made available to Black pupils in rural areas. This discrimination in per capita educational spending only came decisively to an end under an ANC government in the course of the 1990s. But because the ANC government inherited a huge backlog in the provision of quality education, this contributed to a lingering perception of poor delivery (as discussed in Chapter 7).

Until the late 1960s, the prevailing legislation and conditions had not prevented economic development. Yet skilled labour had been in short supply from the beginning, constituting an important opportunity loss of even faster growth and development (always difficult to appreciate and quantify). Less-skilled Black labour was also in the process of becoming scarce where it was wanted most, as the industrial expansion was focused on the relatively few metropolitan areas, with government policy aiming to obtain a different social dispersion from the one dictated by natural economic development. And the first effective stirrings of Black discontent, in the 1950s and early 1960s (see, for example, Joseph 1998), had led to the modern phenomenon of capital flight, foreign disapproval and the first strains of foreign financial disengagement. A fundamental growth constraint had come into being, in turn contributing to the slow strangulation of the old political dispensation.

The Economic Struggle Decades, 1970–1993

The pre-1994 White political regime, in wanting to maintain and bolster its historic hegemony, made some clear choices in terms of economic and social policy. In economic terms, an early and widely accepted development model for developing commodity exporters favoured active import substitution as the industrialisation strategy of choice. In South Africa it meant that behind protective import tariffs and quotas, a heavy manufacturing industry was created, with increasing forward and backward linkages into agriculture, mining, industry and infrastructural activity. The isolation of two World Wars helped to give impetus to this development policy, as did rich natural resources providing a ready-made export base.

In addition, as political isolation began to be applied from the 1960s, an economic policy of autarky (self-sufficiency) was a natural successor to such an import substitution strategy. Another policy overlay was provided by social ideology (apartheid or 'separate development'), attempting through active regulation to achieve a certain geographic spread of people and economic activity. These policies distorted the natural, integrating, specialising growth of our market economy, stunting its expansion and reducing the economic returns to be had from our rich resource base and capital investments generally. At the same time, they massively institutionalised human underachievement.

By the mid-1960s, according to Scheepers (1982) and Du Plessis (1965), any limited potential for import substitution had already been fully exploited. From there onward, the returns on investment steadily declined, and the economic growth rate with it. Growth in real Gross Domestic Product (real GDP—the value of all goods and services produced in the economy in a year, adjusted for inflation) started to progressively lose momentum.

From an average of 5.7% real GDP growth annually in the 1960s, the country's growth rate halved to 3.3% in the 1970s, halved again to 1.5% in the 1980s, and became as little as –0.4% in the early 1990s, before recovery set in, as set out in Table 1.

Throughout this period, further specialisation of economic activity became steadily obstructed. Industrial activity was retained that should have been surrendered to imports, and the country increasingly failed to enjoy the development impulse from trade competition that would have encouraged deeper specialisation and more efficient deployment of scarce capital and labour skills. Worse, there was the inclination to pour scarce resources into misguided infrastructure projects, fight foreign wars and uphold a political ideology at the expense of a social dispensation more supportive of political stability and economic development in the long-term.

Table 1: The Unwinding of Economic Growth, 1960–2002

	South Africa's average annual GDP growth (%)
1960s	5.7
1970s	3.3
1980s	1.5
1990–1993	–0.4
1994–2002	2.8

Source: SARB Quarterly Bulletins.

If it was not enough to have made debilitating policy choices, our natural resource endowment left us temporarily in the lurch. After a burst of windfalls in the 1970s as the gold price rose spectacularly from $35/oz to over $800/oz, gold mining became burdened by high costs, dwindling returns and a changing world environment. Gold mining reached a peak of just over 1 000 tons produced annually in the early 1970s, contributing 8% of GDP, 12% of government revenue and over 50% of export earnings by 1980 as the gold price rose. Thereafter, the gold price fell rapidly by more than two-thirds in dollar terms and physical output declined by 60% in a matter of 25 years. The only grace was that this industry's decline could be managed gradually rather than abruptly, mostly due to a steady weakening of the rand, limiting the economic and social impact of this major change of fortune.

Internationally, the period of reconstruction and high growth following the Second World War also ended in the early 1970s. It had provided a high demand for the commodities easily mined in South Africa and therefore was a mainstay of its exports. But as high global growth faltered, so did the demand prospects for South African commodity exports.

The energy shocks of the 1970s did two unfavourable things to South Africa. They accelerated industrial change internationally (reducing the commodity-intensity of GDP), while they simultaneously gave South Africa a false sense of security through temporary gold price windfalls.

The 1970s saw a global move away from energy-intensive physical product with a high commodity content towards technology-based services, thereby exposing the entire foundation of South Africa's century-long modernisation. For we were commodity-based, off which we had leveraged a protected industrial superstructure. Yet the world was ending its industrial phase (the post-industrial era loomed, except for still-industrialising emerging countries, especially in Asia), while also increasingly becoming an integrated market place. The loss of global integration that had begun in 1914 was rapidly being undone. Protectionist features were on the wane. World markets were coming into being—no longer only in commodities, but in manufactures and especially important, in finance. Global competition was increasingly becoming the driving force behind all change. This impacted on technological change, cost structures, market pricing, labour behaviour and public policies generally (encouraging deregulation, privatisation, a lesser public burden on the economy, lower taxation and market-based monetary policies).

Apartheid became increasingly unacceptable to a sceptical world. As isolation and alienation proceeded, while domestically the ideological commitment deepened, foreign capital started its long process of disengagement. Private risk capital (that is, foreign direct investment) was the first to dry up in the late 1960s. Its absence was initially not sorely felt, as during the 1970s the country had embarked on an ambitious programme of infrastructure expansion (electricity generation, port and railway expansion), financing this in part with long-term public borrowing from select financial centres overseas at the time of a rising gold price. When this development had run its course by the late 1970s, the country increasingly came to rely on short-term trade finance and other borrowings in the early 1980s. This option finally ran out with the so-called foreign debt 'standstill' of 1985. Trade sanctions were not directly effective, except in the sense that they indirectly forced a misallocation of resources (a lethal process in the manner that it eroded economic returns over time). However, financial isolation *was* effective in the sense of closing off access to stable foreign capital in stages. Fundamental change was required in order to regain a more viable development route.

Because of dwindling economic growth and a stagnating tax base, and in the face of rising demands for public funds, the public finances became overburdened. Public sector debt was rapidly run up and the tax burden was allowed to rise. Deficit funding was condoned, inflation rose, the currency became unstable and weakened progressively, and interest rates were kept artificially low. Financial destabilisation progressed in stages, though it never reached the hyperinflation phase. External debt did increase, but not unduly so, for political isolation simply denied South Africa that option. Throughout the period exchange control (imposed in 1961) came to be relied upon to keep the economic prisoners inside the political prison of their own making.

Ideological bankruptcy was followed by a financial hollowing out, which contributed greatly to social decay. Whereas labour absorption had progressed more or less satisfactorily in line with the growth of the urban population and labour force up to the late 1960s, the foundation for modernity was simply not being built adequately. The education effort was skewed and inadequate with a modern post-industrial society in mind. Employment generation faltered along with economic growth. Mistaken capital allocation (encouraged by artificially low interest rates as noted) favoured capital-intensive over labour-intensive activity. Unemployment started its long rise. Social decay, in the rural as much as in the urban areas, followed even as population growth was still accelerating (see, for example, Marais 1998).

A modern and well-functioning economy, infrastructure and export-base had been systematically distorted, while preventing a more sustainable social dispensation from coming about. Three growth constraints combined to lay us low.

Firstly, economic activity became distorted through mistaken policy choices, causing economic returns and economic growth to dwindle.

Secondly, slowing growth internationally in the 1970s reduced our export growth potential, even as gold became less generous in its yield, necessitating structural adjustment.

And thirdly, our policy choices (apartheid and self-sufficiency) and fate (gold's decline) progressively came to destabilise the current account deficit over the balance of payments. This imposed a growing current account shortfall as we increasingly exported too little relative to our growing import appetite (the corollary being that we increasingly consumed too much out of our income relative to the funding needs of our investments). This made the current account deficit increasingly unsustainable and thereby ended the viable basis on which our industrial development through import replacement had been based for 50 years. Consequently, for the first time there was an indisputable need for a sustained inflow of foreign capital in order to continue with the *status quo*. Yet it was at this very moment that the years of strong capital inflows started to come to an end. A balance of payments constraint on the capital account came into being as we made ourselves politically unacceptable abroad, while our failing economic performance increased the financial risk to foreign providers of capital, making them progressively unwilling creditors and investors.

With our external accounts increasingly in disarray, this constrained balance of payments condition became the main weakness in South Africa's armour. It forced a rapid fall-off in our economic growth as we could pay our way less easily, and the more frequent interruptions of business cycle upswings that then followed steadily cooled the ardour for expansion-driven investment spending. In turn, the slower pace of economic growth contributed to a deepening deterioration in social conditions, especially the relentless rise in unemployment and the changing character of our urban centres as poverty and informal settlement spread.

Policy reform and reconstruction, although already begun in stages under the old dispensation, had to wait for a new political dispensation to regain legitimacy and vigour.

An Inheritance of Inequality

This history, described so far in all its complexity, evolved a severely skewed income distribution along racial lines, which by 1990 had a structure as shown in Table 2 on page 26.

Table 2 shows that in 1990 only 2% of Black South Africans enjoyed income in the top 20% (quintile 1), while two-thirds of Blacks had incomes placing them in the lowest two income quintiles (Q4 and Q5).

Chapter 9 reveals (in Table 16) that Blacks only comprised one out of seven of all South Africans in quintile 1, a remarkably low number, given that Blacks make up 77% of the population. In contrast, Blacks comprised nine out of ten in the lowest quintile (Q5). So both within their own community, and within the larger population, Blacks were mostly poor.

According to Table 2, two-thirds of Coloureds were in quintiles 3, 4 and 5 (on average better off than Blacks, but not much). In contrast, three-quarters of Indians were in quintiles 1, 2 and 3. And over 90% of Whites were in these three quintiles, too.

Table 2: Composition of Income Quintiles by Race, 1990

	Q1% (High)	Q2%	Q3%	Q4%	Q5% (Low)	Total %
Black	2	10	23	31	34	100
Coloured	8	28	33	20	12	101
Indian	17	36	27	12	8	100
White	51	30	12	5	3	101

Source: Statistics South Africa (StatsSA).

A survey done in 1998 by the South African Advertising Research Foundation puts some rand values to the numbers in Table 2. The data for claimed household income for various population groups shows that some 70% of Black households had less than R1 400 of claimed income per month. In contrast, over 60% of White households and over 45% of Indian and Coloured households, as opposed to only 3% of Black households, claimed income of R6 000 or better per month.

Given that the population is 77% Black, 11% White, 9% Coloured and 3% Indian, and with the ANC government having achieved political majorities of 66% in the two democratic general elections of 1994 and 1999, the future evolution of the income distribution is the focus of much political attention. With a number of East African countries having driven out their Indian communities in the 1970s, and Zimbabwe in recent years apparently driving out its minority White population in stages, the central concern among South African White, Coloured and Indian minorities focuses on their potential downslide. At the same time, many previously disadvantaged South Africans remain on the lookout for gains, now that the political balance has shifted in their favour. These hopes and fears are mirrored in confidence surveys, prominent among these the RMB/BER Business Confidence Survey (see Graph 1) and the FNB/BER Consumer Confidence Survey (see Graph 2), both undertaken by the Bureau for Economic Research (BER) in Stellenbosch and discussed in the next section.

Confidence in South Africa

Besides its natural beauty, the unequal distribution of income and wealth is the most striking aspect about South Africa. This situation has preyed on foreign and local minds for a long time. Can something this unequal be fixed peacefully? History is full of less than peaceful transitions. What would make South Africa a candidate for peaceful change?

But it is not as if there is no confidence at all in South Africa. In parts the level of confidence has shifted, sometimes dramatically so. The real question concerns whether this shift reflects a permanent breakdown and confirmation of an irretrievable negative condition. Or, is this merely a temporary phenomenon—with different people driving change and others now being mere participants—that will eventually yield a positive outcome?

Confidence is a matter of perception, laced with emotion. The more uncertain the environment, the more brittle the confidence. When change is fundamental, and 'big' events impact with great regularity, lack of confidence can become palpable, just as euphoric moods can also show up visibly in opinion surveys.

Over time, opinion surveys have noted patterns of change, which tie in closely with the cyclical behaviour of the economy. But it is not only such economic cyclical behaviour that can show up clearly in these surveys. For when structural change becomes very intense, this also can become reflected in apparently more permanent shifts of opinion. Interestingly, considering popular impressions, two features stand out about sentiment in South Africa in recent years.

Whereas business confidence surveys show a fairly normal cyclical pattern up to 1980, with business downswings reflected in 'low' confidence readings and upswings in 'high' readings, the pattern post-1980 changes noticeably (see Graph 1). Recession lows in business confidence remain mostly unchanged, but upswings record lower and lower peak readings, as if stagnation was gradually undermining growth prospects.

In contrast, consumer confidence surveys show little evidence of significant deviations from traditional cyclical behaviour throughout the 1990s, except (perhaps temporarily for very specific reasons) at the very end when such data have tended to become unprecedentedly volatile, reflecting the remarkable financial and geopolitical turbulence of those years (see Graph 2).

Graph 1: RMB/BER Business Confidence Index

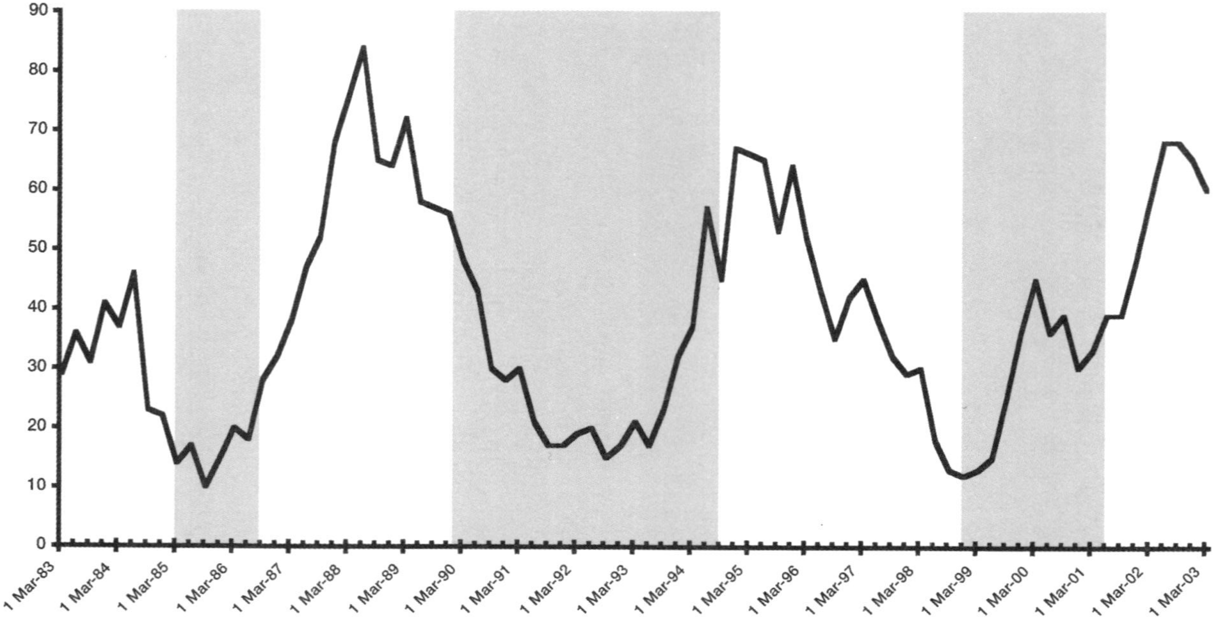

Technical note:
The BER business surveys, covering manufacturing, retailing, wholesaling, motor trade, as well as building and construction, are conducted quarterly among some 3 000 company executives in South Africa. Business 'confidence' is then measured as being the number of respondents indicating 'satisfaction' with present business conditions, expressed as a percentage of total responses.

Graph 2: FNB/BER Consumer Confidence Index

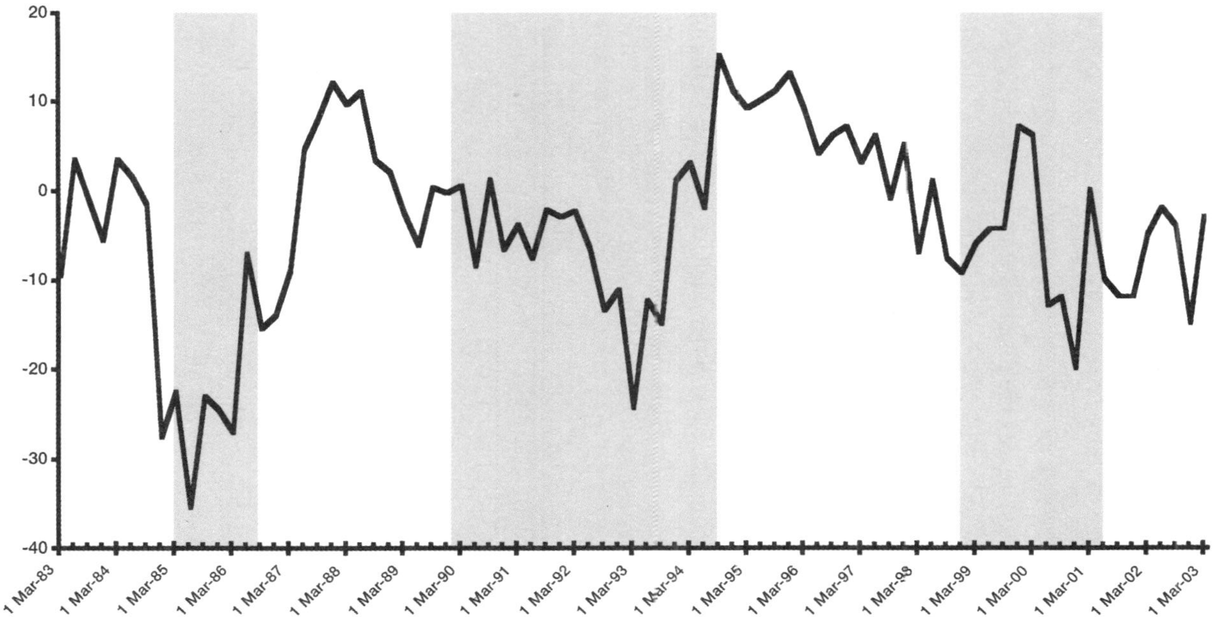

Technical note:
The FNB/BER Consumer Confidence Survey is conducted quarterly among some 2 500 heads of households by way of personal interviews. Consumer confidence is then measured by deducting the number of consumers indicating a lack of confidence from those indicating confidence, and expressing this net number as a percentage of total responses. The long-term average in this measure is not zero (50% confident minus 50% lacking confidence), but instead runs slightly below zero (–4%). The technical note following Graph 3 contains more detail as to how consumer confidence is determined.

While business confidence data can be broken down by economic sector, and certainly has relevance for conditions in those sectors, greater nuances about the country's overall progression can be obtained from the consumer confidence detail. For this reason it may be instructive to delve a little deeper into the consumer confidence data, for it brings out more clearly the experiences of various population groups during this lively transformation period. In contrast, business confidence data merely confirms the existence and condition of the business cycle, and little else, as we would intuitively expect. In this respect it is perhaps important to note that business confidence is quite 'colour-blind', unlike the unique experiences reflected by each of the major population groups when questioned as consumers.

Contrasting Black and White Consumer Confidence

When we go into the consumer confidence data, the most eye-catching structural change in the 1990s is the watershed discontinuity marking 1994. The various population groups did not experience the political change in the same way. What is startling is the mirror-image change experienced by especially Black and White consumers as reflected in their expressed confidence (see Graph 3).

Whereas prior to 1994, there was not all that much of a difference in expressed 'confidence' between Black and White consumers, the moment of the democratic election saw a dramatic widening in a very short period of time (less than a year). As far as can be ascertained, on average 20% of Black consumers became 'confident', where they in normal times would not have so indicated. And about 20% of White consumers no longer expressed themselves as 'confident' where previously they would have done so. It constituted a break of some permanence, which lasted to 1999 (that is, over five years). There was more volatility in the White measure of confidence over this period, very much still tracking the business cycle, if on a lower absolute level of confidence. It would appear that a significant number of White consumers had become less confident because of the political, social and economic (structural) changes.

In contrast, Black consumers come across as having reached a permanently euphoric high after the 1994 election, from which nothing could apparently budge them, and showing less of a correlation with the business cycle over this period. This step up in their confidence could mostly be explained by political euphoria, but other features played a role too. The financial position of many Black consumers improved greatly. Educated and skilled Blacks gained easier access to jobs and to credit than in the past. The Black population increasingly benefited from social delivery, gaining greater access to social goods such as electricity, water, housing, healthcare and education. (See Chapter 7 for a more detailed analysis of improved delivery in social services and Chapter 9 for changes in income distribution over this period.) So while part of the changed Black view can be attributed to perception, a large part stems from real changes in their financial position.

Black South Africans tend to see their financial position very much in the same way they see the economic position of the country over the next twelve months. They have this trait in common with populations as diverse as those of Greece, Spain, Sweden and Ireland (see comparative data in the Euro-zone Consumer Confidence Survey).

This is very much unlike White South Africans, who in times of stressful events show a much greater disparity between confidence about their own financial position (fairly stable) and the economic position of the country (subject to much greater volatility). They have this in common with citizens of the United States (compare data for the Michigan Consumer Confidence Survey), Germany and France (amongst others, as can be seen from Euro-zone data).

In the course of the 1990s, Whites on average moved away from being better-than-average confident about their own finances, as was the case prior to 1994, to being less-than-average confident (by a similar margin) about their finances thereafter. Many Whites remain dissatisfied about many things (including non-economic features, crime being one). This apart from very real economic changes adversely affecting the financial position of White consumers, for example, the sustained high real interest rates during 1996–1999 and the loss of job security in the private and, especially, the public sector.

White consumer sentiment about the short-term outlook for the country shows a similar structural break since 1990, only with many more people expressing themselves negatively. In contrast, Black consumers since 1994 became more confident about the country, until things started to go wrong from 1997 (see Graph 3).

Graph 3: FNB/BER Consumer Confidence: White versus Black

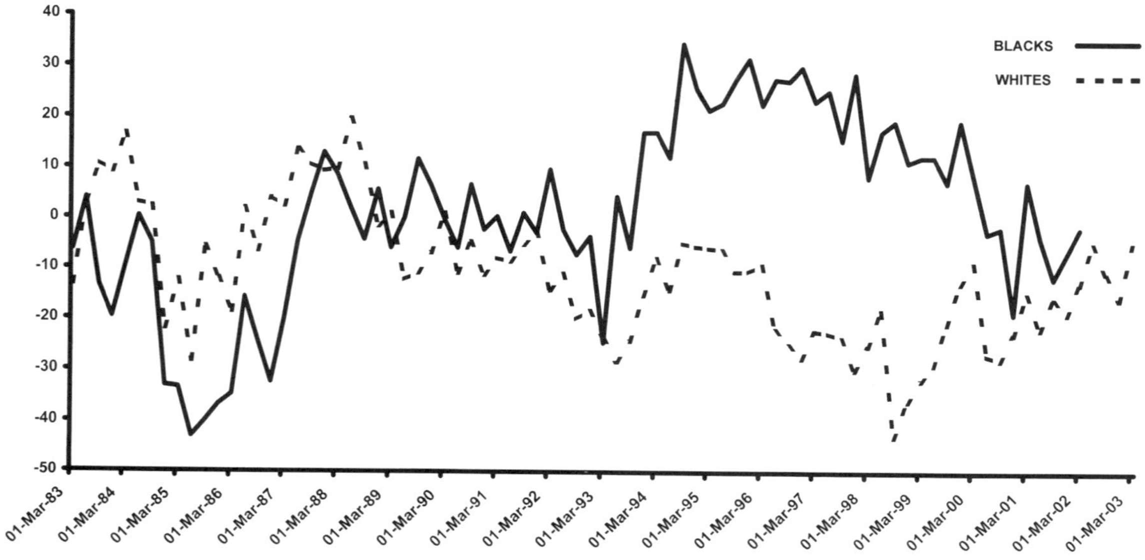

Technical note:
White and Black consumer confidence, as reflected here, is calculated in each instance in exactly the same manner as the overall consumer confidence shown in Graph 2. Three questions are asked, concerning own finances over the next twelve months, the outlook for the economy over the next twelve months, and whether or not it is now a good time to buy durable consumer goods. The answers to each of these questions are processed by deducting those indicating a lack of confidence from those indicating confidence, and expressing this net number as a percentage of total responses. A composite confidence index is then calculated by taking a simple average of the results of the three questions. This applies to White and Black consumers separately as reflected in Graph 3 (and it applies to overall consumer confidence as shown in Graph 2).

Convergence of Black and White Confidence Post-1997

Most encouraging are the tentative signs of convergence in the opinion survey results for 2000–2003 among Black and White South Africans (see Graph 3). This result may still reflect radically different underlying conditions and opinions, yet it could be the first sign of 'normalisation' (defined for now as a return to pre-1994 average opinion readings) and the beginning of the end for more extreme readings of confidence. In turn, this may be reflecting developments in the economy and society at large. The attempt at structural reform may be more advanced and more successful than generally acknowledged. Despite a very unfair history, and a very unequal distribution of income and wealth as a consequence, processes have been set in motion, which may be beginning to succeed in making South Africa more viable than in the distant past or during the interregnum of stagnation and reform.

The first evidence of this was the relatively peaceful nature of the political change in the early 1990s. The follow-through may now be observable in subsequent political, economic and social reforms that are steadily repositioning the country for a better future performance. Instead of non-performance and decay, and subsequent demise, along the lines observed with regularity elsewhere on the African continent since the 1960s, it could be different here. This is hardly yet accepted by all (judging by the ongoing emigration), but subsequent chapters will discuss the mounting evidence, and especially the implications for future performance.

2 POLITICAL PRE-CONDITIONS FOR CHANGE

The Many Crucibles of South African Nationalism

Seen from a Black perspective, South Africa's modern political history goes back over a millennium in time. In those far-off days, the ancestors of most of today's Black South Africans came to settle here—the Nguni-speaking people mainly on the coastal plains of Natal and the Eastern Cape and the Sotho-speaking people in the eastern interior. These pastoralist migrants from the north settled down to a rustic way of life, which for centuries thereafter would seem to change little in this land of plenty (Ritter 1955).

In contrast, from a White perspective, modern political history started five centuries ago with the arrival of the first Portuguese seafarers in the southern Cape in 1488, before long supplanted by more permanent Dutch arrivals in the Cape peninsula from 1652. For Indians, the experience stretches back well over a century, to their first arrivals from India during the 1860s, most at the time destined as indentured labour for the Natal sugar farms.

Throughout this modern period there was to be conflict aplenty in the subcontinent. The Black migrants found the land thinly occupied by indigenous hunter-gatherer people, so-called 'Bushmen' (San) and related Khoikhoi ('Hottentot'), the latter also having become pastoralists. Where their paths crossed, assimilation or dispersion of the original inhabitants (westwards) resulted in a gradual process of displacement.

The White settlers interacted far more ruthlessly with the original Khoikhoi occupants of the Cape. An uneasy coexistence set the scene from the start. Within a century this would see growing displacement and subjugation: the Khoikhoi numbers rapidly dwindled and their freedom was mostly lost, as Whites, Blacks and half-castes ('Bastaards', subsequently renamed Griquas) followed an active policy of extermination or absorbed lingering Bushmen and Khoikhoi elements. Together with slaves imported from Asia and elsewhere in Africa, as well as the offspring of White miscegenation, these disparate elements gradually coalesced into a distinct population group of their own, today recognised in their own right as the Coloured people (see, for example, Mostert 1993).

Besides inter-racial conflict, intra-racial clashes would reach deep into the South African consciousness over the centuries as well. The early

Cape colonists collided with Dutch authority. It took over a century for them to migrate far enough eastwards to make their first contact with the Xhosa. Meanwhile, the French, who had temporarily occupied Holland, clashed with the British who took over the Cape permanently from 1806. For the first time the free ways of White frontier life came to be disciplined, while the first of a series of attempts was made to 'settle' the eastern frontier militarily, a process that would take a century to complete fully and eventually was also extended to the Black tribes of Natal.

The Nguni people knew inter-tribal conflicts of their own during this period, among the Xhosa and their neighbours, and most spectacularly in Natal, where the Zulu nation gained ascendancy for the first time under Shaka in the 1820s. Meanwhile, White Afrikaner colonists had become restless under British imperial rule. They eventually started a migration into the north-eastern interior during 1834–1840 in an attempt to escape British influence. Unable to avoid conflict with British Imperialism, these Boers (farmers) won the first skirmish but lost the second 'White' civil war (the Anglo-Boer War of 1899–1902), yet by constitutional means eventually gained overall power at Union (1910). This same arrangement deepened political dissatisfaction among the subjugated indigenous population, ultimately leading to general civil war in the second half of the twentieth century. This condition ended less than a decade ago in a globally hailed, peacefully negotiated, political settlement. South Africa had come of age, creating a fully inclusive democracy.

For many, the achievement of democracy must rank as the biggest experience of a lifetime, the defining moment that shapes all else. For the political 'winners' it provided a reason to celebrate joyfully after centuries of repression and denied opportunity. And for those who disagreed with the course of events it was apparently reason enough to say 'adieu' in untold numbers of ways. The nature of the political change being experienced in South Africa is certainly fundamental. Its essence has been captured by Huntington (1998):

> Prior to 1949 both South African and Western elites viewed South Africa as a Western state. After the apartheid regime took shape, Western elites gradually read South Africa out of the Western camp, while white South Africans continued to think of themselves as Westerners. In order to resume their place in the Western international order, however, they had to introduce Western democratic institutions, which resulted in

> the coming to power of a highly Westernized black elite. If the second generation indigenization factor operates, however, their successors will be much more Xhosa, Zulu, and African in outlook and South Africa will increasingly define itself as an African state (95).

It is this progression of events—what lies behind us as much as what may lie ahead—which makes many local and foreign people concerned about the future, for themselves as much as for the country at large.

Such anxiety appears to have been part of White population subgroups from the earliest times. For example, authors such as Boonzaier et al. (1996), Mostert (1993), and Sparks (1991)—describing White interaction with the Khoikhoi from earliest times in the late fifteenth century to today—have highlighted the suspicions, misperceptions and misrepresentations that lingered over centuries.

The collision between Dutch and English cultures, in what Smuts termed 'the Century of Wrong' (Paton 1965), created a fundamental hostility between British imperialistic arrogance and Afrikaans nomadic trekboers. The latter's striving for survival and longing for cultural independence was systematically constrained over a long period of time. This process started in earnest with the manner in which the unconstrained lifestyle of early frontier living came to be more conventionally regulated as 'civilisation' took the Eastern Cape region more firmly into its grip in the opening years of the nineteenth century. This was shortly followed by the 'unjust' manner of slavery's abolition in 1834 in the Cape, and culminated in a series of imperial land grabs involving the Transvaal and Free State that subsequently led to the bitter war of 1899–1902.

Such imperialism from the outside, and the large Outlander contingent residing in Johannesburg from 1886 on the inside (see Crisp 1974), fuelled the steadily developing Afrikaner nationalist fires to ever greater intensity.

When self-government came (again) in 1906 (for the Transvaal) and 1907 (for the Free State), before long enshrined in the Union of four South African territories in 1910, along with the franchise, the opportunity was there for self-assertion, and General Hertzog took it. His 'two-stream' policy, favouring Afrikaner separateness, initially had an uphill battle against the instincts and policies of Generals Botha and Smuts, who favoured a united White front within the British Empire (see, for example, Armstrong 1939; Meiring 1975; Smuts 1952).

Nevertheless, the differentiation process among the White subcultures proceeded systematically. From the 1920s onwards the racial card was increasingly played by White Afrikaner nationalists, with scarred emotions from the past and future trepidation—about English cultural and Black ethnic domination—always as the main keys. The future was supposed to lie with racial (and cultural) segregation rather than unity despite heroic dissenting attempts by, for example, Hofmeyr and others (see Paton 1965).

Indeed, after a short period of United Party rule under Hertzog (1934–1939) and once more Smuts (1939–1948), Afrikaner nationalism flourished and finally won through overwhelmingly under Malan and his successors—Strydom, Verwoerd and Vorster—in stages driving the segregation option to its eventual extremes.

By the mid-1960s, Paton (1965) could lament that more than a generation had gone by in which fear had essentially prevented Whites from engaging in constitutional reform imaginative enough to admit fellow South Africans on an equal and liberal footing. Another full generation would have to pass, in the process having the politics of segregation destroy the financial health and modern underpinnings of South Africa's economy, before the political leap of faith would finally be attempted in the 1990s.

Many of the anxieties expressed, particularly by Whites through the ages, remained vibrantly and abundantly in evidence as the adventure of inclusive democracy began in mid-1994. In this respect, the FNB/BER consumer confidence surveys discussed in Chapter 1 tell a cogent story that is worthy of thoughtful consideration but is too often ignored.

Unlike Algeria in 1962 or Zimbabwe in 1980 (or other instances in history where losing minorities decided to leave in a hurry, actively encouraged by their new masters), South Africa's modern story appears more to be one of survivors of all kinds making a go of it. Many people fall by the wayside over time, but many more stick it out. Consequently, the nation's shape and identity is changing all the time. Emotions, on all sides, run deep and tend to deflect attention away from more fundamental changes that will be the more startling once their impact starts to dawn.

When it achieved political power in 1994, South Africa's new dispensation was confronted with choices as to which direction policy should take. Clearly, the emotional damage of the past had to be addressed, in the process incurring fresh trauma for those people who felt themselves to be newly dispossessed politically. Theirs was not a unique experience. In the mid-twentieth century, there were apparently Americans still deeply troubled by their civil war of a century earlier. Similar phenomena occurred at different times in Holland, Britain, France, Russia and China. The First and Second World Wars redefined the way Europe thought and felt about itself (and the way the world saw Europe).

The four defining historic blights for South Africa were:

- the partial extermination and subjugation of indigenous Cape people by Whites (and others) in the seventeenth and eighteenth centuries;
- the subjugation of Black tribes by British imperialism in the nearly 100 years of war that started in the 1780s;
- the 'Century of Wrong' culminating in the Anglo-Boer War (mainly for Whites) during the nineteenth century;
- as well as the protracted apartheid struggle (this time for all South Africans) in the second half of the twentieth century.

The associated trauma goes deep and is likely to linger for a long time. But such conflict is inevitably a source of renewal, too. Seeing through the trauma, and valuing the positive and necessary changes, is something that few, if any, among us succeed in doing sufficiently.

When the evidence is considered, South Africa's civil conflict of the twentieth century was not a 'hot' war. Too few people died for it to earn this label. And the political deal, when it was done, apparently was guided by a meeting of minds. The country was to progress, not digress, and the crucial political ingredients were at hand—including an apparent maturity not often displayed on the African continent during the last century.

Inevitably, however, there are parallels, and to some observers these carry in them the potential for future disaster in South Africa. The early African progression to independence elsewhere on the continent in the course of the 1960s had in many instances ended unfavourably for the White and Indian communities, along with a general loss of modernity and development momentum. Similarly, South Africa's formation as a sovereign modern entity on gaining self-government at Union in 1910 was shortly followed by a disastrous detour as Afrikaner nationalism gradually took centre stage and the Botha and Smuts ideal of a unified White nation progressing along liberal lines failed to materialise.

The modern and far from convinced observer, looking back from the beginning of the twenty-first century, presumably has every right to question why history should not now repeat itself in South Africa. Why should Black nationalism not want or need a detour too, to learn the follies of its more extreme thinkers, before a century of realism would teach them differently, as has happened to Afrikaans nationalists—as much as to Latin American nationalists during the twentieth century—and is currently still in progress in many other African countries?

The real tragedy of White rule in South Africa over the past two centuries has been the steadily evolving nationalism of Afrikaans-speakers, based on fear, clashing with the idealistic liberalism of English-speakers. The former was overly realistic, to the point of not acknowledging the humanism and ability to progress to modernity of Black South Africans. In contrast, the latter was largely informed by a missionary utopia whose values originated far from these shores. Their concept of the 'noble savage', as formulated first among French philosophers in the eighteenth century, did not allow for or attempt to address the fundamental economic and social underdevelopment they encountered. What was missing from these positions was a simple pragmatism, one that continental missionaries had already shown to a far greater degree, but whose practical influence, aimed to impart useful skills, remained limited in the presence of greater fears and ideas.

Yet would the damage inflicted on human relations by Afrikaner nationalism and British imperialism poison the well from which a common future would ultimately have to draw its vitality? This did not seem to be the case at the end of the first transition decade, but then so far South Africa has only had the benefit of the first generation of Westernised Black modernisers. What second and third generation leadership still lies ahead, and what values will they be defending against what imaginary adversaries? Alternatively, will pragmatism win out this time, with two centuries of learning behind us, locally and continentally as much as globally?

The early twentieth century was marked by great poverty among especially the Afrikaans community, just as much as among Black South Africans today, particularly those in rural locations. Perhaps there has been no equivalent of the Anglo-Boer War, but the cultural repression of the past century has surely been equivalent to, if not far worse than, the Afrikaans 'Century of Wrong'. Consequently, if economic argument does not succeed in encouraging a Black nationalistic detour in the twenty-first century, could an emotional appeal to cultural fundamentalism—as can today be observed in some parts of the Middle East—still succeed (the big fear among many Whites)?

Not unlike a century ago, it seems that it will all crucially turn on political leadership and vision. Human choice can create an enabling environment in which other forces can thrive, just as it is capable of destructive detours. China's modern history since 1949, for example, saw such detours, as Mao launched his misguided revolutions and purges in the 1950s, 1960s and 1970s, from which there has been a rapid recovery only since 1978, initially under Deng Xiaoping. South Africa appears destined to side-step such detours, for a number of reasons:

- Early twentieth-century White nationalists did not have the benefit of hindsight, or the international exposure, that our Black nationalists have today. Social engineering ideologies the world over have been found wanting, increasingly making way for more decentralised 'natural' change processes (known as free markets).
- The majority of White people are led by a leadership ready to see sense (recognising what eventually went wrong elsewhere in Africa, and why its own behaviour had no moral foundation). And thus did Whites in 1994 surrender to the idea of political wisdom, namely that the present and future generations of Black leaders would be wiser than their White predecessors had been.
- Black leaders (and people) will not want to commit the same social injustices perpetrated under earlier regimes, having themselves and their forebears been victims of thoughtless policies (echoing Mandela's famous words 'never again').

Furthermore, the world's collective experience of the past century may be such that South Africa's modern political leadership will be better placed to pursue what we now term sustainable economic and social development, which has at its core a fundamental political revolution (inclusive democracy) and the magnanimity and clear-headedness to use this opportunity wisely.

It was not as if preceding generations were ignorant of what needed to happen politically for South Africa to be able to develop constructively. Few, though, predicted the process correctly. Some, locally as well as abroad, understood the need for change, if South Africa were to become politically viable for the long-term.

In 1960, in an address to both houses of the South African parliament in Cape Town, the United Kingdom's Prime Minister Harold Macmillan spoke of the 'wind of change blowing through the [African] continent'. His words were memorable enough to reflect on once more. Anthony Sampson (1967) was there to record Macmillan's speech:

> The most striking of all the impressions I have formed since I left London a month ago is of the strength of this African national consciousness. In different places it may take different forms, but is happening everywhere. The wind of change is blowing through the continent. Whether we like it or not, this growth of national consciousness is a political fact. We must all accept it as a fact. Our national policies must take account of it (185).

As Sampson records:

> with courtesy but firmness, (Macmillan) came to the nub of the speech, the dissociation from South Africa's policies:
>
> What we think right derives from long experience, both of failure and success in the management of our own affairs. We have tried to learn and apply the lessons of both. Our judgement of right and wrong and of justice is rooted in the same soil as yours—in Christianity and in the rule of law as the basis of a free society. This experience of our own explains why it has been our aim, in countries for which we have borne responsibility, not only to raise the material standards of living but to create a society which respects the rights of individuals—a society in which men are given the opportunity to grow to their full stature, and that must in our view include the opportunity to have an increasing share in political power and responsibility; a society in which individual merit, and individual merit alone, is the criterion for man's advancement whether political or economic (186).

A previous South African Reserve Bank (SARB) Governor, Gerhard de Kock, made it clear in the mid-1980s that only a fundamental change in political conditions would make it possible for South Africa to develop more normally and to its full economic potential. Political change was a precondition for economic development to be able to resume its interrupted journey. With the political change a reality after two successive democratic general elections since 1994, and international acceptance regained, it is the manner in which we choose to capitalise on this condition that will determine our performance going forward. The political choices underlying our economic and social policies are to be our proactive contribution.

The Inheritance at Democracy, 1994

What then was the inheritance bequeathed to the nation when it finally made its political peace in 1994?

South Africa was socially deeply divided and unbalanced, as reflected most poignantly in its sharply uneven income, wealth and job distributions. This was due only in part to the deep educational and skill deficits, making the larger part of its labour force unemployable in a modern sense. The country's finances were in a poor state, too. Fortunately, there had not been a hyperinflation, and external debts had remained limited, but there were few foreign reserves (indeed none). Capital flight was serious, as exchange controls proved only partially effective in preventing capital from leaving. Government finances had imposed a large budget deficit, a high and growing public sector debt as well as a heavy tax burden, contributing to a high inflation rate and a weak currency. Economic growth was low (indeed negative in per capita terms already for over a decade), and the economic structure inefficient. Political expectations among the managerial and professional class were low (with many seriously contemplating emigration), while economic expectations among the lower income groups and unemployed about obtaining higher income and access to social goods were high. Crime flourished and was considered a major blight.

Nevertheless, South African society and its economy had not been devastated on any grand scale; 'weathered' is a more appropriate term. Modernity had not been lost. There was a modern infrastructure in place (though unbalanced, favouring White communities, while much less supportive of the Black population). The institutional fabric was modern and effective. A pool of skilled labour was on hand (although it was demoralised). And the economic structure was not distorted beyond redemption. Essentially a market economy, it would be able to respond well to better price signals and would not simply fail for want of its protective shield. The absence of new foreign direct investment for decades, and the social, trade and financial isolation, had not noticeably degraded the productive apparatus. The main reason for this was that most foreign companies operating in South Africa had stayed during the years of troubles, keeping their productive capacities modern by reinvesting where this seemed sensible in terms of financial returns. South African companies had similarly been capable of gaining state-of-the-art technology internationally. It was not entirely efficient, but the premiums involved were effectively minimal (a feature of globalisation). So whereas the inheritance in many respects looked tainted and financially weak, a precursory dusting-off showed that what was in place could be made to perform in the shortest possible period. This presumably was not a negligible feature in the political decisions being made about how to position the country going forward.

The Challenges Facing Democracy

What then was required to resume South Africa's development? Clearly, social expectations had to be met, if only as a down-payment on what would be possible in the longer-term. The country's finances had to be sorted out (the budget, tax incentives, inflation, exchange rate, foreign reserves, exchange control). The economic inefficiencies had to be reduced, to get a better economic performance but also to reposition the country strategically. We also had to leave commodity and industrial bases behind and become more services-based as was happening elsewhere, even while earning our way export-wise, and hopefully attracting foreign participation to make this effort less arduous than it would be otherwise.

Social spending and the financial cleanup were to be government and SARB responsibilities. But getting the economic structure to become more efficient was a matter of allowing competition in. Both management and labour were to be introduced more seriously to global competition by opening up the economy, and ending subsidies and privileged access. This change in the 'rules of the game' may have been the most confusing of all for many people. In the past, rigidity used to be handsomely rewarded and irrational demands were possible, irrespective of their economic impact. Now all were to be increasingly confronted by global competition and economic practices geared to development.

Apart from the key decision to hold a democratic election in April 1994, a few other things stand out in demarcating change. These include:

- ending foreign wars;
- the reduction in import protection;
- allowing labour to organise freely;
- the determination to regain control over the budget;
- lowering inflation by trade liberalisation and by maintaining real interest rates and keeping the real effective rand stable; and
- the relaxation/abolition of exchange control.

Still to be implemented is the large-scale privatisation of state assets (discussed in greater detail in Chapter 4). Anyone who has been through an organisational restructuring (today including many of those working for quoted companies, parastatal organisations and most state departments and quasi-state institutions, such as universities) will recognise all the signs and symptoms of change: the confusion, uncertainties and risks stretching into the future. It is a condition in which discouragement easily gains the upper hand, for change is not a simple process.

Yet there comes a point when the pieces start to fall into place—not perfectly, but nonetheless in working order. The hungriest of the social demands have been met, and though few are satisfied, the country has bought time. Political structures have been democratised. Freedom of movement has created much change previously obstructed. The finances have been sorted out, yet the monetary side awaits completion, dependent as it is on privatisation (and global conditions—an uncertain aspect). The structural inefficiencies have been greatly reduced in the sense that employment rationalisation has progressed, though some of this not purely in response to external competition but also because of excessive labour demands (relative to actual labour productivity), worsening an old problem (unemployment).

Some skilled labour has emigrated, but because of the rationalisation in employment there is a reservoir of surplus skills from which the economy can draw for a while (see Chapters 5 and 9). This gives the country some time to get its education effort sorted out and this is obviously an urgent priority.

Foreign capital is not yet on board to any significant degree. This statement needs some qualification as there are many foreign companies operating in South Africa. A significant number of them have been here for many years already, and their operations continue to function well.

Furthermore, some foreign portfolio investments have been made since 1994, but these are not much more than what has flowed out of South Africa through asset swaps by local financial institutions, thereby denying the country much of a net gain of foreign capital. What we need is some new additional capital. This is not a particular need in the area of short-term bank credit (our trade financing needs are adequately served) or with regard to government bonds (budget deficits are adequately funded locally, with foreign bonds mostly raised for the purpose of establishing an international market presence—'benchmarking').

The real need remains for foreign commercial participation in our economy, for this will strengthen our economic structure immeasurably (as it has done in waves these past 100 years). Foreign commercial participation would bring not only capital, but also specialised technology. The economy is not doing badly without such infusions, apparently capable of generating up to 3% of real GDP growth, but the country could always use more such inflows. In addition, they would bring in more specialised skills—that is, if we let them enter, which we should as these skills are not acquired easily, as shown up daily by our education effort (see Chapter 9 on skilled labour).

Our need for foreign capital comes mostly because we have decided over the years of hardship to consume more of our income, thereby reducing the rate of national saving as a share of GDP. In a way, this has been extremely short-sighted, as it has greatly increased our reliance on supplementary inflows of foreign capital to still be able to fund needed fixed investment. Companies have not reduced their savings flows much (being commercial enterprises), but they have been tempted to divert their cash flows overseas in order to diversify and expand. We need new foreign entities to come in and augment a shrinking domestic pool of such commercial talent. There is nothing special about this (it is a global phenomenon), but it is still very urgent nevertheless.

Government is doing more than before. It has allowed the tax-take to rise gradually compared to its own spending, thereby reducing consumers' ability to consume while dissaving less itself. It has also started to increase its spending on infrastructure. But private savings have yet to show any resurgence of note, probably a reflection on the times and the concomitant personal financial strains, but also reflecting the strong redistributive nature of fiscal policy over many years now.

Consequently, our national savings rate remains very low—only about 16% of GDP. We need to increase this or remain dependent on foreign suppliers of capital to give us the means to fund our capital formation. Faster growth should generate more domestic savings as well as draw in more capital from overseas. If our economic growth rate is to be higher than 3% p.a. our investment-to-GDP ratio will again have to rise to well over 20%, and savings with it, either from local sources or from external ones. These are not simple things to achieve.

Nevertheless, we are a going concern. Much structural change has already been effected and our new form is becoming recognisable. More needs to be done, but it is in the nature of things to be always a work-in-progress. We are certainly no longer slowly grinding to a standstill as happened in the 1970s and 1980s. With the political change of early 1994 apparently so effortlessly—if perhaps a little deceptively—taking hold, and with the external pressures off, the economy nearly immediately bounced ahead. It entered on an impressive growth 'run', non-agricultural GDP averaging 3.5% real growth in 1994–1995 on an apparently accelerating trend.

That we ran into renewed financial interruptions in the second half of the 1990s, was due to incomplete financial reform at home and occurrences abroad (Asian contagion in 1997-1998, American adjustment in 2000–2001), discussed in greater detail in Chapter 4.

Importantly, this growth episode (1994–1995), though short-lived—indeed, cut short—showed the extent to which economic growth could accelerate once confidence took hold again. Equally important, the financial events of the years 1996–1998 showed up the nature of disruptive intrusions, which have the ability to dampen our growth and which need to be decisively overcome if we are going to succeed in achieving a sustainable growth momentum.

What the country does not need now is a major stumble: a financial market event globally, or a change in policy direction domestically that would endanger the continuation of structural reform, even undoing what has been achieved.

Summarising South Africa's Historic Condition

At this stage it is useful to summarise the main constraints on economic growth facing our policymakers during the twentieth century and to describe how a start was made with transforming these through the political and economic reforms of recent decades. This should allow a greater appreciation of the policy mistakes that were made during this period and the real potential for better performance going forward, once reform is more complete, as discussed in further chapters of this book.

The manner in which South Africa industrialised had a major bearing on the policy constraints that materialised over time. South Africa's modern economy was started as a commodity play, in terms of which international demand governed both the demand for and prices of our export commodities. Increased export earnings stimulated domestic spending, output and imports, with imports rising until a current account deficit took shape. In earlier periods, political acceptability and high investment returns stimulated large capital inflows, which allowed a substantial current account deficit to be run as it was easily financed because of our economic and political attractiveness. Over time, this balance of payments condition of chronic current account deficits and capital account surpluses came to be near-permanent for a variety of reasons. South Africa's industrialisation was mainly encouraged via import replacement through a policy of import protection and stimulated through periods of isolation during the World Wars.

Though import substitution did replace imports with local production, this did not result in a lower current account deficit due to a lesser import need, as this policy did not encourage a high level of efficiency and trade competitiveness. Indeed, to a remarkable degree this policy accommodated the political choices of the period, in terms of which costly social choices were made, such as a labour policy giving preference to cheap labour (particularly in agriculture), and later on to high-cost labour in manufacturing, as well as capital investment in projects with low economic returns. Though the industrial economy that came into being this way was not hopelessly inefficient, it essentially did not attempt to earn its way. The new local production would still need imported inputs, while it would not attempt to export, having little incentive to do so (thus becoming a net absorber of foreign exchange). Instead, everyone looked towards mining as being the great earner of foreign exchange. Efficient mining operations produced export commodities coupled with favourable spillover effects into manufacturing, while manufacturing industry (with a few exceptions) effectively produced for local consumption, rather than trying to generate foreign exchange too, and covering the costs of its imported inputs.

Relative prices were sufficiently distorted (the exchange rate was too highly valued), and the resource endowment fabulously rich, for this condition to continue immoderately for decades.

Thus a balance of payments condition that should have progressively eased in terms of a development model favouring trade competition, in effect was indefinitely maintained in terms of a rich natural endowment, the preference for trade protection and the peculiar South African political choices governing the allocation of resources. An economy organised in a manner that encouraged a balance of payments deficit on the current account could continue to grow indefinitely as long as a surplus was being maintained over the capital account. From 1970 onwards, though, in a matter of 30 years, this picture would be fundamentally transformed.

From the late 1960s, a capital constraint started to operate. This did not initially tighten the balance of payments constraint, but its presence can be observed from the steady change in the nature of the capital flows. From a condition of large foreign direct investment flows prior to the 1960s, the reliance shifted to long-term foreign borrowings in the 1970s, to short-term borrowings in the early 1980s, culminating in the so-called debt standstill of 1985, after which in the late 1980s large capital outflows had to be financed. This 'closing' of the capital account ended the easy financing of the chronic current account deficit. A capital account constraint over our domestic economic set-up had come into being. In the absence of discipline elsewhere in society (fiscal policy was in the process of being systematically overburdened), a more stringent monetary policy had to be imposed, aimed at reducing domestic demand and economic growth in order to engineer current account surpluses.

This complex situation became confused for a while by the short-lived gold booms of 1974 and 1979–1980, but (as discussed in Chapter 1) physical gold production peaked at just over 1 000 tons annually in the mid-1970s, after which a steady decline set in. The gold price peaked in 1980 at $800/oz, after which it started its long-term decline too.

With our main export price faltering, and gold becoming more difficult to mine economically, and political risk foreclosing on the capital account, the balance of payments constraint tightened sufficiently for it to choke the economy into stagnation in the course of the 1980s. Industry was mostly unable to ease this situation, its operations not being efficient enough to start trading competitively on any scale and to export itself out of these deepening constraints. The effective ending of economic growth further deepened South Africa's unattractiveness to foreign capital.

In this manner, South Africa approached the moment when a number of switches needed to be thrown:

- The political constraint over the capital account needed to be eased.
- Growth needed to be restored for the country to become attractive again to outside capital and to encourage rising domestic fixed investment (the traditional pull-factor).
- Growth could only be restored if the current account condition could be eased and the business cycle be extended once again into longer, stronger growth runs, with import needs adequately accommodated.

In principle, dumping apartheid and White rule in favour of inclusive democracy and Black rule relaxed the political constraint over the capital account from 1994. However, this change heightened risk perceptions and risk aversion, which would require (much) time to be reduced. Black rule initially introduced uncertainty and some policy choices—especially political activism—created great unease, given Africa's track record and the unnerving example being set next door in Zimbabwe in the late 1990s and early 2000s.

Furthermore, economic growth had to be speeded up from within in order to restore the attractiveness of investing in South Africa. The political breakthrough and the restoration of faster economic growth together would determine the full lifting of the capital account constraint.

The needed economic transformation was as dramatic as the political changes, if less visible. In order to change the current account condition and its constraining influence on economic growth, in the absence of renewed commodity windfalls, the domestic economy needed to be freed from its protective cocoon and be made to earn its way in the world. As with any poorly managed inheritance suddenly put on a better footing, this would yield two benefits: better returns from invested capital, and the ability to pay our way—exports expanding sufficiently to cover import expenses—to the point of attracting new capital to invest productively and further strengthen our position.

This transformation would come about by lifting the protection of decades through progressive trade reform and by way of a forced change in relative prices (through a falling real exchange rate), in any case underway in the mid-1980s under pressure from the increasingly constrained balance of payments. This change would both boost exporting and temper importing.

Since these measures were instituted from the mid-1980s onward, the change in the performance capability of the South African economy has been much more formidable than the modest economic growth performance of the 1990s would suggest. This has occurred for various reasons. As suggested, the capital account constraint would take time to ease effectively, despite the political embargo being lifted, because of lingering risk perceptions and slow growth. Indeed, the capital constraint would be last to ease, in response to better performance. But the better growth performance would take time materialising, as the reform policy was not implemented without making some unfortunate choices. Some of these reinforced capital account volatility and its constraint over domestic policy freedom, restraining the economy's growth performance relative to its capability at the time.

This complex set of interlinking features is considered more closely in Chapters 3, 4 and 5.

Chapter 5 (micro-economic restructuring) highlights the extent to which trade reform, and political activism, stimulated the private sector to become more efficient and trade-competitive. This was to be the key in transforming the current account condition by increasingly showing evidence of better economic returns (higher productivity) and an ability to earn our way externally (increased industrial exports), rather than to be solely dependent on a rich endowment or windfalls.

That this process did not lead to much faster economic growth than was achieved in the 1990s, and a more complete transformation of the capital account constraint, has had everything to do with the reform choices and policy stumbles of the 1990s. The main missteps—essentially of a monetary or financial nature—were reform sequencing (preferring early exchange control liberalisation and only late privatisation, rather than the other way around), and monetary policy's slow switch from focusing on rand stability to domestic stability. These policy issues are discussed in detail in Chapter 4 (financial restructuring).

The opportunity loss involved (slower growth than bargained for in terms of the reform agenda, and a longer-lasting capital account constraint remaining in effect) are discussed in Chapter 3, where the ANC government's main macro-economic policy choices (Gear) are discussed and its disappointments highlighted. However, also coming into focus is a belated foundation on which the lifting of the balance of payments constraint on current and capital account can be contemplated. As this is achieved, business cycle upswings should become less interrupted in coming years, and should become more reinforced through future government actions, including belated privatisation, a greater monetary policy focus on domestic stability and more public capital spending.

In the absence of global shocks impacting on trade and capital flows, the South African economy has therefore reached the stage where it is near to completing its structural reforms, achieving finally a fundamental easing of its external constraints, and attaining a faster sustainable economic growth performance than it has for decades. This will still only remain a midway station to an even stronger performance (with many people wanting to know why we cannot aim for 6% average growth compared to merely 3.5% to 4%). Realistically, though, in the course of improving its economic performance in coming years, South Africa is bound to encounter new constraints to its growth performance, particularly with regard to its store of human capital, with government policy likely to play a pivotal role in transforming this longer-term constraint or maintaining it in place through its chosen education and training policies (see Chapter 7).

South Africa's full rehabilitation will not be complete until this social dimension has been adequately transformed too. Improved education and training, in particular, are the keys to improved employability of labour and its role in achieving an even faster rate of economic growth.

In the course of this development, greater redistribution of opportunity (jobs) should make for less inequality and greater political stability. A more efficient labour market, allowing more rather than less competition, will be an important ingredient in achieving a broad-based rather than a narrowly-based middle class.

3 A PLANNED ECONOMIC REVIVAL

Prior to 1994 the apartheid government attempted to give itself some 'wriggle room' through a series of feeble, though broad, attempts at reform—constitutionally, socially, economically and financially.

Starting in the 1970s in the private sector, certain mining groups made a beginning with narrowing the wage gap by increasing the real wages of the lowest paid. Labour unionisation was allowed to take hold and job reservation was phased out. More public funds were allocated to provide social services to Coloured, Indian and Black communities. But the racial inequalities remained glaring in every sphere, and access to economic opportunity was unequally divided.

Nevertheless, the basis for a more efficient functioning market economy was being created in this period. Labour was granted greater freedom of association. Monetary policy was placed on a market footing by abandoning credit controls in favour of a market-based interest rate policy and a more flexible exchange rate regime. Foreign trade was freed gradually as various reforms scrapped quantitative import restrictions and began the arduous process of lowering import tariffs. At the same time, a start was made with reforming the parastatals, forcing a greater financial discipline on them. This led to the first large-scale shedding of public jobs in the late 1980s (a fifth of all parastatal jobs disappeared). The gold mining industry also began the process of rationalisation (nearly a tenth of all mining jobs were lost). Between 1985–1987 and 1990, some 125 000 jobs were lost this way—an unprecedented change in modern South Africa, but still only a small step compared to what was to come during the 1990s, when such job losses were to happen *annually* in the core of South Africa's formal sector (see Chapter 5 for further discussion).

The real transformation of the South African economy and social dispensation got underway from 1994 onwards. The initial policy framework was known as the Reconstruction and Development Programme (RDP), which was mainly an idealised political agenda seeking to mobilise broad support for the newly installed ANC government's still-evolving approach to economic policy and social delivery. Implementation of the RDP fairly quickly showed the difficult balancing act demanded of the new government, which was expected to meet the increasingly vocal and growing demands of its core constituencies, while also having to reassure domestic and foreign investors regarding its willingness to adhere to internationally accepted economic policies.

The Origins of Gear

In early 1996 the country was faced with external pressures and the need to gain credibility regarding its commitment to sound macro-economic policies. Consequently, the government launched its Growth, Employment and Redistribution Programme (Gear). The new programme retained broad social objectives but essentially represented a political watershed for the new regime in favour of an outward, market-oriented policy framework.

For reasons that were far from generally clear at the time, a major rand depreciation commenced in mid-February 1996. The 1996 Gear document mentions the rand being 'somewhat overvalued in response to a temporary capital surge' (in 1995), but the decline 'was also the result of increased concerns regarding policy trends and economic prospects' (10). This might be so, but Chapter 4 provides an interpretation that more fully describes the process and reasons why the currency gave way in the manner and at the time that it did.

Meanwhile, this February 1996 'rand event' acted as a wake-up call to the government and its policymakers. The quick economic rebound post-1994 had reflected the political euphoria, but now had fizzled out and potential growth remained on a low trajectory.

The Gear document (1996) states very plainly that government saw this rand depreciation as representing a threat and an opportunity. It signalled a worse crisis and contraction to come if nothing was done and it also suggested a danger of further capital outflow and a balance of payments crisis. Growth would then be abruptly curtailed, and structural adjustment under terms set by international agencies would become unavoidable.

Put this way, there was everything to lose and nothing to be gained from doing nothing. It was an opportunity which provided a springboard for growth. According to the Gear formulation, there were apparently only two real options, that is, a domestic-oriented policy or an outward-oriented one.

The domestic-oriented policy option (as formulated at the time) entailed an 'expansionary fiscal strategy' (that is, cutting taxes and/or increasing government spending). Gear (1996) acknowledged that this would boost growth, but only in the short-term, after which it would reproduce the historical pattern of cyclical growth and decline:

- Growth above 3% would be choked off by a rising current account

deficit, higher real wages and the curtailment of investment.
- Higher fiscal deficits would lead to higher inflation and interest rates, further increasing the fiscal deficit through a higher interest burden.
- Uncertainty could cause a balance of payments crisis (through an outflow of capital).

None of this could have appeared attractive. Consequently, it opened the way for what in retrospect remains a leap of faith, namely, that only deep-rooted reforms would allow faster growth without descending into the kind of disaster guaranteed by fiscal expansion.

It was this logic that convinced the government 'to break the current constraints and catapult the economy to higher levels of growth and employment' (Gear 1996, 2). A transformation towards a competitive, outward-oriented economy was needed. The balance of payments stranglehold over economic growth needed to end.

The Gear document provided a short summary of the progress that had been made to that date, what was evident about then current trends, and then led on to prescription as to what should be done to create a 'competitive outward-orientation'.

As background, Gear noted that since the 1980s:
- GDP growth had been restored in excess of population growth (if only by a narrow margin).
- The budget deficit had been reduced, the tax system reformed, and government spending reprioritised (far from complete reforms at the time, more in the nature of down-payments, but real nonetheless).
- Inflation had been reduced (by at least a third in underlying terms) and the balance of payments constraint had eased (a contentious claim as the 'rand event' indicated unsustainable pressures).
- The economy had been opened up through trade reform.

Notwithstanding these achievements, it was evident that:
- Job creation as primary vehicle for income redistribution had remained inadequate.
- GDP growth of 3% going forward would fail to reverse the unemployment crisis; would limit funds for social delivery; and would yield insufficient change in the income distribution.

When projecting economic trends as they had manifested themselves up to that point and allowing for certain minimal aims of government policy, the team formulating the Gear strategy in early 1996 came up with what it termed its Base Scenario Projections 2000 (that is, what would happen if no additional policy changes were made).

The expectations for 1996–2000 with and without Gear are contained in Table 3:

Table 3: Economic Policy: With and Without Gear, 1996–2000

	Gear target	Without Gear
Fiscal deficit (% of GDP)	3.7% p.a.	4.0% p.a.
Average tariff (% of imports)	7.6% p.a.	8.8% p.a.
Average real private wages	0.8% p.a.	1.4% p.a.
Real bank rate	4.4% p.a.	5.2% p.a.
Real government investment	7.1% p.a.	2.4% p.a.
Real parastatal investment	7.6% p.a.	2.7% p.a.
Real private investment	11.7% p.a.	5.6% p.a.
Real non-gold export growth	8.4% p.a.	6.9% p.a.

Source: Gear (1996).

The Base Scenario assumptions about 1996 2000 yielded the following projected results:

- GDP growth averaging 2.8% p.a.
- CPI inflation averaging 9.5% p.a.
- Formal job growth in the non-agricultural sectors to average 1% p.a.
- New formal jobs averaging 104 000 p.a.
- Current account deficit as % of GDP averaging 1.4%.
- Real manufacturing export growth to average 8.5%.

The government considered such prospects to be inadequate compared to the needs of the country. Population growth of 2.5% p.a.; unemployment projected to climb to 37% of the economically active labour force (on the expanded definition—see Chapter 5 for a closer description and contrast with 'official' unemployment); huge social backlogs and a very unequal distribution of income and wealth required a better economic performance and a change in policy direction was required.

The Main Policy Objectives of Gear

Gear restated the government's economic policy objectives to be the achievement of:

- higher economic growth and job creation;
- redistribution in favour of the poor; and
- increased social delivery.

Gear then articulated the belief that higher growth required the economy to become more competitive and outward-orientated. This required in turn:

- faster growth of non-gold exports;
- rapid growth of private fixed investment;
- rapid growth of public fixed investment;
- increased labour absorption; and
- increased social delivery.

These desired outcomes required in their turn:

- competitiveness in exporting;
- greater labour market flexibility; and
- increased labour skill development.

To achieve all of this, the following actions were proposed:

- budget deficit to be reduced faster;
- state spending to become more redistributive;
- gradual exchange control relaxation;
- consistent monetary policy to contain inflation;
- real trade-weighted rand to be kept stable at the now competitive (depreciated) level of 1996;
- further trade reform by way of reduction in import tariffs, encouraging more efficiency;
- tax incentives to stimulate investment;
- privatisation;
- increased public investment aimed at social delivery;
- structured flexibility in collective bargaining;
- training levies; and
- social agreement to wage/price moderation.

Accordingly, Gear proposed certain adjustments to economic policy for the period 1996–2000 (set out in Table 3). An additional $0.5 billion of foreign direct investment was on average expected to flow in annually.

These changes, had they been effected in full as envisaged, were expected to generate the results for 1996–2000 as summarised in Table 4.

Table 4: Expected Outcomes: With and Without Gear, 1996–2000

	Gear target	Without Gear
GDP growth	4.2% p.a.	2.8% p.a.
CPI inflation	8.2% p.a.	9.5% p.a.
Formal job growth (non-agricultural sectors)	2.9% p.a.	1.0% p.a.
New formal jobs created	270 000 p.a.	104 000 p.a.
Current account deficit (as % of GDP)	2.4% p.a.	1.4% p.a.
Real manufacturing exports	10.8% p.a.	8.5% p.a.

Source: Gear (1996).

Relatively small changes to the fiscal deficit, real bank rate and average import tariff, and somewhat bigger changes to public fixed investment growth and export growth, were expected to boost GDP growth materially (from 2.8% to 4.2% on average p.a.). An even more ambitious expectation was exercised with regard to job creation, where the faster GDP growth and slower average real private wage growth (0.8% instead of 1.4% p.a.) was hoped to be boosting job growth threefold annually (to 2.9% instead of 1% p.a.).

None of these objectives was especially challenging, except perhaps for the aim of tempering real private wage growth, that is, keeping wage growth down in order to increase labour absorption (widening the employment base), with the government not being a disinterested political onlooker to this process.

However, besides the real wage growth question, quite a number of these policy objectives did not come near implementation, some as a matter of government policy. Consequently, neither did the results match the earlier Gear expectations.

Examining Gear

There appear to have been five main process steps by which Gear sought to achieve its objectives.

Firstly, the rand's early 1996 depreciation to what was judged to be a more competitive level was considered a major opportunity for promoting exports and import substitution. It was government's intention to utilise this opportunity to the fullest (to eventually end the current account constraint over the balance of payments).

Secondly, in order to maintain this trade advantage, policy adjustments were needed to avoid erosion of the rand's newly acquired trade competitiveness through higher inflation. To this end:

- Government spending was to be restrained.
- Overall wage increases were to be kept in check.
- Import tariffs were to be reduced, lowering domestic costs for producers, compensating them for higher costs due to the rand depreciation.

In addition, with an eye on higher inflation once faster GDP growth materialised (due to demand pressures), there was a need for a tight monetary policy and above all productivity-linked wage increases. Inflation had to be kept below 10%, preserving the competitive advantage of the rand depreciation.

Thirdly, reduction in government consumption would:

- reduce dissaving;
- increase gross domestic saving from 18% to 22% of GDP, as;
- gross fixed investment was expected to increase from 20% to 26% of GDP; and
- the difference (that is, 4% of GDP) was to be provided by way of capital inflows.

Fourthly, through stronger export growth and additional tax incentives, a major aim was to create conditions for a substantial shift in the private fixed investment function, to be reinforced through higher real public fixed investment.

Fifthly, higher employment was to be achieved through:

- higher economic growth;
- real wage growth moderation;
- public sector fixed investment; and

- greater regulatory flexibility for labour.

These were Gear's main intentions, but from 1996–2000 things worked out quite differently.

As discussed earlier, in 1996 the government expected a mediocre economic performance through to 2000 if nothing was done and it proposed Gear to achieve a better performance. The eventual outcome, however, was considerably worse than either the original expectations without a proactive change in economic policy, or with Gear's intended results. The discrepancy is summarised in Table 5.

Table 5: Gear Objectives: Prior, Targeted and Actual, 1996–2000

Policy objective (annual average)	Prior to Gear	Target Gear	Actual
Export growth	6.9%	8.4%	6.6%
Real private investment	5.6%	11.7%	2.4%
Real public investment	2.7%	7.6%	3.8%
Real GDP growth	2.8%	4.2%	2.5%
CPI inflation	9.5%	8.2%	6.7%
Current account deficit (% of GDP)	1.4%	2.4%	1.0%
Private wage growth	1.4%	0.8%	2.5%
Formal job growth	1.0%	2.9%	–0.3%
New formal jobs ('000)	104	270	–30

Sources: Gear (1996), SARB Quarterly Bulletins.

What happened during 1996–2000? In nearly every aspect, things did not seem to turn out as expected, for a number of reasons, including:

- mistaken assumptions (regarding the export response);
- unintended consequences (the anti-inflation budget bias restrained public investment);
- mistaken policies (the monetary defence of the rand, giving rise to debilitating interest rate shocks); and
- an inability to control events (high wage growth), leading to more unintended consequences (formal job shrinkage).

Let us review these various factors in more detail.

Exports disappointed

In the event, the real trade-weighted rand not only depreciated by 9% in 1996, but then kept on depreciating—a full 20% in real terms between 1995 and 2000 (and an estimated further 30% in 2001 alone). Yet the real non-gold export performance during 1995–2000 disappointed, relatively speaking. It grew by 6.6% on average, compared to the expected 8.4% annually as intended by Gear.

This happened for three reasons. Firstly, the global economy encountered the Asian contagion during 1997–1998, deeply cutting emerging Asia's GDP growth and imports. As a result of this, Europe also experienced a fall-off in growth. With these two regions by far the biggest of our export markets, their weakened domestic and import demand reverberated onto our exports.

Secondly, the structure of our exports (and our industrial base in its entirety) is as yet not able to respond to real currency depreciation effectively. This is because over half our exports remain commodity-based and their demand internationally is income-driven and not price-driven. Rand depreciation therefore does not succeed in expanding global demand in these instances, nor are market share gains possible (as any price cuts are met by competitors defending their share, a 'world' clearing price being established for all suppliers).

By contrast, export demand for our industrial manufactures is price-sensitive, so it should benefit from rand weakness. Unfortunately, another more fundamental problem presents itself here. Globally, according to Strydom (2000), such trade is not so much 'inter' as 'intra', that is, it does not take place so much 'between' countries as that it takes place 'within' multinational (global) sourcing networks. Many of our industrial companies are not part of such networks, or their foreign affiliates see them as serving purely the African market. And yet it is such contracts that make exporting most dynamic. South Africa's lack of these trends/arrangements must be seen as part of our apartheid legacy of isolation, and export contract arrangements like those that exist in the motor industry remain for the moment the exception rather than the rule.

Thirdly, private fixed investment (as discussed further below) also disappointed for domestic reasons. This had implications for the export performance, as the decision to embark on investment projects, even if primarily domestically-oriented, tends to have an export component as well. Thus, increased investment activity in a competitively trading market economy, in which capital and labour have been rationalised and have become more efficiently organised (see Chapter 5 on the progress made with micro-economic restructuring), tends to reinforce exporting, and may henceforth far more easily pay its way in terms of imported input needs.

That our export performance still disappointed during 1996–2000 was therefore not only a reflection of global conditions and the nature and responsiveness of our existing exports to currency depreciation. It also importantly reflected the failure of private fixed investment to respond more vigorously to the envisaged Gear policy actions.

Real private fixed investment

Apart from real export growth not becoming quite the growth driver that it had been envisaged to be for private fixed investment growth, a bigger disappointment took place elsewhere. The rand eventually depreciated by more than ever expected (for reasons, see Chapter 4). Gear had not foreseen this nor did it anticipate the SARB's high interest rate defence, and the implications of this for growth.

The SARB responded to the 1996–1998 currency events by pushing real interest rates to a much higher level during 1996–2000 than 1990–1995 (on average they doubled). This had the effect of greatly slowing the economy during 1997–1999, lowering average GDP growth to 2.5% for 1996-2000, compared to the 4.2% annually hoped for by Gear. The demand-pull envisaged by Gear simply was not there. Besides, existing assets were used ever more efficiently (see Chapter 5), thereby still further reducing the need for expansion. Thus the desired drivers of real private investment growth remained in abeyance, and it only averaged 2.4% instead of the expected 11.7% annually as per Gear.

Real public fixed investment

This was expected to grow by 7.5% annually from 1996. There was a burst of activity at parastatals focused on Telkom in 1997–1998, but thereafter this tailed off again and growth in such investment only averaged 3.8% annually for the period. Real fixed investment by the government showed little inclination to accelerate much throughout the period, in part reflecting the budgetary constraint. Thus, such investment spending failed to provide the support for social delivery as intended, but it also did not augment overall demand in support of faster private investment and GDP growth.

The balance of payments

From the vantage point of mid-2001, the balance of payments performed much better than expected, for the current account by that time had entered into surplus (amounting to 0.7% of GDP annualised during the first half of 2001). This must be compared to the high GDP growth and 3% of GDP annual current account deficits expected by Gear. Reasons for the difference include a modest export windfall in late 2000 and early 2001 (partly on account of favourable global conditions of a very temporary nature). Mainly, however, it was the slow domestic economic growth (and subdued importing as a consequence), with the weak rand probably encouraging some import substitution (but see the 'Inflation' section below).

Gear had assumed in terms of the savings/investment balance that foreign capital to the tune of 4% of GDP would be flowing in on a consistent basis over time. This has not happened as yet.

Inflation

The real achievements of the 1996-2000 period turned out to be financial discipline and considerable efficiency gains. CPI inflation reduced structurally, averaging 6.7% during the period, and falling to 4.6% by late 2001. This was due to:

- fiscal discipline (budget deficit reduction);
- slow GDP growth (the high real interest rate regime);
- trade competition; and
- slowing unit labour cost growth due to an increase in productivity (mainly, but not exclusively, through labour retrenchment in the core of the formal sector—see Chapter 5).

Slow economic growth and budget restraint as inflation suppressants explain themselves. The remaining two factors need more focus: something fundamental—which has implications for the years ahead—was going on.

Firstly, let us look more closely at foreign trade. Gear proposed to maintain the 1996 depreciation of the real rand in order to retain the acquired advantage for exporters and import-competing local producers. To this end it had to prevent an acceleration of inflation, which would have eroded the rand's newly gained trade advantage.

Gear intended to contain inflation partly by reducing import tariffs further for domestic producers using imported inputs. As it turned out, the rand's real depreciation doubled between 1996–2000 while, according to Lewis (2001), import protection was not greatly lowered further from 1996. Domestic producers should therefore have been burdened by a sizeable increase in import costs on account of the depreciated rand and would have passed this on by raising their domestic prices, thereby giving inflation a strong boost.

This did not happen to the extent warranted by the extensive depreciation of the rand and we need to explore why. The first thing to note about the currency environment during this period was that it was marked by a major strengthening of the dollar, underperformance by the euro and shock depreciations in parts of the emerging world (especially in emerging Asia).

South Africa's exports are predominantly dollar-based, so a strong dollar was good news on this score. South Africa's imports (excluding oil) are primarily sourced in Europe and Asia, so the weak currencies of those regions were more good news as they limited cost pressure for us. The extent of the overall trade-weighted rand depreciation therefore overstates considerably what the rand's movement was against those currencies in the countries from where we mainly import. (On the whole we have to ignore the rand/dollar depreciation, except for oil imports, after which a much less severe trade-weighted depreciation materialises, in turn having a much lesser imported inflation effect than perhaps initially assumed.)

Moreover, if the rand did on average depreciate in real terms against importer-currencies, was that the end of the story? Or did those foreign producers defend their market share vigorously? Given the global trauma of this period—the 1997–1998 contagion, the loss of economic growth, increased global competition in shrivelling export markets—it was not unexpected that a ferocious defence was mounted by foreign producers. Anecdotal evidence suggests that our importers did not experience much of a currency shock other than against the dollar. Besides, they were also shopping for the cheapest suppliers in these years of stressful global conditions, lowering rather than increasing their costs.

But the scenario described above suggests something radically different. Instead of the rand depreciation granting local producers a protective shield behind which they could increase import substitution, this may not have been the reality. Instead, the very ferociousness of global competitors may still have put downward pressure on our local producers.

This was not to the point of these foreigners taking market share (for our imports did not increase to any extent other than explained by GDP growth), but mainly by simply creating market pressure on many of our local producers. In the old South Africa, this would have led to despair and increased market share for imports. In the new South Africa, something else apparently happened: our domestic producers responded to outside pressures by becoming more cost-effective.

In addition, they were under pressure from within and they reacted to these sources of cost-pressure (that is, labour demands and non-wage cost-enhancing labour legislation) with vigour. Instead of average real private wage growth of 0.8% and average public wage growth of 1.3% annually, as intended by Gear, these actually increased by at least 2.5% and 1.8% p.a. respectively during 1996–2000. These may seem small deviations, but they reflect enormous pressures (and even greater expectations about future developments).

With foreign competitors putting them under pressure and domestic labour unions and legislation increasing their cost structures, our producers were required to become proactive in order to survive. This they did with apparent aplomb, but with one unwanted outcome from a national perspective—a decline in formal employment (instead of the gains envisaged by Gear as one of its main objectives for the 1996–2000 period).

Jobless growth

According to Gear, real wage moderation along with faster GDP growth was to generate a cumulative 1.4 million formal jobs during 1996–2000, increasing these from 6.8 million in 1996 to 8.2 million in 2000. Instead, there was actually a decline to 6.7 million formally employed by 2000. This means that 1.5 million jobs (some 20% of an envisaged expanded formal sector) were eroded away by events not foreseen or proposed by Gear. What happened during those years?

We know that GDP growth averaged only 2.5% annually (and not 4.2% as predicted). This explains much of the jobless condition, but factors other than slow growth were a contributing factor. Real private fixed capital stock increased by 2.5% annually during the 1990s, probably further enhanced through the addition of IT consumables (software applications) not accounted as investment spending, yet greatly adding to the capital deepening in especially the services sectors.

GDP growth in the 1990s was therefore entirely generated through capital additions and productivity growth. No new formal labour was added—indeed it was reduced by 4% during the decade. Existing resources were used more effectively. Why and how did this happen, after decades devoid of such achievement? (See Chapter 5 for a more in-depth discussion of the extent thereof.)

In an economy such as South Africa's, which had been shielded for several decades, inefficiencies had probably accumulated over time, even as the world outside our borders became progressively more aggressive and productive, using technology, global economies of scale in trade and organisational change to force the productivity pace in response to increased deregulation, competition and innovation.

This impact of globalisation probably came progressively ashore in South Africa in the course of the 1990s, and this development is likely still deepening. It is manifested in a growing, 'revolutionary' productivity performance in the formal core of the economy (discussed at greater length in Chapter 5). Its main driver is not final demand and it is only to a limited degree contributed to by fixed investment (the traditional 'pull' factors of economic growth). Instead, some things appear to be pushing very strenuously.

Those things are trade (global producers of all kinds exerting market pressure), labour (organised labour demanding higher wages and benefits, along with legislation pushing employment equity), and technology (new, productive, innovative technology—see Chapter 8). The result is a much more intense use of existing resources to produce a unit of GDP. At a time of slow GDP growth, it means only moderate growth in fixed investment and even a small decline in formal employment.

As Chapter 5 will show, the core of the formal sector (the large, established employer organisations and companies) has reduced its employment by some 17% since 1990, yet according to the SARB (2001) the real private fixed capital stock increased by over 20% during this period. This implies a very sizeable increase in the capital/output ratio for the formal private sector during this period (that is, increased capital deepening per employee).

In terms of income distribution, the 1990s did not record a decline in capital's share in the national income, or an increase in labour's share. Despite the considerable pressure by the unions and affirmative action generally, private capital succeeded in maintaining its relative share of national income over the decade.

This had various impacts, with ramifications for the distribution of income:

- The high real wage gains indicated that employed ('insider') labour succeeded in increasing its real income. Yet the slice of national income going to labour did not change much (it fell slightly towards the end of the 1990s), and formal employment actually declined.
- This suggests that the distribution of income (between haves and have-nots) worsened: more people were without formal income, while fewer people were earning steadily more.
- As the majority of those benefiting from union and affirmative action were Black, the distribution of income within the Black community became more unequal. Chapter 9 contains data for 1990–1995 that highlight these shifts, which are expected to have continued through 2002.
- Both public and private sector affirmative action (that is, Black, Coloured and Indian preferment) displaced Whites, many of whom emigrated, with the remainder either retired or redeployed into the formal periphery (see Chapter 5). The latter feature probably was one of the main explanations for the observed change in income distribution in the 1990s, at the expense of the relative position of Whites and to the advantage of Indians, Coloureds and Blacks (see Chapter 9).
- Finally, there was the impact of redistributive fiscal policy, increasing the tax burden and changing the public spending bias. There was an even greater after-tax effect as fee-charging (for example, for education, healthcare, local and provincial services) impacted on higher incomes (see Chapter 7).

These tendencies, as described so far, also appear to have imparted a structural change in the balance of payments, where a lesser import propensity is probably developing. This should not be confused with a decline in import penetration, which in fact is still increasing, yielding trade efficiencies. Instead, what is being referred to is the spillover into imports as the GDP expands, finding local producers unable to meet such demand. If more output could be generated with existing resources, a lesser spillover into imports could develop. This would explain the manner in which unit labour cost has barely increased since 1999 as productivity growth reached 5% annually in the core of the formal sector, where most of the labour shedding was taking place, and staying over 5% p.a. through 2000. This, along with the impact of a reduced budget deficit, is the main explanatory force behind the structural decline in inflation. And up to late 2001 it had barely been checked by the weak rand or non-tradable administrated prices that were still holding out.

Structural changes are therefore at work in the South African economy on a considerable scale, so far without the benefit of much higher economic growth or an increase in formal employment. What are the future implications?

Policy Choices Going Forward

Gear proposed an export and investment strategy, which—as already discussed—disappointed on both these fronts.

To the extent that it favoured exports, Gear was also a strategy that proposed making us more dependent on other countries' growth. World trade in dollar terms grew by 6% annually in the 1990s, which comes across as an attractive source of high demand growth. Such a strategy, though, needs two qualifications:

- Firstly, our economic structure still has a heavy commodity dependence, while our exportable manufactures tend to be first-stage beneficiated products or based on relatively simple technology. The former go mostly into the global market (but due to their nature enjoy a slower rate of growth than overall world trade), while the latter are mostly exported into Africa (which due to underdevelopment and slow growth has a limited absorption capacity, once our exports had captured a 'natural' market share in the region). Either way, most of our export markets do not grow as fast as the global picture suggests.
- Secondly, such a dependence on external demand involves risk over which we have no control. If the economic growth of the other countries falls off cyclically, so too will our export demand, without our being able to take corrective action.

On the domestic front, our private demand growth disappointed because of macro-economic developments (the 1996–1998 rand events and subsequent increases in real interest rates). A repeat of such an occurrence has been made less likely by a change in policy (the conversion to a 'cleaner', purer float of the rand and inflation targeting as the anchor for interest rate policy, see Chapter 4).

This proposition was stress-tested following the precipitous decline of the rand in late 2001, when it reached R13.85 to the dollar from a level of R8.45 to the dollar four months earlier. This excessive rand undershoot succeeded in getting another imported inflation impulse going from early 2002. The subsequent inflation bulge was reinforced by a steadily rising oil price (Brent crude increasing from $18 per barrel in late 2001 to over $35 per barrel by March 2003); and a major rise in the maize price (white maize in early 2002 rising to over R2 100 per tonne).

Together these three events reversed the steadily declining inflation rate of preceding years. From a secular low of 5.8% in late 2001, CPIX inflation rose to 12.7% in late 2002 before starting to subside again. This was due to a strong revival in the rand (falling below R8.00 to the dollar again by March 2003), while the price of white maize also more than halved (to below R1 000 per tonne on the expectation of an excellent maize harvest), suggesting that a much lower inflation rate would prevail by late 2003.

Instead of triggering another disruptive interest rate shock aimed at containing the inflation eruption—as had happened on occasion in the past—this major 2002 inflation setback resulted in a much less severe interest rate response. The prime interest rate was raised by a relatively modest 4% in the course of 2002 at a time that inflation rose by 7%. In effect, this allowed a temporary drop in real interest rates to take place. Such a mild interest rate response was appropriate given that the inflation setback was of a temporary and supply-side nature, and not really amenable to interest rate treatment. Whereas exporters and import-competing local producers did gain from the rand's decline, the overall economy was denied a major net growth impulse from the rand depreciation, with the rise in interest rates sufficiently constraining domestic activity. Unlike previous such episodes, this policy tightening remained moderate enough to prevent a major economic pullback, as had happened in 1996–1998. Thus, the real economy sailed serenely on through it all, achieving real GDP growth of 3% in 2002, on a par with the 2000–2001 performance.

Besides monetary policy becoming less anti-growth biased during external currency disruptions, fiscal policy has also apparently effected a fundamental change in its anti-growth bias of recent years. Starting in 2002–2003, with the budget deficit down from 8.5% of GDP in 1992–1993 to 1.5% of GDP a decade later, and with tax revenue growth strong, due to GDP growth and more efficient tax collection, government finally permitted fiscal policy to become more growth-supportive. It has done this by allowing the planned budget deficit for 2003 to widen (aiming for 2.5% of GDP), and heavily increasing its social as well as infrastructure expenditures. This fiscal stance appears to be sustainable in coming years.

At the same time, fiscal, trade, labour, technology and global influences are all combining to make our economy more productive, more responsive, less prone to inflation and with less import spillover on current account than in preceding decades. We know that our exports continue to have their limitations, but we also have reason to believe that future investment decisions will lead at least partially to higher exports as well, if the currency were to remain attractively priced (see Chapter 4 for the progress with financial restructuring), and given the more competitively organised factors of production (see Chapter 5 on the progress with micro-economic restructuring).

We expect import demand to retain a certain income elasticity, linked especially to fixed investment. Nevertheless, its role has been changed by the productivity performance. This is possibly only temporarily, but exactly how much so? The test will come when we approach 4% GDP growth on a sustained basis once again. Along the way we are likely to find, as we have already seen since 1999 in the latest economic upswing, that a moderately growing economy no longer automatically tightens the current account condition unsustainably, provided the world economy is performing benignly and our currency is undervalued and supportive of exporting. Few people as yet want to buy this proposition that South Africa, through its many reforms, has succeeded in already fundamentally repositioning its economy with regard to its current account condition. Similarly, just as many have difficulty with the proposition that its inflation is steadily easing and is far advanced in its convergence with its major trading partners. Such a change in underlying inflation conditions and similarly the various reforms addressing the capital account constraint, should not be confused with the temporary inflation bulges following rand shocks, themselves still primarily a reflection of externally weak finances, and something not as yet fully addressed (but very much remaining on the reform agenda).

Most importantly, has Gear achieved its intended leap, not in growth (so far), but in financial discipline—budget deficit reduction and inflation—and in structural efficiency (productivity)? Are external and domestic finances to be further strengthened by belated privatisation and finally bolstered by exchange control liberalisation? And what kind of attractiveness would this create for foreign capital, once growth does begin to accelerate? South Africa's credit risk must be reducing, as reflected in the increased country credit rating from international rating agencies, with another series of positive outlooks granted in early 2003, suggesting an actual upgrade later in 2003 as we steadily move up the investment grade scale. On a three-to-five year view, South Africa will probably become the first big sub-Saharan country to win an A-credit-risk rating. Botswana, which is smaller, is currently the only sub-equatorial African country to be ranked in that way, while Australia, for example, enjoys an AA-rating.

Growth has upward potential if interest rate disruptions like those in 1998 are not repeated. Our present and changed policy mix makes such disruptions less likely in the future. Currently, the rand is allowed to take a greater share of any adjustment burden in the case of external pressures, and price stability is enhanced (to a far greater degree than in the past) by structural reform in the public and private sectors.

The SARB, though, will want to maintain its traditional vigilance over demand pressures, for which reason the level of real interest rates bears watching. As excessive rand volatility can trigger inflation bulges, the SARB remains inclined to counter rather than to condone these by way of moderate, neutralising interest rate responses, going by events in 2002.

Gear as formulated did not necessarily push exports for growth's sake only. Clearly, an outward-oriented development policy should also succeed in transforming any balance of payments constraints on sustained growth.

Gear's proposed currency undervaluation promoted export growth and import temperance, potentially transforming the current account condition and preventing exponential deficits from accompanying faster economic growth, though Gear still did project modest current account deficits. Gear also expressed the ambition of going back to higher fixed investment growth, a part of which would be for export production, prompted by attractive relative prices (due to the undervalued rand). Only a portion of such investment spending would be domestically funded, with a needed annual capital inflow of at least 4% of GDP assumed (equivalent to the expected savings shortfall and current account deficit). Thus, through better economic performance and reduced financial and political risks, Gear envisaged the capital account constraint to be ended as well.

An outward-oriented policy, aimed at promoting greater efficiency in the economy, would welcome strong export growth as a source for demand growth, but most of all to break the balance of payments constraint on growth. There would be room for domestically generated growth in demand as well, that is, consumption-driven and investment-sustained demand as accelerator effects come into play (the modern story behind Australia's high-growth performance since the early 1990s). Such domestic demand growth is a function of appropriate interest rate levels, tax rates and government spending that at least are not anti-growth in their impact.

Thus, Gear essentially sought to promote growth by putting the economy on a healthier footing, thereby making the current account condition more manageable, and boosting our attractiveness to foreign providers of capital sufficiently for the capital constraint on our development to be lifted. In making these proposals, we retained some of our traditional approach to economic development, as we continued to presume a domestic savings shortfall, current account deficit and capital account surplus, presumably a reflection of our emerging country condition (where heavy infrastructure needs warrant such an approach under 'normal' circumstances in which such access to foreign capital exists).

This is, of course, still a risky development approach, as it implies dependence on the outside world to augment our shortfall of capital, needed to fully fund our fixed investment effort. This is akin to the Latin American, American and Australian approaches to economic growth and development, which tend to rely (heavily) on access to global savings inflows over many years.

The alternative to these global risks is to become more self-sufficient, *not* like in the apartheid days of substituting imports through trade protection (thereby encouraging inefficiency), but by exporting more, saving more out of income, and funding all our investment needs domestically. This would be akin to an Asian approach of favouring a high savings and strong export regime, with such self-sufficiency minimising any balance of payments constraint on the current account, and thereby also reducing reliance on foreign capital inflows.

Such a development approach is still dependent on the world, this time for access to export markets. In an open global trading system, such access is as much a function of the ability to deliver, as is the creditworthiness requirement of the net foreign exchange absorber. These development models are just differently organised domestically.

To achieve an Asian-type development approach, the South African economy would have to become even more fundamentally transformed: lower cost structure, less consumption-inclination, higher savings and investment for exports. The necessary changes to achieve this condition, focusing on the exchange rate, supply of skilled labour, demands by organised labour, the costs of political activism, and the export orientation of our companies, amongst others, perhaps remain hard to attain, as they have proven to be in Latin America, America and Australia. The latter, though, could only afford their development approach because other countries were prepared to be net savings generators.

A further issue to consider is labour. What is going to happen to jobless growth? Faster GDP growth will create some jobs, but clearly labour needs to take cognisance of foreign competition and technology and our producers adjusting to these and other pressures on them.

Organised labour's membership rose spectacularly during the 1970s and 1980s as Black workers were for the first time allowed to organise too. Total union membership reached a peak of 3.8 million by 1998 (out of 10 million employed South Africans, and union membership at the time represented nearly 60% of the formally employed). Yet, some two years later, union membership was already down to 3.3 million (some 50% of the formally employed). Union-heavy sectors (such as mining, manufacturing and parastatals) shed labour most dramatically during these years, even as the sectors absorbing labour (mostly services and smaller businesses) were by their nature much less unionised (if at all), with pay-differentiation for more-skilled work also discouraging union membership.

With employment rationalisation not at an end in the older, better organised core sections of the formal sector, union membership can be anticipated to drop below 3 million and to 40% of the formally employed by 2003–2004 (see, for example, the Labour Force Survey from StatsSA for September 2002, which estimated only 2.8 million unionised workers in the economy).

New jobs can be expected to be created in less organised parts of the economy (smaller firms, services-based and higher-skilled labour being more pay-differentiated). These tendencies augur well for higher productivity gains as well as more market-related real wage growth, and therefore greater potential for new job creation. But they also suggest a learning curve for organised labour, something that can be observed as having taken place in other parts of the world already.

According to the International Labour Office (ILO 2001), reform should aim to make our labour market more flexible. For instance, reforms aimed at making labour markets more flexible in Austria, Denmark, Ireland and the Netherlands have reduced unemployment rates and have contributed towards lower youth and long-term unemployment. Successful reforms appear to be those measures that take the needs of workers and firms into consideration. The modern approach is as far as possible to apply information communication technology (ICT) in creating and sustaining high levels of employment. A new ICT-induced change in the labour market of especially OECD countries is the gradual termination of long-term employment with a single firm. People tend to change jobs frequently while working for multiple employers. Temporary and self-employed workers are on the rise. The low barriers to entry for online businesses encourage self-employment. Freelancing has become popular in the United States and the United Kingdom. Non-standard work agreements such as temporary jobs and part-time jobs have become significant in industrial countries. Countries reluctant to open their labour markets to accommodate these new flexible contracts are likely to retain higher levels of unemployment. The modern, ICT-exposed work environment contradicts single task jobs that are typical of inflexible labour markets. In the modern economy, job boundaries are disappearing and the work environment is gradually moving away from long-term repetitive tasks in favour of short-term, project-oriented assignments. Thus, flexible working times and flexible work locations and organisation are becoming increasingly important in defining work opportunities (see Katz and Darbishire 2000).

Gear expressed great hopes about education. Yet so far there is scant evidence of any significant improvement in education results. Indeed, rather the opposite impression currently prevails (see Chapter 7). In the short-term this does not matter too much, as there is a surplus of skills because of the same economic events that have prevented formal job growth since 1990. This also explains why it has been possible to absorb so relatively painlessly the large-scale emigration of skilled labour of the past decade. But any such reservoir of surplus skills will not be around indefinitely. Time is running short on the education front to do something effective about increasing the supply of skills, given the long lead times needed to produce an impact in the labour market. This effort will in all likelihood determine whether the economic growth rate now within reach will become sustainable, and indeed will be outdone by a yet more impressive development effort in the longer-term (see Chapters 7, 9 and 10).

Criticism of Government Policy

Three criticisms can be levelled at the government's economic policy of the late 1990s. Firstly, the slow pace of preparing for privatisation did more damage than perhaps sometimes realised. It may have kept political disagreement down, but earlier privatisation would have assisted in correcting our domestic savings imbalance more quickly. It would thereby have put less strain on the budget during the 1990s, achieving the same result compared to a more restrictive fiscal policy that ended up being less supportive of final demand and GDP growth than it could have been. Government consumption spending (social delivery) and public fixed investment (infrastructure) could both have been more supportive of growth.

Despite this criticism, it is not as if we have lost this option forever. Instead, privatisation seems more than ever a support for strengthening both our budgetary and external finances. The potential pay-off in support of the macro-economic balance (savings), risk perceptions, social delivery, infrastructure development and growth, thereby assisting in lifting the capital account constraint on our economy's performance, may still be considerable, if the government continues to proceed with privatisation as it claims to be its intention following the Telkom listing in February 2003 (see Chapters 4 and 9).

Secondly, economic growth was unnecessarily held back by the interest rate shocks that followed the rand events of 1996–1998. Thereafter, the rand was apparently expected to carry a larger part of any external adjustments, putting less pressure on interest rates and domestic growth compared to what happened in the late 1990s. Thus, following this change in policy emphasis, our domestic growth 'runs' should be able to lengthen, providing 'pull' incentive to fixed investment growth, just as trade competition and the new technological opportunities provide 'push' incentive for cost-reducing investments.

Thirdly, along with delayed privatisation and the learning curve in monetary policy, the demands by labour unions and the non-wage cost-enhancing nature of labour legislation have powerfully combined in contributing to jobless growth over a long period of time. Despite active forums such as Nedlac, where these things could be discussed, there has only been limited progress in recent years in slowing down real private wage growth.

'Gradualism' and the Future

Government's conduct of economic policy in recent years has known a certain 'gradualism'. It has taken time to prepare for privatisation. It took time to reduce the budget deficit and anti-growth bias of fiscal policy. It took time to adopt a more flexible attitude to the exchange rate in conjunction with an independent SARB. And on the wage front there was no visible political objection to high private wage growth even when accompanied by formal employment stagnation.

These labour demands made a powerful contribution to encourage producers to become more efficient. They perhaps unintentionally intensified the survival drive of producers, leading them into strong productivity gains that became the main force reducing inflation. This has improved financial stability and has become an important cornerstone of our attractiveness to foreign investors (lower risk) once faster growth can be had as well.

With the growth suppressants in our economy now weakening, and global market pressures and technology making it possible to enjoy high productivity growth, our labour unions should rethink their priorities. Instead of insisting on high real wage growth in its own right (encouraging labour shedding), let the coming of faster economic growth absorb all the available labour skills first and then put pressure on producers by creating labour (skill) shortages. Such resource pressure would create the needed incentive for greater labour training throughout the economy. The decision by employers to train more workers (new and existing) is a process akin to deciding on fixed investment. It will not happen in a vacuum, only in response to growth and resource scarcity.

If unions do not take this reality to heart, growth is likely to remain more jobless than is necessary, with less of a gain in income redistribution than may otherwise be possible. South African unions may take a long time to come around to this view, though labour unions nearly everywhere else in the modern world have. By contrast, government has already shown signs of thinking along different lines, by switching to a policy of wage moderation in the public sector as of 1998 (interrupted by events during 2002), and the attempt since 2000 to ameliorate some of the 'unintended consequences' of the new labour legislation in smaller businesses. The real force, however, is likely to be global trade competition, the 'economies of scale' efficiencies that accrue to exporters, the market pressure bearing down on local producers from abroad, and the technology alternatives that allow more efficient production through capital deepening. These forces are more powerful than the labour unions. They force producers to make survival adjustments to their operations, in the process shedding labour on an unprecedented scale, thereby weakening the influence of organised labour over real private wage growth.

In time, therefore, jobless growth may turn out to have been a temporary phenomenon only, characterising the 1990s as economic restructuring proceeded at full tilt at a time of slow growth and strong trade and labour pressures. Going forward, the trade pressures and new technologies will still be there to force further productivity gains, but the higher growth will see more net formal job employment.

Whether unemployment is then reduced quickly through high resource pressure, skill scarcity and the willingness to train available labour, will depend on the attitude of unions and government. The more the latter stay with favouring elitist outcomes, the more limited the job creation process will remain. The 'insider/outsider' phenomenon of the 1990s will probably remain with us for longer, and evolve under the influence of forces as discussed. On balance, we are likely to remain a high-wage economy, with high residual unemployment, and only slow progress in reducing this, despite progressing towards a higher rate of growth than seen in the 1990s. To the extent that this happens, it will reflect the balance of forces within society, and the remaining economic and social imbalances (such as a very unequal distribution of income, wealth and jobs) driving them.

The Cost of 'Gradualism'

It depends on how we see the political capacity of South Africa to absorb change as to whether the gradual implementation of certain crucial aspects of economic policy and the condoning of a high-wage policy constituted 'Big Mistakes' in an overall context. The government opted to put into place the 'right' principles for long-term development as embodied in Gear (especially fiscal restraint and inflation reduction). It then chose to meet some of its social objectives immediately, some of them through its labour initiatives but bearing in mind that it largely inherited rather than created the labour dispensation making for high real private wage growth. It more specifically allowed privatisation to be implemented gradually rather than radically. These actions were political decisions that represented trade-offs between short- and long-term delivery and provide an indication of what the country can forbear.

Does South Africa have the staying power to continue with its chosen course? The government (as the ultimate insider) presumably has made its political calculations and its domestic and global audiences have questioned these choices. So far, there is no indication of a change of mind on the side of the government, or of its being unable to deliver its chosen policy mix. The country's largest labour union Cosatu (with 1.8 million affiliated members) has regularly over the intervening years suggested a reopening of the Gear debate, but so far with no noticeable success, at least not up until early 2003. If anything, in late 2001 Cosatu appeared to be jeopardising its continuing political alliance with the ANC government by insisting on being heard on the privatisation issue.

In every dimension (budget, monetary, privatisation, trade, public fixed investment, and even in some respects, labour), economic policy reform appears to be more than halfway to finality in terms of the Gear objectives. We can include in this estimate the intended privatisation of public assets in terms of their preparation phase. In other words, the hardest part of the long reform process actually already lies behind us. The last push may coincide with a steadily stronger economic upswing, which should be the easiest time to absorb the final adjustments and to encourage private economic agents to increase their risk-taking.

The country, though, is paying an economic price for such 'gradualism' (especially the many unemployed and underemployed, the so-called 'outsiders'—see Chapter 5). But presumably the government did buy political time with gradualism in at least one part of the social sphere, especially among the up-and-coming new labour elite—the new 'insiders'. But the labour laws remain a sticking point, much more modelled on inflexible parts of continental European policy (with its vast welfare systems) than the more flexible market approaches of English-speaking countries. They will not necessarily prevent economic policy in the years ahead from delivering higher growth, but the growth may be more jobless than intended, and skewed in favour of skilled rather than less-skilled work. This remains a problem, with such a large part of the labour force less skilled and with a change in education performance not something simply to be achieved overnight.

It would have been better if the economy had retained a larger component of less-skilled labour for longer, allowing time to recast the education effort. The chosen route of transforming the economic structure has encouraged capital deepening and favoured skilled labour, finding both the labour force and the education effort unready and incapable of making this transition quickly. In this respect, at least, some of the mistakes of the struggle decades continue to be repeated. The outcome has been a very large increase in unemployment and its associated social ills (for example, crime). The policy of allowing labour 'insiders' for too long to gain high real wage increases and be favoured by new cost-increasing legislation regarding labour practices had consequences, which were perhaps not adequately thought through. Unless, that is, we wish to be politically cynical and claim that symbolically it was a political imperative that a new Black labour elite was going to be favoured for a while. That this apparently came at the expense of less-skilled labour was incidental, if unintended, but entirely foreseeable.

Future political and social imperatives will decide whether the country creates a narrowly based 'small' Black middle class, or whether it succeeds in building a broad-based large one. The keys to this question are partly the promotion of faster economic growth, partly a structural deepening of our productive base (especially an increase in the number of small and medium-sized enterprises) and partly the future education effort. Primarily, however, it will be decided by the labour dispensation in the sense of distributing available income among the relative few 'labour insiders' as opposed to among the many 'labour outsiders'. A more efficient market allocation will favour the development of a broad-based Black middle class, thereby expanding the democratic base. In contrast, strong unions, little competitive restraint and proactive legislation will favour the development of a small Black middle class, with attending social ramifications.

4 PROGRESS WITH FINANCIAL RESTRUCTURING

In the early 1960s, South Africa's national finances were impeccably Swiss in nature. There was a low tax burden, strong currency, low inflation, low government indebtedness, minimal foreign debts, a high savings rate, strong capital inflows, few balance of payments problems, and strong foreign reserves. Only exchange control marred an otherwise impressive record. Given the political situation at the time it was impossible to maintain such exemplary financial stability, but this should not deflect from its existence before the apartheid troubles started to weigh more seriously on the country and its finances. South Africa was attracting copious inflows of foreign capital and it was achieving a historically high economic growth rate built on a strong natural resource base, half a century of industrialisation (based on import substitution), the stimulation afforded by the isolation of two World Wars, and an inclination to being financially strict and working hard.

This strong financial legacy was frittered away in the space of three decades. By the early 1990s, the tax burden had more than doubled to over 20% of GDP. This was perhaps not high by global standards, but it was severely penalising in a country without a social security system worthy of the name. The corporate tax rate had been raised to 50%, the budget deficit reached over 8% of GDP, government debt had topped 50% of GDP, and there was panic talk of being in a 'debt trap'. Externally, the net foreign reserves dropped to (nearly) zero in the run-up to the general election of 1994. The situation was actually worse than this, as the SARB at the time was sitting on a net forward book position that was relentlessly rising and would peak at near $25 billion in the course of that year (this in an economy with a GDP of barely $125 billion).

With a new government about to come into power, whose main support base was the country's poor—nearly half of whom were unemployed—the palpable fear was of greatly increased taxation, spending and deficit borrowing: in short, the kind of short-sighted populist policies that in other countries at other times had led to financial ruin.

The ANC government, however, turned out to be financially conservative. For some this reflected inexperience ('wait until they find out how government works'), while others perceived a genuine sense of discipline.

Given the collective experience of its diverse leadership, it was perhaps not so surprising that the government proceeded cautiously. Civil conflict had exhausted the country financially and economically—though not beyond repair. The challenge was to keep the country a going concern while effecting the changes that were overdue, readying it for stronger performance in time. Only this would generate the means by which South Africa could be developed successfully, and the poor be uplifted eventually.

Policy Stances Prevailing in the Mid-1990s

Government policy of the mid-1990s was clothed in politically correct terminology and programmes. The Reconstruction and Development Programme (RDP) was heavy on promises of social delivery, and in some respects it did deliver. Glaring inequalities were addressed by reducing the subsidies for previously privileged constituents (mainly Whites) in, for example, education, health care and local taxation. Government wages and salaries were boosted sharply (especially at the lower end of the pay scale), mainly at the expense of service provision and infrastructure maintenance and expansion. In addition, the transformation of the public sector was pursued with great vigour with the aim of achieving a more representative racial balance. Thus redistribution gained its strong emphasis.

These were not small changes, but they were not allowed to devastate the public finances. Financial conservatism was an early hallmark of the ANC government, in the manner in which the budgets of 1994 (drafted in consultation), 1995 and 1996 were crafted. Subsequently, in early 1996, such fiscal discipline was formalised as a strategic component of the government's macro-economic Gear (Growth, Employment and Redistribution—see Chapter 3) strategy. Gear made explicit what until then had come to be understood implicitly, that is, that the budget deficit as a share of GDP was to be gradually reduced by various means.

Initially, economic recovery from 1993 onward had boosted revenue growth. The tax burden had also at first been allowed to rise by not fully compensating for bracket creep in a still-high inflation environment. Despite increased expectations and widespread calls for greater social spending, departmental spending budgets were not allowed to go out of control. Indeed, wage moderation became the norm from 1998 onwards once a better salary dispensation had been enacted. And throughout the

ANC government's period in office, better tax collection has been achieved.

Much was therefore accomplished in a relatively short space of time. As Chapter 7 on social delivery will highlight, the government did succeed in making a serious down-payment on its promises to political supporters of greatly increasing social delivery. At the same time, the public service was reconstituted and salaries greatly boosted, benefiting a large group of middle-class supporters of the government. This was achieved while simultaneously reducing the budget deficit from over 8% in 1992 to 1.5% of GDP by 2001 (see Graph 4), reducing long-term interest rates on government debt from over 15% to 10%, and reducing the outstanding public debt from above 50% to 46% of GDP (admittedly in part by quite legitimately revising GDP higher in the course of periodic reassessments).

It is generally recognised that this achievement by government to date is only a modest midway station on a journey that has much further to go. The government's eventual aims are to:

- reduce the public debt to well below 40% of GDP (mainly by way of privatisation proceeds);
- maintain the tax burden just below 25% of GDP (with the top personal income tax rate already reduced to 40% in early 2002); and
- further lower long-term interest rates into single-digits, reflective of inflation eventually falling to a level in line with our main trading partners (2% to 3%).

Economic incentive should improve considerably through these efforts, and there should simultaneously be a reduction in the debt-servicing burden of the government. If this were to be accompanied by even higher economic growth (approaching 4% p.a. on average), it would open up considerable scope for greater social delivery. It would be the cumulative improvement thereof over time, which would constitute the true social transformation that the government is seeking to effect in South Africa.

After a 50-year detour, the country would have regained both its Swiss finances of old as well as the ability to sustain healthy economic growth, while supported by a viable social dispensation. This pay-off is within reach, provided financial reform continues to progress as now foreseen and here projected.

Although the economy had already cyclically troughed in early 1993, the new upswing was delayed by the political uncertainty ahead of the

Graph 4: Government Budget Deficit*, 1993–2006

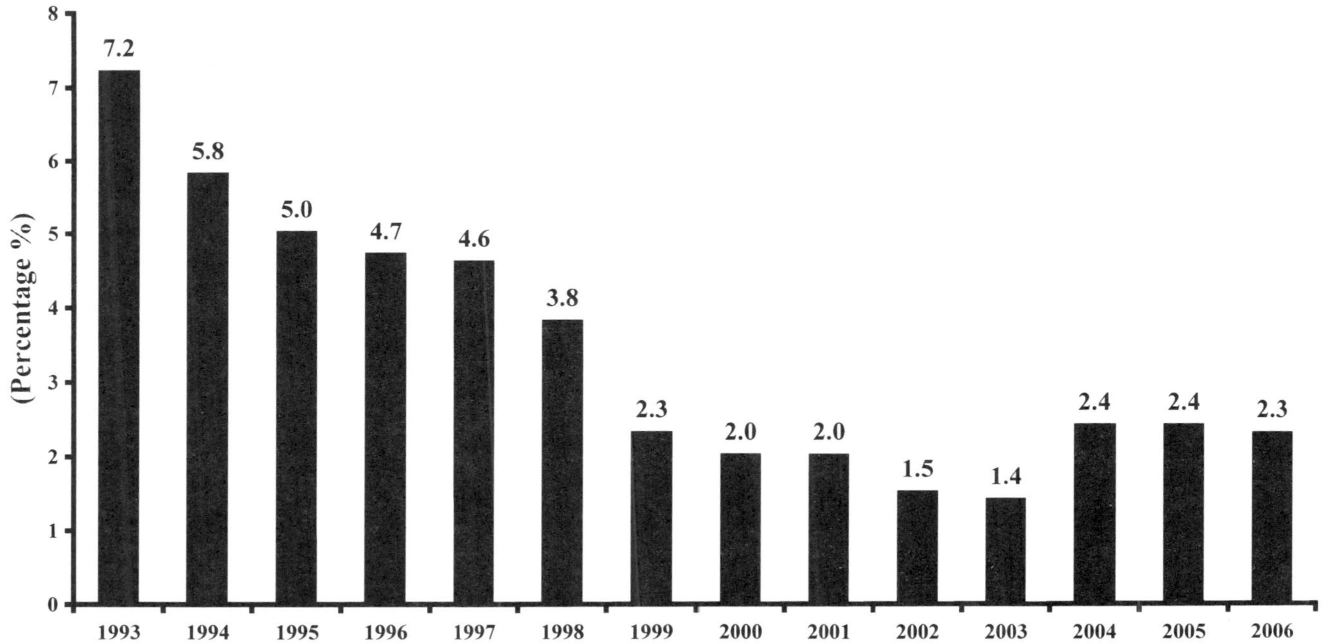

Source : Ministry of Finance, Budget Speech, 26 February 2003

* Year to March

democratic election in April 1994. When the outcome of this election was peaceful, a euphoric mood gripped financial markets as much as boardrooms and consumers.

Established consumers became easier in their spending, while many others enjoyed large wage increases for a while and gained access to credit for the first time. Many businesses, which had pared down inventories and limited their expansion plans, suddenly found themselves on the wrong side of a vigorous business upswing. Their belated response, in boosting inventory demand and dusting off investment budgets, further reinforced the acceleration in GDP growth during 1994–1995. Following the 1994 election, there was a return flow of capital (most of it of a portfolio nature that had departed during 1992–1993 ahead of the democratic election), which allowed the net foreign reserves to be modestly replenished and the rand to recover. In turn, it resulted in an improving leads-and-lags situation (the ability of exporters and importers to accelerate or slow down their payments or receipts of foreign exchange within the strict confines of exchange control regulation) as 1994 progressed, allowing the forward book to be rapidly reduced through 1995 even while funding a moderate current account deficit. It also set the scene for the next attempt at structural reform, now that the election had been successfully traversed, and a new political regime had started to make its policy intentions known.

At this remove, in early 2003, the policy mistakes that were made stand out clearly, for we know what subsequently transpired. However, we should not forget the realities facing the policymakers when the reform choices of the early and mid-1990s were made. In looking back, three crucial decisions were made which are understandable in terms of the tenor of the times, but whose combination proved a mistake:

- Early exchange control reform was favoured by all.
- The SARB retained its central aim of achieving macro-economic stability by targeting both interest rates and the rand, even while integrating more closely into the global financial system, yet with very limited foreign reserves at its disposal.
- Privatisation was kept over for the long-term.

Exchange Controls

For a country engaged in a war—even a war with itself as in the case of South Africa—the imposition of exchange controls will always be a temptation in order to strengthen its national defence. For those who for years proposed that it would be better to lift South Africa's exchange controls as quickly as possible, this was just another way of saying (though not at all consciously in too many instances), that the White regime should see sense and capitulate as soon as possible. Coincidentally, it would free the way for those who wanted to escape the coming of Black government. Obviously, exchange controls are not an efficient economic policy tool. But they are a means to keep a political dispensation afloat, if only a little beyond its sell-by-date, in the process contributing in diverse ways to the further undermining and hollowing out of the economy and its finances. For the longer such a conflict continues, the bigger the structural damage tends to be.

While exchange controls are in effect they do grant a partial degree of freedom to the monetary policymaker. This can be seen in China today, where its currency (the renminbi) is not yet fully convertible (capital account transactions remain controlled). This fact helped China to survive the Asian contagion of 1998 as domestic capital could not become mobilised to destabilise the currency in response to outside speculative pressures.

Something similar applied to South Africa between 1960 and 1995, when a parallel currency dispensation existed for non-resident investors in various guises. What was first termed the 'blocked' rand, then the 'securities' rand and eventually became known as the 'financial' rand, isolated capital account transactions by non-resident foreigners, separating them out from the commercial rand transactions of residents on both current and capital accounts. This mechanism allowed the SARB to conduct the monetary policy that it did. As will be shown, its lifting turned out to be a more traumatic experience than understood by most at the time.

Early Reforms

Monetary policy was one of the earliest reform arenas—along with labour reform—possibly because it was subjected to enormous strains as the political death struggle of the lingering old regime overburdened the national finances. Furthermore, best global practice was changing during this period, confronted as it was by more rapid inflation and greater exchange rate volatility worldwide on account of growing international capital flows and economic imbalances. As money supply growth and inflation steadily gained momentum in the 1970s, the SARB switched to a more flexible exchange rate policy (allowing the rand to lose value gradually in recognition of changed circumstances).

Eventually, the SARB proposed to move away from an ineffective policy of credit controls that merely distorted the credit and pricing channels, in favour of a market-based interest rate policy. This was effected in stages from 1979 onwards, yet it could not undo the general drift to greater financial instability. This was partly due to the distorting influence of the gold boom of 1979–1980. But even more important, was the systematic deterioration in fiscal policy as government faced a rising tide of social demands and conflict—internally as well as externally—at a time of a deteriorating growth performance and a tightening balance of payments constraint.

It was a poorly kept secret at the time that the SARB was independent in name only. In reality, the SARB governor would check with the head of government when he wanted to change interest rates, and for a period was not able to do what an independent monetary policymaker would have done. The misguided interest rate cut ahead of a by-election in late 1984, which immediately and derisively became known as the 'Primrose Prime', was the most flagrant example. Less visible were the moments when interest rates should have been raised, but were not, blocked by political fiat. SARB Governor Gerhard de Kock never knew the luxury of independence that his successor Chris Stals apparently knew from day one in office. This *status quo* remained applicable under the new government for Stals, and is still true for his successor, Tito Mboweni.

The government had two political expectations of monetary policy in the 1970s and 1980s:

- keeping the rand more stable than warranted by underlying conditions (causing it at times to become overvalued); and
- preventing higher interest rates from retarding economic growth.

To allow the rand to weaken was seen as a loss of national esteem (still thinking with Swiss standards of a bygone era in mind, with especially the Bretton Woods arrangements—rigidly fixed exchange rates—remaining an intellectual anchor). More practically, as related years later by a senior central banker, exchange rate depreciation was seen technically as fanning inflation, apart from politically eroding the living standard of the elite middle class, much of whose 'prosperity' was supported by imported goods. Consequently, the government found itself under attack from all sides, from the left as much as from the right of the White political spectrum, regarding a currency trending down and interest rates trending higher.

The disengagement of foreign capital from South Africa (described in Chapter 1) effectively ended the continuation of foreign support that had accommodated domestic arrangements for many years. The high national savings rate of the 1960s had been eroded away as stagnation had taken hold. In addition, the rand became overvalued and the global environment deteriorated in the 1970s and early 1980s (outside of temporary gold booms in 1974 and in 1979–1980). Taken together, these developments structurally increased the balance of payment deficits (due to higher import inclination combined with an eroding export base). Such deficits were no longer easily financed by supplementary inflows of foreign capital. It was a stressful condition that led to periodic attempts at cutting back the domestic economy via higher interest rates (when disaster loomed), even as the rand was systematically weakened over time.

The misguided social (apartheid) and autarkic (self-sufficiency) policies of the White government ensured a misallocation of scarce investment capital and dwindling economic returns. Simultaneously, equally unsound macro-economic policies contributed to a deepening balance of payments constraint, heightened susceptibility to inflation, and led to increasingly frequent interruptions of business cycle upswings, shortening the latter's duration and negatively affecting private investment decisions. This caused growth momentum to be lost steadily as stagnation (cessation of growth) took centre stage, gradually becalming the economy during the 1970s and 1980s, with short-lived gold booms constituting only temporarily confusing diversions.

Interest Rate Policy

For a while during the 1980s, interest rate policy in South Africa, which should have been more effective in controlling inflation and contributing to a better-performing economy over time (the aim overseas), became pro-cyclical rather than contra-cyclical. In other words, it amplified the swings of the business cycle rather than assisting in smoothing out such volatility. It similarly worsened financial instability via a more volatile rand exchange rate and inflation.

The best illustration of this can be seen in the large fluctuations in nominal and real interest rates during the 1980s. By keeping interest rates too low during upswings (indeed, heavily negative in real terms), and by moving them too high before long in order to abort a dangerous situation developing on the balance of payments (in the process triggering deep business downswings), monetary policy worsened cyclical volatility. This progressively damaged expectations with severe implications for foreign capital flows, fixed investment and savings behaviour.

The end came with the so-called debt standstill of August 1985. Even though the politicians would still need another decade to come to an agreement, the room for manoeuvering had been greatly reduced. The economy did recover from the recession of 1985–1986, but essentially had lost all forward movement on the production side. Keeping interest rates low could revive demand, but the balance of payments could not stand this for long with a debt standstill negotiated and in place. Economic stagnation had become an accomplished fact as the severe balance of payments constraint strangled all attempts at growth revival.

With the political watershed came greater effective independence for the monetary policymaker. Whereas the closing years of De Kock as governor of the SARB had seen yet another steep cyclical increase in interest rates during 1987–1989, it was the change in state presidents in August 1989 that opened the way for a change in policy. State President Botha had frequently dictated terms to the SARB, but State President De Klerk gave incoming SARB Governor Stals the breathing space he needed to make the switch in monetary policy that he considered necessary. Consequently, the real monetary policy revolution got underway, belatedly but still in time to make a huge difference to what transpired in the 1990s decade.

This monetary revolution was to have its ups and downs. The clear initial winner was a policy of imposing adequate, yet stable, real interest rates on the economy in line with its structural realities. This meant that interest rates should be higher than inflation at all times, while taking into account the country's low savings rate, still undisciplined fiscal policy and distorted economic structure, and the implications thereof for a constrained balance of payments and inflation behaviour. The current account deficit simply could not be allowed to become too big at any time, besides which there was the aim of reducing inflation as well as transforming exchange control.

During 1989–1995, Stals succeeded in imposing a fairly stable real interest rate on the economy, which for the prime overdraft rate (the main benchmark for commercial bank lending to their 'prime' corporate and individual customers) turned out to be 5.5% on average for the period.

Inflation

Much has been made of how SARB monetary policy has contributed to lowering inflation during this period, from an all-time peak of 21% Consumer Price Index (CPI) inflation in 1986 (mostly a reflection of the massive rand depreciation in the preceding two years), down to 15% CPI inflation in 1990, and from there down to 10% by 1995. However, as has been discussed in Chapter 3, micro-economic developments probably played the greater role in this process.

Unwinding inflation from its 21% peak in 1986 was a matter of stabilising the rand after its massive 1984–1985 fall. This the SARB did by pushing the prime rate to 25% and effectively keeping it there for a year while the economy entered an unforgettably sharp recession. But this monetary policy 'squeeze' only brought the economy back to its underlying, by now embedded, long-term inflation level of around 15%. The breaking of this inflation momentum—which dates from 1989–1990, as Chris Stals became SARB governor—marked the beginning of structurally lowering the inflation rate.

The period 1989–1995 witnessed both a protracted economic downswing (and eventual recession) during 1989–1993 as well as a vigorous post-election upswing in 1994–1995. Insufficient demand (and drought impacting heavily on agricultural production) became a debilitating factor in pushing the economy into recession during 1992–1993, but abruptly disappeared from the scene as of early 1994 as the outcome of the general election ignited a broad-based economic and financial euphoria.

Throughout 1989–1995, money supply growth equalled or exceeded nominal GDP growth. Therefore, if monetary policy during this period did do anything favourable, it was to prevent even more lively credit expansion than would otherwise have happened if interest rates had been lower than they were allowed to be. In other words, the SARB conducted a policy of monetary 'containment' rather than one of curtailment. As to lowering inflation, the SARB's macro-economic policy of restraining credit growth may have made a contribution, but was probably not the primary factor.

The rand was volatile during the period, though no longer deteriorating, as its massive undervaluation after the mid-1980s episode, together with stagnant economic growth and a neutral balance of payments, helped to re-establish a semblance of stability in the economy.

In the lead-up to April 1994, few people were thinking of a stable rand and lower inflation ahead. Instead, expectations were fixed on the coming political change and the likely further withdrawal of foreign capital.

It would seem, therefore, that inflation became eroded mostly for micro-economic reasons, but against the background of a stable financial system. In particular, greater trade reform and thus increased import competition played a leading role as import quotas were abolished and tariffs reduced. In addition, lower global inflation (indeed disinflation) and the beginning of wrenching structural change in our domestic economy were being felt. The latter implied shedding of especially less-skilled labour, in part in response to trade changes, in part to bigger labour demands regarding wages, benefits and working conditions, but even more so in response to technological deepening. The consequent labour market pressures contained the wildest demands made by organised labour in the post-1994 euphoric period, while simultaneously greatly boosting productivity growth, especially in the formal core of the economy.

It does not appear to be a generally recognised fact that labour productivity in this formal core had only grown by 3% for the whole of the 1970s decade. The 1980s decade was even worse: productivity improved by only 2% (in other words, at most 0.2% annually for twenty years). This started to change with a vengeance when trade reform was introduced, at a time which closely coincided with State President De Klerk's opening of parliament speech in February 1990, heralding the political watershed to come.

Both these changes appear to have had an electrifying effect on the country's private sector, with labour shedding outside mining and the public sector seriously taking off from 1990. In retrospect, it comes across as a proactive business response aimed at competitively surviving these fundamental changes. The economy was going to open up to outside competition, at the very moment when organised labour was supposedly going to be favoured by an incoming Black government. As the new government did nothing to inhibit these responses in any way, the structural change underway since 1990 has favoured capital deepening as well as more trade specialisation. It has seen labour productivity steadily accelerate, especially in the formal core. There it averaged 3.4% p.a. during the 1990s decade and 5% during 1998–2001, even as annual wage settlements decreased from over 17% (nominally) in 1990 to 7.5% (nominally) a decade later. Despite a weaker rand during the 1990s, faster increases in non-tradable service prices (especially certain administered prices), and a mini-oil crisis during 1999–2001, inflation was steadily being pulled lower throughout the decade. From levels exceeding 15% in 1990, headline CPI inflation by late 2001 had reached 4.3% (and CPIX inflation had fallen to a cyclical low of 5.8%), with the potential of being reduced towards the 3% level on a permanent basis over the course of the 2000s decade. This process, though, was likely to be periodically interrupted, as it was already during 2002, as inflation rebounded on the back of another short-lived 'shock' rand depreciation and rapid maize and oil price increases were brought on by unfavourable global conditions.

Exchange Control Liberalisation

Apart from maintaining real interest rates at what was considered a sustainable level, and maintaining a healthy banking system via its regulatory role, the SARB was deeply involved with the currency. Exchange control reform was supposedly the responsibility of the minister of finance, but clearly SARB advice was sought at all times. It was the management of the currency and the liberalisation of exchange control that turned out to offer the most vexing policy challenges of the 1990s, also because both had ramifications for domestic interest rate policy.

The SARB leadership of this period had been steeped in monetarist thinking, in terms of which there is no inflation without excessive money creation. Furthermore, currency stability as an anchor for containing inflation expectations was a hallmark of this generation, a legacy of the Bretton Woods arrangements. This must also be understood against a backdrop at the time of an as yet unreformed budget and economic structure, which maintained an inflation bias. 'Defending' the currency was thus a natural inclination. It would, in fact, be more correct to say, for a currency that was forever backsliding, that the operational term was 'dirty' (that is, managed) floating, with a bias in favour of stabilisation.

This inclination was not to remain without repercussions as reform was implemented.

It was a mindset that operated naturally within the confines of exchange control and with the undeniable luxury of having non-residents ring-fenced by a financial rand. Non-residents were the only people enjoying the benefit of a freely convertible rand (in their case, the financial rand). By contrast, transactions by residents were very much governed by exchange control (and conducted in the commercial rand only). This meant that the SARB was at worst confronted with the structural deficiencies of the economy as these determined the level of exports and demand for imports transacted in the commercial rand, and did not also have to take into account foreign currency speculators. A special complication was the so-called 'leads-and-lags' phenomenon discussed earlier. Nonetheless, this ring-fenced reality gave the SARB considerable power to influence the demand and supply of currency, in the process allowing it to impact on the level of the commercial rand, and on domestic arrangements (demand, growth, and inflation).

When financial liberalisation got underway, this mindset was not adjusted equally fast, with certain consequences for which the country paid a price. Perhaps the most important consideration here was that despite the political breakthrough of 1994, with South Africa being 'welcomed' back internationally, the scepticism of foreign providers of capital maintained an effective capital account constraint that would take time to be unwound.

The big move was the abolition of the financial rand in mid-1995. This brought the financial transactions of non-residents into the ambit of the commercial rand. A big gorilla was taken on board, so to speak, without the SARB apparently being sufficiently aware that its own influence had commensurably been reduced. Worse, too many domestic players appeared to be blissfully unaware of the increased currency risks, even after the experience of 1985 that should have provided plenty of warning, apart from experiences in other emerging countries similarly situated.

At the same time, exchange control was being relaxed. It affected individuals, companies and institutions in different ways but with the same net overall effect—a steady outflow of capital. In certain years this was rewarded by an even bigger net inflow (mostly of a portfolio nature), but in other years it was not.

The idea with financial liberalisation is to strengthen the country's economy. But if the timing or sequencing of reform is only slightly unfortunate, either because of global conditions, or because a different sequence would have been better, we can expect to pay a steep price. The country was not bankrupted by the events of 1996–1998, but the changeover in policy emphasis could have been undertaken in less costly ways.

When a country makes its currency more convertible, as South Africa did when it abolished the financial rand, it must allow for the fact that the currency market broadens and deepens. The new players will have something to say over what they encounter along the way. For the SARB, with still very low foreign reserves, wanting to continue as if nothing had changed, came close to wanting its cake and eating it, too. Modern central banks, in fact, need to surrender power to markets as the latter get bigger and stronger, especially so if the country in question is a small one (at least, that is the international experience).

Perhaps more fundamentally, the budget reform and micro-economic changes, already underway for some years, were reducing the country's inflation inclination, while the force of globalisation internationally was assisting in lowering global inflation pressures. Provided it would not be exceptional (as happened in late 2001), currency volatility would potentially impart less of an inflation shock pass-through than before, allowing a more general anti-inflation approach to be successful. Acceptance of this idea would take time to vest. As yet, the capital account constraint had not demonstrably been lifted.

Within six months of abolishing the financial rand in July 1995, the country was basking in a heavy inflow of foreign (portfolio) capital as part of the post-1994 euphoria. The SARB was assiduously fine-tuning the rand to an 'anchor' level of R3.60 to the dollar; and local companies were responding to this policy in the presence of double-digit forward interest rates by electing to go increasingly uncovered on their foreign exchange transactions.

Something was bound to happen, and it duly did: one really big order, selling rand in favour of foreign currency, and our first post-modern currency crisis was underway in the early part of February 1996.

In essence, the technical nature of what happened in early 1996 was no different from what had happened in 1985. Then there had also been such a major rand event, similarly taking place against the background of a unitary rand (the financial rand having been temporarily abolished in 1983). Large numbers of exporting and importing companies with uncovered foreign exchange rate exposures found themselves suddenly losing money as a few big (speculative) transactions depressed the exchange rate just enough for potential losses to be created on such exposures. It was enough, given the sense of shock and uncertainty about what would come next, for panic to take hold.

As exposed companies tried belatedly to cover in, they found no willing counter-parties (except a beleaguered SARB). Their sheer volume of rand-selling depressed the exchange rate even further. Only once this frenzy subsided, generally a matter of weeks to months, would the rand stabilise again, but now worth 15% to 30% less than before the stampede commenced, with no way back.

Of course, an officially floating currency should not experience a crisis. Instead, it should 'float'. The rand did not 'float', because though the SARB was claiming that it was floating, it was also 'managing' the level of the rand in an attempt to use it as an anchor for stabilising inflation expectations and as an added bonus to pull in boundless amounts of foreign portfolio capital 'on the cheap'. Perhaps it was being assumed that, given the political change and the post-1994 'euphoria', also fleetingly noticeable among foreign providers of capital, the capital account constraint should already be much less severe as our newly acquired attractiveness was popularly evident?

That is not ultimately how the global currency markets operate. What was called 'dirty' (managed) floating may have worked in a partially-controlled environment where a dual exchange rate and exchange control partitioned market players with regards to origin (that is, residents as opposed to non-residents). With the dual currency gone, it was not only investors in search of high interest returns who were attracted, but also very large international speculators focusing on possible currency plays. With these players entering the arena, the game changed somewhat, enough to rule out 'dirty' floating as a viable policy as it merely attracted powerful speculators for an easy bet against a chronically weak central bank (something nearly everyone internationally appeared to have understood at the time, except apparently the central bank in question).

Currency misalignment is a major risk once controls are surrendered and the whims of the free market start to drive what remains an incompletely reformed economy (and society), however vigilant a central bank. The proof of a capital account constraint having ended, must be experienced in the eating of the pudding, as foreign capital remains easily accessible even in more difficult circumstances. This was, for example, Australia's experience in the 1990s, but had as yet not happened to South Africa at the time.

The country paid dearly for the policy of managed floating of the late

1990s, which did not bring a permanent capital inflow bonanza. We experienced six months of gains in 1995, followed by an abrupt outflow of capital, a 20% rand depreciation, two interest rate increases during 1996 (and more of a rise in real interest rates), even as the solidly based economic expansion of 1994–1995 unnecessarily and prematurely started to falter. This was a steep price to pay for not correctly reading the implications of financial liberalisation as sequenced at the time, or the exchange rate policy then effected.

There was a temporary recuperation in 1997, until the Asian contagion erupted at mid-year (of itself a similar crisis to what we had experienced in early 1996, only on a much bigger scale as various countries were affected simultaneously). We should have been forewarned by that experience, and have realised that in 1998 global sensitivities about potentially weak currencies were going to be heightened.

Instead, the first nudge to the currency by speculators in early 1998 brought the SARB running to its defence, yet with no foreign reserves of consequence to back it up. When the new stampede really got underway, instead of the SARB giving way immediately, there was initially a tepid interest rate response. It was only eventually in August 1998 that prime was taken to 25.5%, as it had been under similar circumstances in 1985. However, this time a marginal-lending rule of 40% was temporarily imposed on the commercial banks. This effectively shut the borrowing window on their corporate clients and thereby ended a major source of financial speculation against the rand (as domestic leads-and-lags financing abruptly ended).

The economy as a whole slowed down steadily as the burden of real interest rates during 1996–1999 became double to triple what it had been during 1989–1995. This just goes to show, if proof is needed, that real interest rates do matter to the economy, especially one as intricately dependent on private credit as ours. And a too high real interest burden is guaranteed to slow our economy down to a standstill. This was a heavy price to pay for another miscall on defending the currency.

The second half of the 1990s was not as successful from a monetary policy point of view as the first half had been, despite the reduction of inflation throughout, the abolition of the financial rand and the steady relaxation of exchange control. The country paid a stiff price for the events of 1996–1998 in economic growth forgone, and expectations (local and foreign) were badly dented, at a time when we could not afford too many stumbles.

The 'Impossible Trinity'

The macro-economic policy dilemmas experienced by South Africa in the course of the 1990s reflect a fundamentally unstable relationship among three critical aspects, namely, capital flows, inflation and growth, as impacted on by the currency and interest rates. This potential instability and its policy implications are briefly examined in order to throw further light on South Africa's experiences in the 1990s and 2000s.

In an ideal situation, a country would simultaneously achieve perfectly mobile capital (no exchange control), monetary independence (the ability to set independently our interest rates with the needs of the domestic economy in mind), and a stable currency (no inflation threat). Unfortunately, in reality these three conditions existing simultaneously are a very unstable proposition, with little chance of lasting, especially for a country with doubtful credentials—and South Africa in the 1990s and early 2000s was still very much an incomplete reform story. Consequently, such an ideal situation is known as the 'Impossible Trinity'.

This fact has not prevented countries from trying. For a long while (smaller) countries tried to run their own interest rate policies with their domestic needs in mind. They also preferred the benefit of having free capital flows, supplementing whatever meagre savings they might have at home and bringing dynamic foreign fixed investment, cutting-edge technology and management expertise in its wake. This was like taking on board a gorilla pillion rider, someone who had an opinion about everything—the politics, the economics and the appropriate interest rate policy—and the muscle to back it up. Indeed, this was the capital account constraint in its full glory. Any deviation by the country's conditions or policy preferences from this gorilla's preferred scenario, and it would start moving its capital on a collision course with the country's central bank (steering its exchange rate with domestic objectives in mind). As the global gorilla grew in stature during the 1980s and 1990s and the influence over events by central banks of especially smaller countries shrank, currency crises became the order of the day.

These crises forced central banks to choose from among three options:

- stick with a 'managed' currency, and eventually get ambushed;
- let the currency be determined by the market by condoning it to 'float', and risk overshooting ('misalignment');

- or fix the currency to something bigger than the market gorilla (for example, a fixed link with the US dollar by way of a 'currency board'), and risk getting hoisted with inappropriate currency and interest rate strength (in effect, swapping a rampant dollar and US interest rates for market forces).

If a country floats its currency, it has the independence of setting its domestic interest rates (supposedly), while benefiting from the mobile capital flows (supposedly). If a country fixes its currency, it retains the benefit of mobile capital, but interest rates are now linked to US interest rates, set by the Federal Reserve with US needs in mind (not any other countries'), as is the level of the currency (determining the viability or otherwise of a country's exports, without it having a say in the matter).

Unfortunately, all these options are less than optimal. Manage the currency, and get periodically hit by currency crises (and find then that interest rates cannot, after all, be fixed with domestic needs in mind). Fix the currency to the dollar, and find that a periodically strong dollar and high US interest rates are the last thing a weak economy needs, lowering growth from two sides by losing trade competitiveness while hurting domestic producers.

Argentina did well out of its currency board in the early 1990s because:

- its own incompetent government was no longer determining policy;
- the market gorilla had been neutralised; and
- the dollar was undervalued and US interest rates were low.

Fast forward to 1997–2000, and the market gorilla was still at bay, but the US had grown into a gorilla of its own via an overvalued dollar *and* high US interest rates. Argentina was being squeezed mercilessly by both conditions to the point where the markets were starting to ask whether Argentina would stay the course and remain linked to the dollar. The markets had assumed this, and bought Argentina's foreign bonds on this assumption. Argentina had placed all its bets on its link to the US. From late 2000, with global markets steadily becoming more sceptical, Argentina had the dubious honour of being burdened by two gorillas: the US and the global markets.

A currency board is thus not an easy option. The sacrifice of monetary independence involves real risks and economic costs, for example, currency devaluation and debt default *if* the world (that is, the International Monetary Fund) is unable or unwilling to underwrite a country's foreign debt, as happened to Argentina in early 2002.

The 'pure float' alternative also has drawbacks. The market gorilla is often unhappy about the way things are going with its host and periodically drives its currency into serious medium-term misalignment. This can have severe consequences for economic growth (if the currency becomes overvalued), and for inflation (if the currency becomes heavily undervalued, requiring corrective interest rate intervention and thus also hurting growth).

Consequently, countries often want to claim to be 'floating', yet use interest rates (surreptitiously) to prevent the currency from getting too far from the ideal position, hoping all the while to fool the market gorilla into thinking it remains in charge. More often than not, such a policy soon gets confronted by another currency crisis as the central bank is 'found out'. In this manner, small countries are often forced from pillar to post and back, underperforming their economic growth potential as financial disturbances rule.

The International Monetary Fund (IMF) prefers countries to go for either extreme (fixed or floating), but experience suggests that a country is likely to encounter difficulties with these options.

Is it better to have a policy that tries to steer the domestic economy even while buying off the market gorilla by 'judiciously' using interest rate policy? This option needs to be managed very carefully. It may mean higher interest rates than we would ideally want domestically for growth, but not as high as a currency board link may imply, thereby keeping capital flows manageable. What such a policy does acknowledge upfront is the existence of a capital account constraint and the need for domestic conditions to reflect this reality.

A 'Genuine Floating' of the Rand since October 1998

The financial crisis of 1998 did bring changes in the way monetary policy operated. These changes were already effective during the last twelve months of the tenure of SARB Governor Stals, corresponding with the views of independent government advisors who were also more inclined to favour a 'genuine' floating of the rand.

This policy shift implied that the SARB ended its rand-support intervention in the currency market. Initially, this did not mean that the SARB became unwilling to absorb surplus dollars from the currency market, thereby increasing the foreign reserves and/or reducing the net forward book, effectively reducing its remaining net open position. Only from October 2001, would the SARB formally indicate that it would no longer absorb such 'surplus' dollars from the open market. This further enhanced the purity of its rand float. From then on, the SARB's net open position (net forward book minus the net foreign reserves) would only be reduced from 'captive' transactions, such as foreign bond issues by the government and the foreign currency component of privatisation proceeds. Other than these exceptions, the currency market was to be a freeplay of private agents.

This change also implied that the SARB would no longer attempt to support the rand by way of drastic interest rate defences that would induce the country to suffer a recession. Instead, the rand would be allowed to take care of external pressures, while interest rates would primarily be set with domestic needs in mind, that is, the reduction and containment of inflation as well as accommodating sustainable economic growth.

Consequently, during 1999–2002, as Tito Mboweni took over as governor of the SARB (from August 1999), the rand was allowed to fluctuate more in line with underlying demand/supply conditions for the currency. This was still only an imperfect 'float', for while non-residents could participate freely over current *and* capital accounts, residents could only do so freely over the current account and in a controlled manner (guided by exchange control) over the capital account.

As a result of this policy change, companies became more inclined to cover themselves protectively (because of perceived currency volatility), in the process lessening their exposure to such volatility, reducing the risk that had made the 1996 and 1998 rand events so virulent. Thus up to mid-2001 there were no speculative binges or consequent inflation surges to which the SARB felt compelled to react with higher interest rates. Instead, the rand was allowed to find its own level. It fell steeply through mid-2001, mainly against the dollar: from R6.05 to the dollar in early 2000 to R8.45 to the dollar in August 2001. This was primarily in response to US events where a deteriorating economic outlook had the effect of encouraging sell-offs in countries with weak currencies. But the rand also declined on a trade-weighted basis, improving South Africa's competitive position without apparently unduly increasing inflation (aside from the impact of higher-priced oil), as discussed earlier in Chapter 3. This development encouraged the SARB to further lower interest rates twice in 2001. Prime fell by 1% to 13.5% in June, and was reduced by a further 0.5% to 13% in September. However, by then a new whirlwind had been unleashed on an unsuspecting public (and SARB).

The Rand Crisis of Late 2001

From early September 2001, in a matter of four months, the rand declined from R8.45 to the dollar to a new low of R13.85 to the dollar. This event was accompanied by a sense of helplessness, for where did this collapse originate from? Economic reform was bearing fruit, the foreign credit-rating agencies were upping South Africa's sovereign credit rating, the budget deficit kept steadily declining (by now comfortably below 2% of GDP), the current account in the balance of payments was only minimally in deficit (since 1999), inflation was approaching new cyclical lows, and the economy was growing modestly at nearly 3%. These conditions did not warrant the kind of massive currency adjustment being witnessed, although on closer examination this speculative attack on the rand appeared to be due to an interplay of forces, very much confirming the Impossible Trinity analysis (as discussed earlier), and a lingering capital account constraint.

Fundamentally, the current account had experienced an abrupt but minor deterioration in mid-2001 under the influence of global developments. From a small surplus condition (+0.5% of GDP annualised), it swung within months to a small deficit (–1% of GDP annualised), as the commodity windfall of 2000 and early 2001 (mainly platinum group metals) and industrial growth overseas and its support for our manufactured exports fell away.

Furthermore, capital flows remained tenuous for a variety of reasons. The US cyclical correction created risk aversion as did Argentina's stressed condition, with South Africa's liquid financial markets offering generous trading opportunities not easily replicated elsewhere in emerging markets.

Taken together, these conditions maintained a mildly pressurised balance of payments condition where there was not a surplus of dollars. If anything, there was a surplus of rands. Companies, individual investors and foreign fund managers continued to search for (any) means to take money out of the country, while the SARB was known as a net absorber of dollars, whenever any became available, in order to further reduce its net open position. These were the main sources of the tension that had seen the rand depreciate steadily since early 2000. In turn, it suggested that a certain downward momentum had come into being, influencing rand expectations which could have a bearing on future developments.

Other currencies, such as the Australian dollar and those of other Organisation for Economic Co-operation and Development (OECD) commodity exporters, had so far also mirrored the change in international conditions, in particularly the deteriorating US economic outlook and higher interest rates, and its consequent adverse implications for commodity demand. Other emerging market currencies, especially Latin American ones, had suffered more from increased aversion towards them on account of the increase in their perceived risk following events in Mexico (1994), Asia (1997–1998), Russia (1998), Brazil (1999), and Argentina (throughout most of the late 1990s and early 2000s).

South Africa had also suffered from this combination of changed international conditions. To this was now added the impact of a further international shock event (the Manhattan atrocity on 11 September 2001). This terror event levelling the World Trade Centre shook financial markets worldwide, heightened risk aversion, and may in the case of the rand have been more than just a coincidental development (coming across here more as the straw that broke the camel's back). Although 9/11 did contribute to currency volatility elsewhere—for example, in the Australian dollar—it did not apparently trigger shock currency depreciations elsewhere in the world. In South Africa's case, an even more rapid rand depreciation may have been set in motion by a combination of events, including:

- the intense shock of 9/11, which saw global risk aversion increasing;
- the cumulative rand depreciation of the preceding twenty months;
- the collective interest rate cuts of that period;
- the shortage of surplus dollars as the SARB continued as net buyer to reduce its net open position; and
- the new policy determination not to intervene in support of the rand.

A series of additional ingredients were added to this already overwrought market condition. Just over a week after 9/11 the SARB cut the interest rate by another 0.5%. This was shortly followed by an exchange control directive which appeared to have been aimed at limiting speculative pressure on the rand by requiring all market agents to confirm that their dealings were all strictly based on commercial transactions, as required by exchange control regulations. This SARB move may have had the unintended consequence of encouraging the exit of those international participants who would have been willing to and capable of speculatively supporting the rand early on as its decline became excessive (the natural role of speculators being to identify value and by their action serving to limit misalignment and promote stabilisation). The apparent withdrawal of many of these agents from the rand currency market at this crucial juncture may have given more unrestrained momentum to the forces speculating against the rand.

All of these factors increasingly hinted at one-way risk for the rand in favour of depreciation. This may have encouraged all our market agents, especially exporters and importers, to intensify their currency positions against the rand. In the process, this provided greater momentum to the rand's decline and, in turn, probably ignited more and wider (as much small-scale domestic as big-time foreign) speculation against the rand.

This process may have been given further (unintentional) momentum on two other occasions that followed shortly thereafter. In early November 2001, President Thabo Mbeki and SARB Governor Tito Mboweni separately made public statements, explaining that there would not be SARB intervention in support of the rand. These well-intentioned declarations (doubtless with the origin of the 1998 rand crisis in mind), offered remaining market participants a clear vision of uninterrupted opportunity to stay with rand depreciation strategies, thereby likely inviting greater such position-taking against the rand.

The final official act in the rand depreciation drama was the manner in which exchange control permission was granted to South African financial institutions to remit capital overseas. It had been policy to limit such outflows to a percentage of the increase in assets at such institutions. Instead of granting permission throughout the year as investible funds accumulated, thereby limiting the pressure on the rand, such requests had built up during the year. Final approval apparently belatedly materialised in December 2001, unleashing a year's worth of institutional outflows abroad, thereby giving a special twist to the rand's accelerating weakness in late 2001. In a matter of only four months, the rand had depreciated by a further 60%: from R8.45 to the dollar in late August to R13.85 to the dollar by 20 December 2001.

By Christmas the rand finally started to recover. The currency was clearly deeply oversold and rumours were starting to fly that the government might arrange a huge dollar loan ($5 billion to $10 billion) from the IMF or elsewhere in order to be able to enter the currency market. Though without foundation, this rumour probably persuaded exporters to moderate their trading positions, locking in some of their currency profits. As they did so, importers likely became less concerned to cover their future transactions. Together, these actions assisted the rand back towards R11.50 to the dollar where it gradually stabilised through February and March 2002. A suggestion about improper trading practices, and a call for a government commission of inquiry (subsequently appointed under Justice Myburgh) further restored two-way risk during this period, allowing the rand to stabilise as exporters and importers eased their leads-and-lags. The sense of crisis (typical of a financial bubble condition) gradually proceeded to unwind from April, allowing the rand to recover more lost ground. By early July 2002 it was trading at R10.00 to the dollar, and gradually stabilised around this level through August 2002. After renewed weakness, the rand's recovery became more pronounced from November 2002, reaching R7.85 to the dollar by early March 2003.

The upshot of the rand's deep depreciation in 2001 was that imported inflation rose steeply during 2002, with CPIX inflation peaking out at 12.7% by November 2002 from a cyclical low of 5.8% in September 2001. In addition, bank credit and money supply growth jumped sharply during December 2001 to 12% and 17% year-on-year respectively. This probably reflected exporters arranging rand financing (in order to keep export proceeds offshore as long as possible within the 180-day remittance rule in terms of exchange control regulations). Furthermore, nervous capital market investors could have been moving into the money market as capital market rates rose. And consumers pre-emptively purchased durable goods on a large scale ahead of any price increases. New passenger-car sales increased by over 18% in December 2001, and by 10% in January 2002 (year-on-year), thereafter steadily easing as the pre-emptive buying pressure in response to anticipated car price increases fell away.

These developments of a monetary and real economic nature were sufficiently disturbing for the SARB to raise interest rates in four instalments of 1% each during January, March, June and September 2002—prime increasing to 17%. It was quite obvious that events had made it impossible for the SARB to meet its formal inflation target of 3%

to 6% for 2002, with serious doubts about 2003. Moreover, there were growing fears that second-round inflation effects would take hold if no response was offered. The full reach of the SARB's response to events would only become clear in the course of 2002. Any new global shocks would hold the potential of creating additional monetary disturbances.

Inflation Targeting

The rand crisis of late 2001 served to highlight the vulnerability of the inflation targeting policy that the government had adopted in early 2000. As of February 2000, the government had tasked the SARB to conduct monetary policy in a manner that would allow it to meet future inflation targets (average CPIX inflation for 2002 to fall in a range of 3% to 6%, subsequently extended to 2003 and 2004 as well). By shifting its focus to the inflation performance, and away from the daily vagaries of the rand and balance of payments, a monetary policy less inclined to be waylaid by such external considerations and more inclined to set interest rates with domestic needs in mind, appeared to have come into being.

The aim with inflation targeting appeared to be to replace a largely discretionary-based monetary policy with a rule-based one, improving transparency to economic agents. While the SARB's instrument independence was to be maintained (it was still to decide when to change interest rates, and by how much), the overall aim was to get away from currency-support actions and to put into place a transparent policy that would attempt to influence expectations in the broader economy and markets regarding sustainable inflation, economic growth and balance of payments conditions.

To expect the SARB to be the sole institution aiming to contain inflation expectations would not be realistic. Its actions were then bound to come at the expense of economic growth, if too many lingering structural rigidities were to sustain inflationary momentum. In addition, monetary lags are notoriously uncertain, making the targeting of inflation through changes in interest rates over a period of two years a challenging task. In a manner of speaking, the inflation target set for the SARB is a target for the government, in that it implements certain structural policy reforms. Thus, the new monetary policy approach of targeting inflation will be greatly assisted by the more disciplined conditions now prevailing in the country's national budget and by the large productivity gains induced by a more competitively-based trade policy and keeping the increase in unit labour costs in check. Administered prices, though, remain a problem, as they do not necessarily respond to competitive market conditions, especially as privatisation plans have made it necessary in some instances to improve the cash flow of these parastatals by condoning higher prices for their services. Finally, there is the influence of the weak rand to consider, which at 'crisis' time directly pushes inflation higher while indirectly easing the pressure for strong productivity gains.

With structural reform well advanced (budget, trade, and labour productivity), South African markets for goods and labour should function more efficiently than in the past. With credit appropriately priced, there should be less overheating of the economy, allowing a lesser inflation bias in time.

Inflation-targeting by the monetary authorities should thus strive to set appropriate interest rate levels that should function as an anchor for inflation expectations among businesses, labour and consumers. By preventing actual overheating of the economy through excessive demand pressures, and by influencing expectations, it should be possible over time to reduce the actual inflation rate without excessive growth sacrifice.

That this process is not without complications has been borne out by the teething problems of 2000–2003. These may cast doubt on the effectiveness of this approach, although they may not prevent longer-term success in achieving convergence with the inflationary performance of the main trading partners (currently already 0% to 3%).

In this respect, we may want to consider some of the problems that have been encountered. Interest rate policy is most effective in influencing demand conditions, and the manner in which these could affect actual inflation and expectations thereof. When it comes to supply-side shocks, as relative prices are made to change by exogenous forces (oil, food, currency), we may want to suspend the inflation target for the duration, because:

- by its very nature the price shock is likely to be temporary;
- interest rates will not have a direct impact on constraining them as they are not demand-linked; and
- expectations will not be permanently disturbed, if the economy is already structured in a flexible manner and no longer suffers from market rigidities that could propagate an initial price shock indefinitely through secondary effects.

Furthermore, inflation targeting should be forward-looking, in that it wishes to influence expectations about future events and because interest rate changes take up to two years to have their full impact.

These features have been mostly lacking from the SARB approach to inflation-targeting. Supply-side shocks have been met through interest rate increases instead of suspending the inflation target temporarily. Inflation-targeting has not been primarily forward-looking. Instead, interest rate changes have apparently taken place by reference to historic (current) inflation rates, and their supposed impact on future inflation expectations.

In the process, monetary policy has given the impression of having retained a far more discretionary bias than supposedly implied by the intention of inflation-targeting. There is furthermore the emphasis placed on possible second-round price effects following a primary supply-side shock, rather than expressing confidence in the economy's ability to adapt to such price disturbances relatively quickly. Price expectations are apparently still seen as relatively inflexible—rigid even—compared to being flexible and competition-disciplined.

Strong labour unions, political activism, the high incidence of administrative prices, and industry concentration in key sectors of the economy are good reasons not to presume perfect competition to rule throughout the economy.

In addition, an excessive rand undershoot can be assisted to unwind more quickly through a moderate interest rate increase. This makes it an acceptable basis for some interest rate intervention, if it means that the unsettled price environment can be made to stabilise, limiting possible longer-term damage.

Besides, if the rand undershoot is heavy enough, as was the case in 2001, the additional trade protection granted to exporters and import-displacing local producers may be so large as to temporarily suspend market price discipline (competition). Secondary price effects due to excessive rand misalignment may then be expected, eventually undoing the currency undervaluation: not through currency recovery, but through higher inflation. This, in turn, could acquire a greater 'stickiness' of its own, if the exercise is repeated often enough (and 2001 was the fourth in a decade-long series of rand shock depreciations with inflation fall-out: 1992–1993, 1996, 1998, 2001). Consequently, for a country with relatively weak external finances to engage in 'pure' currency floating (leaving the rand entirely to its own devices), at a time of still-incomplete economic reforms and market perceptions based thereon, may give rise to unduly long periods of excessive currency misalignment. Its knock-on effects may induce a permanency to high inflation expectations, certainly more 'sticky' than warranted. The SARB should therefore perhaps, for the time being, continue to take into account the reality of a capital account constraint and its implications for the rand and inflation.

Seen this way, there is a case to be made for a flexible response with interest rate changes even in the case of supply-side price shocks, especially when currency-based. Such pragmatism should be extended to include operations in the currency market itself. This should not be seen as a plea for intervention in support of the rand with very limited foreign reserves, as happened in 1996 and 1998. Instead, we think of the SARB maintaining a presence in the currency market, thereby providing greater two-way risk perception rather than encouraging one-way expectations to come into being or being reinforced. Such a presence would function as a braking mechanism, which should allow more balanced rand pricing, inhibiting the start or progress of unduly excessive rand misalignments, compared to a condition in which the SARB remains entirely hands-off.

This idea apparently regained favour in early 2003, when it became obvious that the SARB had again been a net buyer of dollars. The SARB had reduced its net open position in a matter of two months by $0.5 billion to $1.3 billion (half of it through revaluing its gold holdings due to a higher gold price), presumably in part motivated by preventing an undue, or unduly rapid, strengthening of the rand since late 2002. This change in policy should be welcomed in making the currency market more efficient in its price signalling. There is, though, the qualification that, with the SARB again becoming a net dollar absorber, this is a much more fundamental intrusion into the currency market compared to maintaining a daily presence and inhibiting excessive price instability. Indeed, if a moderate interest rate increase is accepted as the least-cost option of ending a rand undershoot and its threat of disturbing inflation expectations more permanently, there is presumably also the case to be made for reversing such interest rate increases as soon as rand recovery is under way, and inflation projections signal the imminent end of the inflation disturbance (given the long lags with which interest rates do their work). Otherwise, undue growth sacrifice may still result, as the rand strengthens too far, undermining exports, while the still-high interest rates weigh on domestic demand.

Interest rate policy remained at the time of writing in early 2003 more focused on current inflation data rather than on future pricing conditions. This may also have a bearing on currency developments, and their feedback potential for changing inflation, in the case of 2003 possibly encouraging too much of a rand recovery into overshoot territory. As currency shocks, such as the one in 2001, highly disturb the real economy as well as financial markets and the pricing mechanism, preventing their occurrence should enjoy a high priority, short of defending an inappropriate value of the rand. As inflation expectations are to be guided to lower levels over the medium-term, the over- and undershooting of the currency is something to bear in mind when setting interest rates (the conclusion of the 'Impossible Trinity' section earlier in this chapter).

Thus the success of the inflation-targeting approach appears to be a function of the structural reforms being implemented, as well as the fleet-footedness of the SARB in pricing credit correctly. While recent years have seen the successful reduction of inflation (from 15% in the early 1990s, to 10% in the mid-1990s, to 5% by the millennium crossover), the exposure to external shocks and their disturbing price effects have apparently not yet been successfully addressed.

The events of 2000–2001 and possibly future events during 2004–2006 should perhaps make the SARB more sensitive to especially overseas developments (for example, the US economy and financial markets). Changed expectations about growth and interest rates there may lead to an unfavourable shift in expectation regarding the outlook for commodity export countries, while risk aversion may become heightened regarding emerging countries. Both types of expectational changes may encourage a change in capital flows. Their temporary outflows from South Africa could disturb the rand, sometimes violently as has been seen before. If this is going to be the source of an inflation disturbance, *early* interest rate responses may well be advisable, not with the objective of defending the rand, but to impact on changing expectations regarding the relative attractiveness of South Africa. In the longer-term, this suggests that perhaps a more preventive, anticipatory policy, going more flexibly with the global flow of events, may lower the likelihood of undue monetary disturbances from taking place here. This seems preferable to a clearly desynchronised approach and an exclusive domestic inflation focus with a historic bias, which appears to invite rand ambushes and imported inflation shocks that then need to be addressed after the event. If our inflation disturbances now regularly start with global changes (in 1998 it was Asian and in 2000 it was US conditions) and the manner in which this affects global capital flows, our forward-oriented inflation-targeting policy should perhaps incorporate this reality in its positioning and in the conduct of interest rate policy. Though apparently favouring aspects of a more fixed currency approach, the practical outcome of such a policy would be more flexible and discretionary actions, and ultimately would be less costly in allowing timely corrective responses.

A Less Disruptive Monetary Policy

Throughout the struggle decades (1970–1990) and the transition period through 1998, monetary policy has often been as disruptive of the business cycle as the underlying economic fundamentals have been, changing for the better only in stages as events induced changes in policy over time.

In the earlier decades, political choices led the South African government to economic decisions that were invariably poor—deteriorating public finances, rising inflation, dwindling foreign reserves, and increased currency volatility—with various negative forces reinforcing each other.

With the political logjam broken, sounder economic policy-making followed in the 1990s. The idea was to transform the vicious cycle into a virtuous one. To this end, many economic policy reforms were implemented.

One decision taken was to make an early beginning with exchange control relaxation, even in the face of very low external reserves, while keeping privatisation and its access to (foreign) capital a distant objective. In essence, this meant that South Africa wanted to earn its way back to sound external finances and macro-stability through wise political and economic behaviour. Reform plus performance was to equal reward in ending the capital account constraint early. However, it did not quite work out that way.

There was to be little reward for starting slowly with managed (step-by-step) exchange control relaxation, as the private capital inflows generally disappointed relative to the outflows, allowing over a decade only a modest restoration of the foreign reserves. In the post-1994 period this reflected primarily the return-flow of much of the foreign capital that had temporarily bolted during the 1992–1993 rand event, reinforced by subsequent government bond issues and privatisation deals. Overall, the net foreign reserves were restored to $5 billion (two months of import cover), but this should be compared to the explosive improvements in the foreign reserves of other countries to gain a relative perception (China $140 billion, India $60 billion, Russia $60 billion, the last two in a matter of three to five years).

Thus for its entire transition period, South Africa retained exposed external finances, apparently a significant feature in not being able to prevent and/or resist major currency shocks. This condition was further reinforced by the SARB remaining wedded to the dual intervention objective of managing the level of the currency *and* the level of interest rates.

This dual policy objective had been possible—though in an inefficient manner—when exchange control and a dual currency regime ring-fenced foreign non-resident capital transactions from domestic commercial ones. However, once exchange control started to be relaxed, and the dual currency regime was ended, the SARB's conduct of monetary policy took too long to make a necessary accompanying change. By not giving up on its dual policy objective, the SARB invited growing market scrutiny as currency market participants sensed an opportunity. Whereas the 1992–1993 rand depreciation could be related back to the sudden uncertainty concerning a looming democratic dispensation, motivating large capital outflows, the 1996 and 1998 rand shocks were more clearly linked to the SARB's preference for defending the rand through currency market intervention, even when handicapped by low external reserves.

The policy changes implemented from 1999–2000 were intended to prevent a repeat of the late 1990s rand shocks, their inflationary consequences, and the need to use higher interest rates and growth sacrifice to restore macro-economic order. The rand was no longer to be blatantly defended. Indeed, discretionary monetary policy was intended to take a backseat in favour of more rule-bound inflation-targeting, with one objective (lowering inflation expectations) and one instrument (interest rates) to achieve this outcome. It was to be expected that currency volatility would still be incurred, but at least it would not be worsened through SARB intervention. By managing inflation lower over time, and improving economic growth, the forces driving the rand should become less virulent as well. Such reforms and achievements were bound to end the capital account constraint some day.

This change in monetary policy did not succeed as smoothly as hoped, as the time of its implementation happened to coincide with the US economy starting a major cyclical adjustment. This event, as well as the SARB's continuing absorption of dollars in order to strengthen its external finances, put substantial downward pressure on the rand throughout 2000 and early 2001. In turn, this was probably instrumental in creating expectations in the currency market which, when confronted with events of late 2001, led to another major rand depreciation shock.

The SARB probably contributed to deepening this rand shock, as related earlier in this chapter, by the manner of its ongoing dollar purchases, interest rate cutting, exchange control directives and public signalling. No doubt this was a searing experience, which has led to further corrective action:

- For the time being, the SARB did not make any further net dollar purchases in the open market.
- There is a greater unwillingness to ease interest rates in the presence of virulent global conditions.
- The government is displaying greater caution with exchange control directives and relaxation.
- There is a major preoccupation with maintaining credibility regarding the SARB's main policy objective (reducing inflation).

The SARB's intense learning curve had some drawbacks, including:

- It displayed an unwillingness to maintain even a simple presence in the currency market, which lasted fifteen months, ending in early 2003.
- The SARB has shown sensitivity about lowering interest rates early in 2003, even with the multiple supply shocks (rand, maize and oil) all reversed relatively quickly, and CPIX inflation projections signalling a major future falling off in inflation and achievement of targets by late 2003 and during 2004.

However unfortunate this sequence of events may have been, sight should not be lost of the bigger SARB achievements:

- There is a greater willingness to allow the rand freedom, focusing interest rate policy on attaining set annual inflation targets.
- Resuming a currency market presence and making net purchases of dollars in the open market has offered resistance to undue rand strengthening in early 2003.
- The SARB has fulfilled the role of honest broker in publicly signalling to government, labour and business the need for discipline in wage- and price-setting.

Going forward, the steady implementation of this policy stance should make the SARB less of a disruptive influence, either in triggering or worsening rand shock depreciations or through its own shock interest rate responses. In addition, its public role in focusing on inflation expectations, alongside government's many reforms in structurally assisting inflation lower, should achieve success in a matter of years in reducing the remaining inflation to closer to that of our main trading partners in a 0% to 3% range (assuming that these countries themselves will remain near these levels, despite global disturbances as seen in the early 2000s).

Thus, by early 2003 monetary policy may have completed its major modern transformation, from being a part of the problem in reinforcing inflation and disrupting the business cycle (as in the 1980s), and inviting or deepening currency shocks and thereby also disrupting business upswings and the country's growth performance (as in the 1990s and early 2000s), to one where it may steadily guide inflation lower while having a much less disruptive influence through its interest rate setting over rand, inflation, and business upswings.

Together with the change in fiscal bias, from anti-growth during most of the 1990s to one of pro-growth in the 2000s, this major change in the tenor of monetary policy augurs well for achieving both lower inflation and longer economic growth runs (business cycle upswings). This, in turn, will be crucial for gaining greater business and consumer confidence, an increased willingness to commit to fixed investment spending, and a greater commitment to hire and train labour.

In order to fine-tune its monetary policy contribution to general macro-economic stability still further, the SARB may want to consider changing inflation-targeting to become more forward-acting, and anticipatory of changes in global conditions, as discussed, and to reflect this in its interest-rate-setting decisions in future years.

Low Foreign Reserves and Savings Rate

A major remaining structural problem is low foreign reserves and a low savings rate, making the country prone to balance of payments instability as growth speeds up. The attendant pressures can be expected to weigh on the rand, and to intensify imported inflation. Unless, that is, adequate capital inflows can be depended upon, and allowing for the beneficial effects of globalisation on the inflation experienced by our trading partners and their willingness to maintain their share of our market through flexible pricing even in the face of rand depreciation. Foreign capital flows are attracted by the promise of faster economic growth, but are inhibited by currency risk. The very fact of a strained current account condition, in the presence of low external reserves, makes it more likely that rand depreciation cannot be resisted. This, in turn, tends to keep capital inflows low and reinforces the balance of payments constraint. Economic growth is thus kept in check and any capital inflows are further inhibited in a vicious cycle of cause and effect.

To ease this constraint, both higher savings and stronger external reserves are appropriate. This should result in a more stable rand, less imported inflation and less constrained growth. These features, in turn, serve to bolster capital inflows, reinforcing growth.

The government has a two-pronged approach to ease this constraint:

- more disciplined state finances, reducing the budget deficit and boosting the national savings rate; and
- privatisation, reinforcing the savings condition as well as raising dollar inflows to strengthen the external finances.

Unfortunately, the redistribution policies of the government tend to work against this two-pronged approach as they appear to prevent much of a recovery in the savings rate.

Whereas the government is well advanced in reducing the budget deficit (now less than 2% of GDP), other forms of savings (that is, personal and corporate) are yet to show any improvement (if they are not, in fact, deteriorating), keeping the overall savings balance persistently near 15% of GDP since 1997. Indeed, the improvement in the budget deficit may, by its very nature (by further favouring redistribution), well have taken place at the expense of private savings rather than consumption. Public dissaving, though, has eased considerably as the budget deficit has been reduced while public sector capital expenditure has been significantly boosted.

The crowning reform would be in the form of privatisation and the financing—internal and external—this would unlock (see below).

Thus, the country still labours under the constraint of low savings and weak external finances. This also fully exposes any inflation-targeting policy of the SARB to external price shocks as discussed, either generated globally or induced by the very weakness of the external finances. Periodically, as we have come to expect, such shock events impact on the rand and trigger a monetary disturbance.

This unsatisfactory state of affairs will continue at least for as long as structural reform aimed at strengthening the country's finances (and by implication the savings quantum and foreign reserves) has not been completed.

However, once completed, a stronger economic and financial structure should be capable of absorbing external balance of payments pressures more adequately, thereby inviting less rand volatility and less of an inflation consequence and interest rate response from the SARB. Whereas in previous decades this phenomenon has periodically contributed to (serious) business cycle interruptions, transformed external finances should in the future be capable of accommodating a more robust (higher) economic growth performance. Given the government's commitment to structural reform—in particular, budgetary, privatisation and foreign reserves reforms—this appears to be a matter of time, thereby significantly easing the severe capital account constraint of recent decades.

Privatisation

In Chapter 3, privatisation of publicly owned assets was discussed as a means to lift the current ceiling on the growth process, by creating greater fiscal space for future social delivery and strengthening the external finances to the extent that such assets are sold for foreign currency. Here we return to the topic in order to provide further perspective on the amounts that could potentially be raised by government through privatisation, and the scope this will provide for improving the financial environment in support of social delivery and economic growth.

Under different circumstances, it might be an interesting intellectual challenge to debate public versus private ownership of what are, in essence, monopolies. However, South Africa:

- is grappling with the financial aftermath of a civil war;
- is confronted by a large economically backward population still steadily urbanising; and
- shows evidence of progressive social and economic decay.

Consequently, the need for faster economic development and a restoration of healthy national finances is paramount. In our condition, theorising about public versus private ownership comes close to being a luxury.

It should be a broad policy aim for public assets to be managed efficiently, not to be over- or underinvested, and not to be overcharging for important services most of the time, in the process yielding an adequate economic return on the scarce capital invested and skilled labour employed. An optimal dispensation is possible whether an asset is privately or publicly owned: it is all a matter of adequate regulation. Of course, the provision of free or subsidised services to the poor, with or without cross-subsidisation, is another matter altogether.

The political dispensation of the 1970s and 1980s was responsible for too much parastatal over-investing, over-manning and poor financial management of its assets. This can be seen in:

- the substantial surplus capacity in electricity generation for decades now;
- the idle capacity of the national railway and port network even as the national roads get overburdened and new ports are built;
- the acquisition of expensive international finance without adequate currency cover for large infrastructural projects, this being carried by the SARB and ultimately the government (for example, in the case of electricity generation and transportation projects);
- subsidies needed (commuter railways, post office); and
- poor service delivery.

In all these instances, improvement has been possible and during the past fifteen years has slowly been coming about. The one major exception has probably been the railways where the economic significance of the national network appears to be fading away.

Today, though, it would appear that capital at parastatals is being correctly priced in most instances, and that foreign loans are being covered forward. As a consequence, there is a scarcity of capital, which is expected to earn an economic return. Subsidisation from the exchequer, long a beloved approach of the previous regime, is only still in exceptional cases taking place (for example, railway passenger services and the post office). For the most part, public assets today are run like serious businesses: over-manning is out, expenses are kept down, and these entities are expected to turn a profit and pay tax.

In future, therefore, we expect better returns on such capital invested than in the past. There should be a greater contribution to economic growth from such entities, whether publicly or privately owned. The manner of their transfer, the powers of any regulators, and the subsequent performance of these assets are important micro-economic considerations, but should be viewed separately from the strategic financial implications.

Such assets are arguably the only major source of free unencumbered capital in South Africa, owned by the nation at large, and one of the few positive contributions by a prolific past to our future well-being. These assets represent scarce capital that was almost frittered away in our recent civil war. They should be utilised to strengthen the general finances of the country, of which the external component is the most worrying (there is not an easy supply of foreign exchange available to us, unlike rand income and assets that can be generated locally).

The government appears to share this view, though it shows considerable concern about assets that can be privatised as potential niches for empowerment. Furthermore, the government appears to be financially conservative, apparently wanting to hold on to a portion of such assets, partly in order to ensure that they are well managed and possibly to ensure that empowerment survives into the long-term. There also appears to be a suggestion of xenophobia, in that all public assets to be privatised are not supposed to be sold 'only' to foreigners (the preferred option from the point of view of raising foreign currency), nor even 'mainly' to foreigners (the second-best option), but only 'at best' to foreign interests. This runs the real danger that foreigners may lose interest or fail to pay top dollar, neither of which we can afford, going by our external financial weaknesses and the influence these appear to have over our economic performance.

In the main, there is little quibble with the government's intentions. The key strategic public assets that can be privatised, should be and urgently so, subject to the above limitations. The only real question is whether we can get these public assets (Telkom, Eskom, Transnet, Denel) market-ready within a reasonable timeframe, and then be able to sell them into a reasonably buoyant financial market. From the country's point of view, buyers of such assets would preferably be paying over the top, rather than government having to off-load at depressed prices at the bottom of a global bear market. Ensuring that this happens will mostly be a matter of astute timing (and readiness).

There is an impressive list of assets to be sold, there is a timetable of sorts, and the relevant government departments have been preparing these assets for the market for ten or so years now. This has meant:

- a cleaning up of pension funds;
- an end to subsidies;
- a more efficient operating structure (implying cost-cutting and labour shedding); and
- charging more market-related prices (which really means fattening the cash flow of these entities in order for them to become viable in market terms).

There are a few big assets that will provide the lion's share of any total privatisation proceeds, with Eskom, Telkom, Transnet, the M-Cell shareholding, Sasria and Denel leading the way. If the government is going to raise between R50 billion (a low estimate) and R150 billion (a high estimate), it is in these assets that 90% of the value is to be found. There is also extensive state property—land, buildings, real estate—but this may take longer to untangle, and some of it might not be for sale or find a ready buyer (for example, the Union Buildings).

Consequently, there remains considerable uncertainty as to exactly what and how much will be sold, to whom it will be sold, and when. The general consensus seems to be an amount of R100 billion in proceeds, two-thirds of it in foreign currency, all of it to be accomplished in the 2000s decade.

Some of the privatisation proceeds are likely to be ploughed back into these public assets by way of future infrastructural expansion. Only the residual flowing to the state will be genuinely free capital that can be applied towards strengthening the state's finances.

The government's intentions with the capital inheritance that privatisation potentially offers up have been spoken about in public often enough for an outline to emerge. During 2001, and again from late 2002, this outline finally made the stalest bulls come to life in our capital market as long-term interest rates were steadily pushed towards single-digit figures.

As the government is financially conservative, it will probably use any proceeds to pay down its public debt, not unlike an individual using an inheritance to pay off the mortgage, thereby gaining peace of mind *and* a better monthly cash flow.

As an additional sweetener, any foreign buyers paying in foreign currency will be surrendering these dollars and euros to the SARB, which will pay the government the going rand exchange rate, while applying such foreign currency to pay off the forward book. In early 2001 that book still amounted to R110 billion, but the government and SARB borrowings raised abroad during 2001 and the Anglo-American take-over of De Beers between them raised over R40 billion. That left R70 billion at mid-2001, which was further reduced to R50 billion by early 2003. The remainder of the forward book will probably disappear on account of further privatisation deals and as an improving economic performance attracts additional private capital to the country in time (global conditions permitting).

Completion of its privatisation plans would allow the government to pay down the national debt, taking the ratio from 36% to 39% of GDP. Together with lower long-term interest rates as a result of a likely improved country credit rating by Moodys and Standard and Poor, it should lower the government's annual interest bill by a conservative R20 billion to R25 billion in the decade of the 2000s (some 2% of GDP), compared to what it otherwise would have remained.

This explains the government's determination to proceed with the privatisation project, despite strenuous objections from some quarters. If the regulatory aspects are handled well, it does not matter who owns the assets, apart from government's reluctance to part entirely with them (which has already been noted). If these proceeds are applied in full in the manner described, the social returns going forward will be immense. Government will have an extra R20 billion plus annually to allocate to pure social delivery (numbers of houses, teachers, nurses, doctors, security personnel, etc.). Furthermore, the strengthening of our external finances will likely yield even bigger returns, for it promises greater balance of payments and currency stability over the business cycle, as well as lower foreign borrowing costs. These considerations are pivotal in considering the future performance of the whole economy (bearing in mind the likely level of inflation and interest rates), where each additional 1% of economic growth means currently R12 billion more in goods and services produced annually, compounded at 1% p.a. into the future. This adds up to a better living standard for many more people over a full generation, as well as higher tax returns and greater scope for social delivery. The potential employment gains from such additional economic growth would also be substantial over time.

Even if job losses are incurred as these public assets are made more efficient, the eventual financial contribution to overall economic performance is the key. It is this that over time will add back many more job opportunities in the wider economy than were ever directly lost.

Why would such an outcome materialise, and be different from the jobless growth of the years since 1996? Firstly, economic growth since 1996 has been interrupted and kept lower than necessary (see Chapter 3), even as our economy was being made more efficient and having to absorb higher wage demands (see Chapter 5). All these features guaranteed jobless growth—the little there was. Secondly, a less disruptive monetary policy, as has now come into being, can allow longer growth 'runs' and thus acquire greater momentum, even as labour rationalisation becomes less job destructive (past inefficiencies having been addressed), and wage demands become more realistic due to trade competition.

Privatisation's contribution to this changeover would be to strengthen both the national and external finances, making the country less exposed to balance of payments crises, and thereby facilitating longer growth runs. The resultant job growth over a period of years would far outstrip what would need to be given up in the process of privatisation.

Will the final effort still be made to sell these few crucial state assets at favourable terms, mostly to foreign interests? If the government fails to deliver on this undertaking, its ability to strengthen the external finances will be weakened, while domestically it will gain less fiscal space for responsibly improving social delivery. There are many cross-currents buffeting this particular area of the economy, and we can consequently expect only slow progress. Yet with a pay-off as promising as that sketched above, it is unlikely that a powerful, well-supported government will find reason not to go through with it all.

Looking Ahead

What if we privatise, pay off the forward book, gain a higher country investment rating, and capital still does not favour us (on balance flowing out rather than in)? If you had gained the impression that either the liberalisation of exchange controls or the privatisation of public assets are ends in themselves, or are actions that will render an entire policy viable, your impression needs to be qualified. The government's *entire* policy attempt needs to be well-founded, or else we will eventually flounder.

This again raises the question (already posed in Chapter 3), as to whether an emerging country should not rather ensure a high enough savings rate from domestic sources—thereby lessening its reliance on foreign suppliers of capital—if it is not prepared to go the extra mile in fully implementing internationally recognised, 'best-practice' economic policies.

In the end, if we are going to continue our reliance on foreign capital inflows, we have to make South Africa more attractive, by way of political stability, acceptable policy choices, and faster economic growth. Only this will guarantee greater appetite among providers of capital (foreign as much as local) to support our growth ambitions. Our attempts at exchange liberalisation and privatisation on their own could never be perfect substitutes for this fundamental requirement.

Exchange control liberalisation on its own may merely facilitate a net outflow of capital, though controlled liberalisation may have reduced perceived risk as many critical role players have succeeded in diversifying themselves, making it more likely that they will continue as local participants in making the planned transformation feasible.

Privatisation, especially when assets are sold for foreign exchange, strengthens our financial structure and should assist in some way to reduce perceived risk too, possibly even more effectively than controlled liberalisation of exchange control.

But the real pay-off awaits the vesting of political stability, and policy choices reinforcing such political stability in the long-term, accompanied by faster economic growth. It will not be government, or the media or society or labour unions or foreign governments that will decide whether an acceptable condition has been attained. Capital (local as much as foreign), will either signal its satisfaction with greater financial commitment, or it will display its displeasure by withholding funds.

The South African government and society need to come into line with global best economic practices in order to win such support. This is the ultimate reality of globalisation, in which global rules of engagement determine who gets favoured with capital and who does not. The more a society wishes to make use of external resources to supplement its own, the more it has to adhere to requirements that apply to all internationally, without exception.

5 PROGRESS WITH MICRO-ECONOMIC RESTRUCTURING

Structural reform in South Africa is taking place over a wide front. The economic dimensions include macro-economic restructuring as discussed in Chapter 4 (fiscal and monetary policy), social delivery (Chapter 7), as well as micro-economic restructuring, the focus of this chapter.

'Micro-economic restructuring' primarily implies the lowering of trade protection (externally) and deregulation (domestically), with private economic agents responding by repositioning themselves in relation to greater market competition. Complicating factors have been that such micro-economic restructuring has taken place during a period of relatively slow economic growth and has had to be attempted against the background of (and was also partially influenced by) greater demands from organised labour and political activism from government, especially since April 1994. Other structural reforms (such as land reform) will not be addressed here.

The result of the micro-economic restructuring discussed in this chapter has been a reduction in formally employed labour since 1990, even though the economy kept on expanding. This was accompanied by a remarkable resurgence in labour productivity in the core of the formal sector (today still employing 70% of total formally employed labour). In turn, this has led to the creation of a (temporary) reservoir of surplus labour skills despite considerable net emigration.

Structurally, the labour rationalisation process appears to be well advanced, especially so in the core formal sector where most of the labour shedding has taken place, mainly at large employers. In addition, there has been a greater creation of new formal jobs during this past decade than has perhaps generally been realised. This has limited the net decline in formal employment, has kept demand for skilled workers high, and has limited their unemployment (see also Chapter 9).

In what follows, micro-economic restructuring specifically focuses on the changes in employment levels as a result of the forces working on employers.

Changes in Employment Levels

One of apartheid's legacies is an inefficient economic structure due to misallocation of capital and labour under the influence of trade protection, public investment and spending priorities, (informal) White affirmative action, labour legislation, physical planning Acts and often desperate attempts at self-sufficiency. Furthermore, the demands on our natural endowment have been changing, examples being declining gold mining and growing platinum mining activity.

With the political change after 1994, came more labour demands and Black affirmative action, as well as a reduction in trade protection and the preparation of parastatals for privatisation. During the 1990s new technology (largely information and communication) became extensively used throughout most sectors of the economy (see Chapter 8). These influences have all impacted on cost structures, encouraging changes in resource allocation. A separate issue has been that relatively high labour costs have encouraged a bias towards capital deepening and higher-skilled labour, and away from less-skilled labour.

This is an incomplete list of structural distortions, market responses and subsequent changes in policy emphasis, all of which tended to impact on existing employment and on new employment generation. The changes observable since 1970 go far to highlight the structural changes that have been absorbed by the South African economy.

Instead of recording structural change by focusing on the changing composition of output in the economy, with supporting evidence from changing patterns in consumption and investment, it is considered more useful to focus on labour and the changes in employment. This would capture the great change in productivity and the labour rationalisation that accompanied it. This ties in with major policy objectives (creating employment, reducing unemployment, providing greater social delivery, changing the income distribution) as well as allowing reflection in later chapters on the effects of migration and HIV/Aids (see Chapter 9).

The employment changes discussed in this chapter have impacted on the perceptions of ordinary South Africans, shaping their views as to the health of the economy and the direction of likely future trends. This chapter aims to explain these changes, thereby throwing greater light on future prospects.

Labour and Employment Rationalisation

For much of its modern existence, the South African economy has been a protected entity. It was marked by limited external trade competition and apparent shortages of skilled labour. Though there was a surfeit of less-skilled labour, apartheid labour policy from the 1950s onwards attempted to limit the flow of such labour to the cities, creating artificial shortages here, too. With the economy's specialisation stunted, its competition limited and the labour market distorted, labour hoarding or overmanning (that is, over-employment of 'scarce' labour) was common during periods of fast growth. This phenomenon existed for political reasons in the public sector and for business reasons in the private sector.

When it came, modern reform intended to open up both society and the economy, giving people freedom of movement and allowing increased trade competition. The outcome was a better allocation of capital and labour through greater specialisation, and improved economic returns. The main vehicle for effecting this change was trade reform. However, the direct impact of trade liberalisation on the deployment of labour was much less than that of technological change in this past decade. Each in turn favoured capital deepening (or organisational changes such as outsourcing), and re-engineering core competencies that further reduced the demand for labour.

We are in this respect reminded of Sadie's work (1983) regarding an earlier period. He noted that in the 1970s there had been a considerable tendency in the South African economy to substitute capital (the scarce production factor) for labour (the abundant factor). This process had been characterised by greatly increased capital deepening per unit of labour in the non-agricultural sectors of the economy. Contributing causes that were identified included:

- the negative real cost of capital (that is, interest rates generally being lower than inflation) and the high real cost of labour throughout this period, favouring substitution of capital for labour;
- sharply increased labour union activity, favouring automation in order to reduce the exposure to work stoppages;
- the shortage of specific labour skills, favouring the transfer of such skills onto machines by way of automation; and
- the type of technology used (that is, First World-oriented instead of favouring the use of South Africa's abundant Third World resource–labour), which is to an important degree also a managerial preference reflecting a First World-orientation, and therefore more often than not highly sophisticated, and by implication imported.

Fast forward to the 1990s, and the only feature no longer present is the negative cost of capital (it has become sharply positive as interest rates have been raised higher than inflation), but that has not changed the trend as the impact of all the other considerations has apparently intensified.

The change from being a highly protected domestic economy, dependent on efficient mining operations to generate most foreign exchange, to being a more open economy encouraging trade competition generally, can be seen in the changing composition of South Africa's exports in Table 6.

Table 6: Changing Composition of South Africa's Exports, 1925–2001

	1925 %	1980 %	1991 %	2001 %
Gold	43	51	30	11
Other mining	12	25	36	45
Agriculture	25	9	5	6
Primary exports	80	85	71	62
Manufactures	20	15	29	38
Total exports	100	100	100	100

Sources: Bruggemans (1984), Customs and Excise Statistics, Jones (2002), SARB Quarterly Bulletin (various).

Throughout this book reference is made to import substitution by way of trade protection as the main impetus to early industrialisation. This kept the manufacturing industry domestically focused. Trade reform from the mid-1980s onwards lowered import protection and gave a major impetus to private business to become more efficient and trade-competitive. This and the stagnating economic conditions in the home markets made exporting more viable, aided by the deepening undervaluation of the rand after 1992. The resulting transformation can be seen in the changing composition of South African exports in recent years (see Table 6 above). This is clearly so, even if the comparative data for 1980 included temporary windfall earnings for gold, while by 2001 South Africa was increasingly benefiting from platinum exports.

What stands out is the dramatic change in the contribution from manufactures. Table 6 shows that export of manufactures have come into their own, reflective of fundamental changes in the economy as well as in the relations with other countries. Africa's share in our annual total export, for instance, has jumped from 6% in 1990 to 13% in 1999–2001, most of it manufactures.

Import penetration ratios provide another way of illustrating these changes. Imports relative to GDP averaged 30% of GDP during 1946–1960 as post-war demand and industrialisation ensured a high level of imports. The ratio then dropped to 24% during 1961–1973 (on account of the import replacement policy), perked up slightly under the influence of two gold booms to 27% during 1974–1982, virtually collapsed to 20% during the isolation decade of 1983–1993, but has since increased again to over 31% in early 2002 as the economy has progressively opened up.

The change in employment has been equally dramatic. We tend to be aware of changing employment conditions through personal observation, specifically announcements of large investment projects that will be creating x number of new jobs, or news coverage about layoffs, or x number of jobs having been lost during the quarter or year, in this or that company or industry. Over time, we believe we understand the labour market well enough, especially if the news is slanted in one way all the time.

However, this approach is unlikely to offer a comprehensive picture of what is actually happening, although it may well reflect general sentiment.

In the older, mainly industrial and mining sectors of the economy, labour shedding has taken place steadily throughout the past decade. Such shedding has been measured accurately and has been widely reported on, in the process influencing perceptions all round. By contrast, the creation of new jobs, primarily in the services sectors, especially in smaller businesses, is more difficult to establish and report on, except in vague unacceptable ways. And even where reporting has been attempted, it has had great difficulty in competing with the bad news about big labour sheddings.

Understanding 'unemployment' is a complicated process. Like individuals and companies, old jobs tend to 'die' and new ones are 'born'. The churn factor (known as staff turnover) can be slow in bad times (when job deaths may be rising faster, making staff insecure) and accelerate in good times (when job births may suddenly increase, making staff eager to look elsewhere).

Consequently, it is quite a challenge to understand how many jobs there are at any one stage, with a job defined as minimally working x number of hours a week, with a further distinction between what we have become used to calling formal and informal sector jobs. There is no central register where people of working age, or any change in their working conditions are recorded. The government is reduced either to guessing what the number is, or doing the scientific equivalent through representative sampling or surveys. Asking some 30 000 people, selected in a certain way, can give a good feel of what the other 26 million South Africans of working age are up to, provided such surveys are done well and are large enough in size to represent the entire population of working age. Equally important, respondents must feel confident to speak out honestly about their employment situation, making it crucial that confidentiality is assured, and accepted as such.

Before we analyse this modern picture, let us look back over the past three decades, as it took a while to change the approach to collecting data—an approach which for too long has inhibited our understanding of structural changes.

Formal versus Informal Employment

During the 1960s, prior to any economic stagnation, White labour was essentially fully employed. Some Black labour worked in sectors of the modern economy, earning industrial wages, compared to a large subsistence economy existing in the rural parts of the country. These were two completely different worlds, but over the following three decades they would become fused into one. Data-gathering was very much a part of this change process.

Labour surveys in the 1960s were focused on the modern parts of the economy. They were also industry-based and undertaken via employers (what so far has been termed the core of the formal sector). The result was a multitude of industry surveys which were consolidated into an overall picture. But this was not a comprehensive picture as there was no attempt to sample the entire population—apart from population censuses—to establish how it was economically engaged.

Even in those days, small independents that were not part of any organised trades fell outside the net (and are hereafter referred to as the formal sector's periphery—still formal sector, but having to be surveyed separately for us to be aware of their existence). In addition, while the formal, or modern, sector of the economy was well organised, informal activity as a sector was not as yet recognised, as it was not significant in scale, except for subsistence farming. South Africa was in many ways a divided as well as an underdeveloped economy and society.

We are told by Bhorat and Hodge (1999) that in 1970 the labour force amounted to 7.5 million people, 2.5 million of whom were in agriculture. The remaining 5 million were distributed in what comes across as a modern industrial economy. A part of these (3.8 million) was being surveyed via employers. The remainder may be classified as formal periphery, but some of these (for example, domestic service workers, who were probably undercounted) would today be classified as informal.

From 1970, things started to change. Population and labour force growth proceeded at an even, high pace, but economic growth faltered and tax rates became very high. Whereas in the 1960s modern sector employment had expanded very quickly, continuously creating the impression of skilled labour shortages in critical areas, and unemployment remained mostly hidden out in the rural areas, a change in rhythm now occurred. Modern sector employment growth slowed somewhat and—at a time of increasing urbanisation—a gap opened up with labour force growth. Labour absorption had started its long decline.

A portion of the slowing in labour absorption can be ascribed to the high tax regime, encouraging more (small) independents to drop from view into what may be termed an 'underground' economy, free of tax. Another group found that there was no longer quite the same job opportunities at large employers. They still found employment, but in activities not captured by the industry surveys. Thus did the formal periphery start to expand. Relatively high incomes were still being earned, both in the underground economy as well as in the periphery, but this was no longer registered as part of formal employment (though some of it was captured as part of national income estimates). The residue that remained became unemployment—not the frictional variety that had always been present, but for the first time modern, industrial (rather than subsistence) structural unemployment. From an estimated 0.5 million or less than 10% of the labour force in 1970, unemployment began its long march outside of the subsistence economy, in the metropolitan cities and informal settlements increasingly dotting the landscape.

As economic growth slowed, so did employment growth. In the mid-1980s, Peruvian reformer Hernando De Soto (1989, 2000) wrote an influential book about informal economic activity. It inspired a closer look at South Africa's own informal economic activity—a part of the subsistence sector but increasingly of an urban, industrial nature rather than farming only.

By 1990, the official labour statistics, still largely being gathered along the lines described so far, registered a high-water mark for formal core employment (see Table 7 on page 134). From 3.8 million people in 1970, it had grown to 5.7 million.

In addition, from 1990, large employers in the formal core started to shed labour at a rate of 100 000 jobs a year. Some of these people retired, some emigrated, some were absorbed into the periphery, some became informally employed, some dropped from view (though still economically active in the underground economy), and some became unemployed. As to the manner in which employees became designated as working in the formal or informal sectors, this was, and apparently remains, largely a matter decided at the discretion of the interviewer doing the survey. Informal work can also be described as a condition of 'under-employment'. The value it adds and income earned is typically one-third or less that in formal work. It is a condition, which in the modern sector of the economy comes close to that of unemployment, being survivalist in nature.

This differentiation of the South African labour force into formal and informal sectors, core and periphery parts, is reminiscent of the modern labour markets in OECD countries. According to the International Labour Office (2001), these markets have become more segmented in the sense that employers explicitly differentiate between fixed and variable market components, with the first as career-oriented and the second with little career orientation and training. In addition, other segments can be distinguished, such as part-time and job-sharing employment as well as short-term contract workers and external groups such as agency temporaries, sub-contracting and self-employed. Anecdotally, we know that all these features can now be found in the modern South African labour market, but a clear breakdown of the labour force along these lines remains absent from official survey results.

Statistics that are available show that in the decade of the 1990s, South Africa's economy generated 17% real GDP growth overall, with 6% less formal labour employed. There appears to have been a major change in the organisation of the workload, and a dishoarding of labour, suggesting a major increase in productivity (as mentioned in Chapter 3).

Table 7: Labour Growth and Composition in South Africa
1970–1990 The Stagnation Phase
1990–2000 The Rationalisation Phase

Millions	1970	1990	1995	1999
Total employed	?	10.0*	9.3	10.4
Less: Informal sector	?	0.5*	0.6	1.9
Sub-total	7.5	9.5	8.7	8.5
Less: Agriculture	2.5	1.8*	1.2	1.1
Sub-total	5.0	7.7	7.5	7.4
Less: Domestic service	0.4*	0.7*	0.7	0.8
Total formal sector	4.6	7.0	6.8	6.6
▪ Employer/core	3.8	5.7	5.3	4.9
▪ Periphery	0.8*	1.3	1.5	1.7

Sources: StatsSA, SARB, Bhorat and Hodge (1999), own estimates*.

During this time a reservoir of surplus labour skills came into being—people who were retired, underemployed or unemployed. A further extension of this reservoir may well currently be living abroad after having emigrated, with a portion of such emigrants remaining potential returnees in the event of South African opportunities improving, compared to perceived opportunities and experiences elsewhere.

The extent of this overall skill reservoir is not known. Lewis (2001), for example, estimates that by 2001 there was no longer a domestic surplus of highly skilled labour (essentially those with a post-matric education and some relevant work experience), while there was still a surplus of over half a million of skilled labour (with some work experience and at least a matric education). Statistics South Africa (LFS September 2002) has estimated the number of unemployed in these skill reservoirs during 2002 to have been 300 000 and 1.8 million respectively, though not all of these may be considered 'practically employable' as highly skilled and skilled labour for a variety of reasons. In addition, some 500 000 to 750 000 South Africans have probably emigrated these past fifteen years, at least half of them being 'older' generation and skilled to highly skilled.

That more labour can be obtained out of this reservoir is certain, but the skill surplus does not appear large and its presence should not be counted upon indefinitely. For the immediate future, it would seem that relatively slow economic growth (3% p.a.) and ongoing labour rationalisation should throw up more surplus skills. But work is steadily being created in the periphery and informal sectors, emigration is still continuing and at some point the large employers in the formal core will end their labour shedding (see also Chapter 9).

Improved Labour Surveys

Statistics South Africa (StatsSA) used to undertake two surveys of employment: a narrow-based quarterly one, the Survey of Total Employment and Earnings (STEE); and a more broad-based annual one, the October Household Survey (OHS). These surveys have been redesigned, with new instruments having appeared on the scene, such as the Labour Force Survey (LFS) being undertaken by StatsSA.

Formal core employment (as per industry-employer surveys pre-1998 and the STEE survey thereafter) peaked in 1990 and has since fallen by 20%—a loss of one million such formal high-paying jobs (see Table 8). The main losses were spread between mining, manufacturing, construction and parastatals. By contrast, the trade sectors were characterised by employment gains.

Table 8: Changes in Formal 'Core' Employment, 1990–2000 Employer-Based and STEE Surveys

	Change in numbers employed	% change
Mining	–375 000	–50
Manufacturing	–250 000	–16
Construction	–200 000	–50
Parastatals	–100 000	–40
Trading sectors	+100 000	+10
Other services	–175 000	–10
Total	–1 000 000	–20

Sources: SARB, StatsSA (OHS).

According to the OHS Survey, the formal periphery employment (now identified as formal employment not covered by the STEE survey, that is, other than core) has been on a growing trend over this period. For example, it rose between 1996 and 1999 from 1.5 million to 1.7 million, and was subsequently revised upward to 1.9 million for 2000 and to 2.4 million in 2002. This suggests that at least a portion of the formal STEE core employment loss since 1990 has been compensated for by an increase in employment elsewhere in the formal sector. The types of activities absorbing such formal periphery labour (and not covered by STEE, with that survey now renamed SEE) include:

- eating and drinking establishments, boarding houses and guest farms (including Bed and Breakfasts);
- water and air transport;
- financial institutions (other than banks and insurance companies);
- real estate and business services;
- private educational services;
- medical and other health services;
- welfare and religious organisations;
- recreational and cultural services; and
- the primary sector (agriculture, hunting, forestry and fishing).

There is reason to believe that there were substantial increases in economic activity and employment in the 1990s in most of these formal periphery sectors, apart from the many people who dropped from view, but remained economically active in the underground economy. This makes talk of one million formal sector job losses during the decade just the visible part of a much more complex change process. These job losses did happen, but new jobs opened up elsewhere, informally *and* formally—apparently enough to limit the actual decline in formal jobs overall to a much lesser number than that perceived as a result of news coverage of these surveys. Indeed, taking into account informal jobs, there has been a net increase in the total number of jobs.

Taken together, formal core and periphery employment shrank from an estimated peak of 7 million in 1990 to 6.8 million in 1996 and to 6.7 million in 2000 (apart from those who dropped from view, but who remained economically active in the underground economy). Since then this number has jumped to 6.9 million in late 2001, and to 7 million in 2002. Though this book's analysis suggests a turning to be near in formal employment conditions, with some proof of this being the case in the core of the formal sector during late 2002, and with the formal periphery in any case more lively with entrepreneurial start-ups already for many years, the formal sector gains for 2001–2002 as per the LFS may as yet not so much reflect genuine increases as being reclassifications of previous informal activity (the latter having supposedly fallen off to a similar extent). For consistency's sake, it would be practical to maintain the labour market profile for 2000 through 2002, until more convincing proof of growing formal *and* informal employment has been established.

In addition, the skill composition of such formally employed labour changed significantly. According to Bhorat and Hodge (1999), the share of skilled labour grew from some 6% of total employed labour in 1970 to 18% in 1995, mostly deployed in the modern formal sectors of the economy. Today, according to Lewis (2001), this share is nearer 20%, and it is still steadily rising, in line with greater technological sophistication and capital deepening. The Actuarial Society of South Africa (ASSA) predicts that it will reach 26% by 2015 (see Chapter 9).

Apart from the apparent shrinkage in total formal employment since 1990 and the skill transformation of formally employed labour since 1970, a very large informal labour sector has come into being over the past two decades. Today it numbers an estimated 2.5 million participants (which is quite possibly still a sizeable undercount), in addition to 0.8 million in domestic service and 1.1 million employed in agriculture. Thus, total employment gives the impression of slowly rising, perhaps from 9.3 million in 1996 to 10.4 million in 1999–2000 (see Table 9 om page 140), rising to an estimated 11 million in 2002. It is possible, though, that larger and better-managed surveys may be more successful in counting the actual employed, especially those informally employed, explaining part of the observed increase.

These structural changes must be seen against a backdrop of incomplete urbanisation as well as rapid population and labour force growth for most of the 1990s. The population nearly doubled between the late 1960s and the early 1990s (to 40 million), and growth in the labour force was even faster. Yet formal and informal employment growth slowed down during this period, and stagnated during the 1990s, as discussed. Data provided by StatsSA and that used by Bhorat and Hodge (1999), for instance, show that total employment increased by only 40% between 1970 and 1999, from 7.5 million to 10.4 million (see Table 8 on page 135). Total formal employment increased by about 45% (but in addition how many of such skilled labour dropped from view while remaining economically active in the underground economy?). As a consequence of this divergence between the still high increase in population and the much more limited increase in total employment, the pool of unemployed surplus labour grew explosively, to as few as 6.5 million by 2000–2001 and as many as 7.9 million in 2002 (on the expanded definition, see below), compared to about 0.5 million in 1970 (excluding subsistence farming).

Taken together these numbers reflect four key factors:

- the relentless force of population growth during these years;
- the stunting of employment growth in the stagnation period between 1970 and 1990;
- the impact of employment rationalisation since 1990; and
- the apparent structural changes in the composition of employment (that is, formal versus informal, skilled versus less-skilled).

The net effect is a steady increase in the number of unemployed labour either 'willing and seeking work' (which is the official definition of unemployment, registering some 4 million or 26% in 2000), or 'too demoralised' and no longer looking for work, but probably willing to try again if there were to be a slim chance of finding work (the expanded definition of unemployment, which adds another 2.5 million to the officially unemployed, for a total unemployment of 6.5 million or 36% in 2000).

The main difference between these two approaches (that is, the official and the expanded definition of unemployment) is that under the expanded definition, the number of unemployed is realistically much higher. As to the remarkable difference in estimated expanded unemployment between 2000–2001 (6.5 million) and 2002 (7.9 million), this probably reflects definitional problems with regard to those people who are considered employed in subsistence agriculture (1 million less so shown by 2002 compared to 2000) and suggested declines in informal and domestic service employment, but with a better than equivalent increase in formal employment. Besides the possibility of reclassification distorting these estimates, domestic service employment probably has suffered from higher legislated wages and other contractual obligations. But for informal sector employment generally to be trending down in an economy growing by 3% annually during this period is somewhat hard to believe, at a time when the total economically active population increased by 0.5 million to 19 million. It could, though, reflect growing reticence among respondents to answer questions about their work activity out of fear of public scrutiny, at a time when tax collection is increasingly being tightened up everywhere in the economy.

Nevertheless, the overall picture is one of grinding change in employment, and therefore in economic structure. This has been underway for some decades now. Formal core employment peaked in 1990 and has since then fallen steadily, by nearly 10% at large employers in the public sector and by more than 20% in the private sector. For the first time in years, though, the second half of 2002 recorded a small gain in core formal employment at an annualised rate of just over 1%. This gain was also independently reflected in BER business surveys. However, only future LFS estimates and BER surveys can confirm whether this is the secular turning point in formal employment levels. On this score, early indications were that 2003 did not start on a promising note, though this may have been only a short-term aberration. A secular change for the better is probably not far away, if it has not already taken place.

After taking into account those elements of formal employment in the periphery only covered by the broader OHS-survey, total formal employment (as surveyed), is today probably on a par with the early 1980s. What remains unknown is how much additional such activity is still taking place that has dropped from view and is not being registered in any survey.

Only the recognition of informal work, and its considerable expansion in the 1980s and especially the 1990s, gives us the impression of the country not having stood still, but in fact having made a little progress in total employment. But when we consider that the economic value of a formal job is at least three times that of an informal one, it is very clear that employment rationalisation has had unfortunate consequences. Progress has been very slim so far in creating new worthwhile, high-value (formal) jobs to any degree that has been surveyed. All the net additions since 1990 have been in informal employment. And there has not as yet been a clear effective reduction in unemployment (whether on the official or expanded definition).

As of February 2000, StatsSA has run a new 'panel rotating' survey, the Labour Force Survey (LFS), which will be undertaken twice-yearly. The pilot of the LFS showed up higher employment levels than the OHS of October 1999, although most of the changes can either be attributed to closer questioning of respondents (agriculture and domestic service specifically) or sampling error (formal and informal sectors). In the main, the LFS offers a better understanding of the subsistence part of the labour market, but no major surprises.

Table 9: Composition of the Labour Force, 1996–1999

Millions	1996	1999
Formally employed (STEE)	5.3	4.9
Formally employed (non-STEE OHS)	1.5	1.7
Total formal employed	6.8	6.6
Informally employed (OHS):		
▪ Informal sector	1.0	1.9
▪ Domestic service	0.7	0.8
▪ Agriculture	0.8	1.1
Total informal employed	2.5	3.8
Total employed	9.3	10.4
Total unemployed (expanded definition)	4.6	5.9
Total economically active (i.e., employed + unemployed)	13.9	16.3
Total not economically active (e.g., housewives, retirees, pupils)	10.8	10.0
Total of working age (15 to 65 years)	24.7	26.3
Unemployment rate (expanded definition, i.e., unemployed/economically active)	33%	36%

Source: StatsSA (OHS 1999), July 2000.

Such improved surveying of especially subsistence farming allows the extent of unemployment to be further narrowed down. On the expanded definition of unemployment, the OHS in October 1999 showed 5.9 million unemployed out of a total of 16.3 million economically active (a 36% unemployment rate). When the LFS is used, however, many more people are stating that they are available for work, thus increasing the economically active to 18.4 million. After deducting 11.9 million in employment, this leaves 6.5 million people unemployed, an unemployment rate of 35.5%. The net result is an insignificant change in the unemployment rate, but a better understanding of the total number of formal and informal employed, compared to the old OHS. However, as later LFS results through 2002 have shown, there may remain a remarkable undercount of informal work, in part perhaps due to reticence among respondents to forthrightly answer any work-related questions.

To appreciate the full relevance of 6.5 million unemployed, this statistic should be compared to the condition prevailing in 1970 when economic momentum started to falter. In that watershed year, unemployment was estimated at 'only' 0.5 million, an unemployment rate of less than 10%. The deterioration over the intervening three decades has been horrific and socially debilitating.

Future Projections for Unemployment

The rising level of unemployment should be approached with care. We should be hesitant to extrapolate the implied trend uncritically into the future. The rising unemployment numbers reflect maximum structural adjustment in the late 1990s, relative economic stagnation, and the least attractive labour dispensation for creating new jobs, occurring under conditions of rapid increases in a healthy population and potential labour force (see Chapter 6).

The main changes in coming years are likely to be that structural adjustment will be completed, relative economic stagnation will end and faster economic growth will resume. Furthermore, the labour dispensation may find its least attractive cost aspects (from a job creation point of view) weakened in the long-term as labour legislation continues to evolve. In this respect, the potential for absorbing lesser skilled people apparently remains considerable.

Unfortunately, the country will no longer enjoy a healthy population due to the HIV/Aids pandemic (see Chapter 6). A relatively major unknown will be inward and outward migration stimulated by all these developments (see Chapter 9).

The main outcome of the above developments is probably that population and labour force growth will become stunted, effectively plateauing within half a decade from now. Given that South Africa is only about 60% urbanised at present, the country's key metropolitan areas (Johannesburg, Pretoria, Cape Town, Port Elizabeth, East London, Durban, Bloemfontein and Kimberly) should still expand considerably in size, but not to the point of overloading the existing local infrastructure. Best estimates for the next 30 years suggest a 30% to 60% increase in urbanised populations, which translates back to a 75% to 80% overall urbanisation ratio at peak development 30 years hence. If population growth were not to be checked as now expected, the mushrooming of the larger city populations would have made for a radically different urban reality, one which today can already be found in many of the poorer developing countries. On present trends, that apparently is not going to be South Africa's future, unless the existing cities are allowed to decay further due to starvation of capital infrastructure budgets. South Africa probably has not absorbed the worst of the ongoing decay yet, but it will be slowing down sooner, and at a higher level of infrastructure intactness, than perhaps some of the more pessimistic are inclined to foresee.

There is a downside, though. The average unemployment data hides enormous gaps between the various race groups, between the genders, and between urban and rural people. These divides, in turn, appear to correlate closely with years and quality of formal schooling. On the expanded definition, African males saw their unemployment rate mostly unchanged at 37% between 1996 and 1999. In contrast, the white male unemployment rate worsened from 4.5% to 6.3%. Female unemployment rates are higher than for males (15% higher in the case of African females and 1% higher in the case of White females). The Indian and Coloured groups are midway between these two extremes, but increasing relatively the fastest (from 12% to 17.8%, and from 14.5% to 19.3% respectively).

Capital deepening in response to increasing labour costs may worsen these trends in the short-term. But the impact of HIV/Aids in limiting population and labour force growth, and the end to structural adjustment and economic stagnation, should arrest these increases overall and eventually turn them around. Improved schooling, along with faster economic growth and a more job-friendly labour dispensation, are the only serious answers to halving the African unemployment rate as it now exists. On present trends, that could take a generation—a 30-year time horizon. However, as schooling is at present still deteriorating (see Chapter 7) and HIV/Aids could impact heavily among existing teachers (see Chapter 6), this is quite a challenge.

Absorbing Change: A Productivity Revolution

It may be the widespread impression that overall employment in South Africa is steadily dropping, but as already shown total employment in South Africa has actually crept steadily higher, from 9.3 million in 1996 to 11 million in 2002 (even if some part of this increase may reflect only better survey sampling). Nevertheless, the composition of such employment is certainly still changing.

Both these observations are borne out by real GDP, which has been steadily rising at nearly 3% p.a. since 1994. Those who have retained their formal employment (or newly gained it in new economic activities) are on average more productive. Those who have been made redundant, have had to compete with newcomers to the labour market for the limited number of new job openings still being added. 'Old-timers' have work experience, but may be more costly than new entrants, some of whom may have better education and who will accept lower pay. These trade-offs generally will determine who wins employment (if it is not self-made) and who does not. But overall labour deployment is more closely in line with skill proficiency and the ability to produce under the influence of ever more intense competitive pressures, from without and within the economy. More often than not, such skill is further enhanced by capital deepening, as the relative cost of labour continues to favour capital, even when the latter's cost is high.

The average GDP growth of 3.3% in the 1970s and 1.5% in the 1980s was achieved entirely by inputting more capital (physical capacity) and labour. The additional GDP growth that could have been had from organising these inputs more cleverly or from some other technical source (see Chapter 8 on technology's more recent contribution) was absent.

Only in the 1990s do we encounter a watershed as the bigger, older employer organisations in the formal core covered by the STEE-survey shed 17% of their labour. This made a 34% increase in labour productivity possible over the decade in this core part of the formal sector. On present trends, the 2000s decade will likely see a further major increase in this sector's labour productivity, as restructuring is not complete, while evolving technology creates new opportunities for organising work differently. After years of protection, the economy has been subjected to a shake-out that on average has made it more productive, in that the labour force has been more efficiently deployed, but with capital deepening explaining much of the change, implying a major sacrificing of labour absorption ability.

These various forces have worked to reduce employment in a formal visible sense, as detailed above. This is not an unusual experience for a protected stagnating economy in transition. Other examples with similar experiences include Australia, New Zealand and the United Kingdom (in the 1980s), all the countries previously under Communist control (including China) in the 1990s, and large parts of Latin America steadily reforming themselves along market-lines over many years.

That we are not employing all our labour resource reflects a still-increasing population (though growth by 2002 was rapidly slowing down on account of the HIV/Aids pandemic), jobs being created at a slower pace than in the distant past and a mismatch between the skills being offered at the wage being demanded. It is not only a matter of mismatched skill supply and demand (too few with the right education, too many with too little education). It is also due to a lack of even faster economic growth that would create more jobs, and especially the features inhibiting new employment (legislation and political demands that create employer expectations of higher future costs, encouraging capital deepening for existing employees instead).

How far the rationalisation forces still have to run is not easily anticipated. Gold mining, the parastatals, central government, agriculture and probably most of manufacturing and services have shed much of their excess labour from the past. A large part of these rationalisations may have been completed and we are not likely to lose another million jobs over the coming decade due to these forces.

In contrast, new entrepreneurial start-ups, especially geared to the new technologies, have further to run. Private security has unfortunately more expansive potential, too. Greater changes in agriculture in terms of land reform will probably absorb more labour. And in the bigger picture, it is not only cost-reduction, but also the culture of doing things differently and better under the prodding of more intense local and foreign competition that will increasingly be driving our labour productivity. Through these structural changes we have actively joined a world trend after decades of being relatively dormant.

Whole new industries have been created where none existed before. Taxis are one example, with 120 000 taxis on the road today apparently giving employment to some 300 000 people (when allowing for multiple shifts, and fare collection). Bed and breakfast tourism is another example.

Private security today counts well over 200 000 employees. Cellphones, especially the retailing network, and the many (new) businesses either servicing computers and their networks, or providing content services for them, in an infrastructure potentially approaching that of the motor industry, are other examples of expanding work opportunities. These are probably all examples of formal periphery rather than informal sector work.

In contrast, for informal work activity we especially look towards retailing, building activity and other examples of private informal services. Furthermore, there is also the informal protection offered by over 100 000 'car-guards' at public parking spaces across the country.

While increasing urbanisation and growing African immigration will still encourage such informal sector activities to expand, population demographics are likely to be the bigger force in stunting its growth overall. Population and labour force growth will shortly come to a virtual standstill on account of HIV/Aids, if nothing effective is done to end this pandemic (see Chapter 9 for a further discussion of the effects of HIV/Aids on labour supply and skills). The scene is being prepared for a change in overall labour utilisation. Less inhibiting legislation and labour demands generally (a learning curve for all concerned), and faster economic growth as the long preparatory reform phase finally starts to pay dividends, should see an increase in the rate of formal job creation (though nothing as fast as the 1960s).

Despite deplorably low educational and skill levels, and despite political demands and expectations about these and empowerment generally, the national unemployment rate is unlikely to climb further, while the employment level should not remain as stagnant as in recent years. Unlike the 1990s, the 2000s decade should see a genuine increase in the formal employment level and an equally genuine falling unemployment rate.

Most of the one-off negative forces should be ending or lose their vigour, while the job-creating forces should gain in strength, even if only slightly, at the very moment that population and labour force growth come to a virtual standstill. In other words, we can look forward to a period where the interplay of forces is going to be different from what has become the norm for decades now.

This reality, that is, an eventual shortage rather than surplus of skills, and of labour capable of acquiring such skills, may over time become the ultimate reason not to give up on a high-wage policy. It should increasingly make sense politically as unemployment shrinks, but it will probably make the ending of structural unemployment unnecessarily difficult to achieve (see earlier comment in Chapter 3).

Expected Changes in Employment

Even as the economy was being restructured, the social implications of these changes suggested steady and widespread social and physical degradation. Increased unemployment worsened rural poverty, urban decay and crime. Slow economic growth, reform that was too gradual and a high-wage policy, at a time of rapid population expansion, offered a vision of progressive structural and social decay.

As recently as 1996, this still led to projections of stagnant (under-estimated) employment levels, (over-estimated) current unemployment of some 8 million, steady population growth to a projected 65 million by 2025, and a more-than-doubling of unemployment in a generation (to over 14 million by 2025).

Trade reform will continue to lower import barriers over the remainder of this decade in terms of undertakings to the World Trade Organisation (WTO), as well as in terms of bilateral trade agreements, such as with the European Union (EU) and the Southern African Development Community (SADC). South Africa can therefore expect more disruption of its labour force as import penetration rises further, economic specialisation deepens, the relative size of agriculture, mining and the public sector declines, industrial activity is maintained and the services activities expand steadily overall. In addition, the country will continue to absorb advanced technology. All such trends will encourage a greater usage of skilled as opposed to less-skilled labour in the economy, and the changes are likely to take place against a background of a steadily accelerating pace of economic growth until some constraint caps the rate of development (most likely the availability of skilled labour—see Chapter 9).

Lurking in the background will be the continued disruptive influence of a high-wage environment, favouring the few while excluding more and more marginal labour, as capital deepening continues to be favoured by all these tendencies.

As mentioned, economic growth has picked up speed since the dismal performance of 1970–1993. During 1994–2002, real GDP growth has averaged 2.8% p.a., by 2002 making real GDP 25% bigger than it was in 1994. The outlook for the first decade of the new millennium is a steady acceleration towards real GDP growth of 4% p.a. on average.

As to the prospects for labour in this outlook, the rationalisations to be completed during 2000–2005 do not appear to be excessive compared to what has been achieved since the mid-1980s. Net labour shedding is likely to continue in gold mining (another estimated 100 000 jobs), and in industry and services generally (another estimated 200 000 jobs). There has also been the expectation of further labour rationalisation in the public sector, but as of early 2003 it would seem that this sector is already experiencing net growth in employment.

Simultaneously, faster economic growth is expected to generate formal and informal sector employment at a rate of 1% to 1.5% p.a. on a 10 million employment base in 2000 as per the OHS (1999), that is, 100 000 to 150 000 net new jobs annually.

This suggests a neutral to slightly positive outlook for net job creation in the formal sector through 2005, and faster net gains thereafter as structural shedding eases. This does not discount the impact of a high-wage dispensation, unless government succeeds in maintaining moderation in the public sector, and trade competition becomes even stronger in its impact on the private sector.

Most of the net job losses are likely to be less-skilled in nature, while most of the net gains in the formal sector will be skilled jobs, though we must allow for the presence of a large and growing informal sector capable of absorbing less-skilled labour (see Chapter 9 for a more detailed discussion of skills availability in South Africa).

Real Wage Growth Going Forward

The impression is easily gained that the ANC government wishes to use affirmative action at any cost, and that going forward it will continue to implement such a policy with full force.

With regards to social delivery, via state taxation and spending, such bias seems to be very much the case (see Chapter 7). However, when it comes to favouring organised labour by way of a high real wage policy, especially in the private sector, the political case is less clear-cut. The flip side of such political backing, as so far seen in Chapter 3, is that there are now more Black unemployed 'outsiders' than employed 'insiders', illustrated by the widening income distribution among Blacks between 1993 and 1999 (compare Chapters 1 and 9). Over time this reality may change the political dynamic in favour of any real opposition claiming to represent the poor. During 2000, there were an estimated 3.6 million Blacks formally employed, and total union membership stood at 3.3 million. In contrast, there were over 6.5 million unemployed, of which at least 6 million were Black. This is in addition to the 5.2 million workers, again mostly Black, informally employed throughout the economy at very low wages. In other words, there were nearly 12 million people either unemployed or barely earning a living through informal work, most of them Black, against 3.3 million unionised labour earning relatively high wages and salaries. Politically, these ratios do not support an indefinite favouring of labour insiders.

The government therefore has an important political incentive to move to the middle of the political road, favouring less of a high-wage dispensation that boosts the few while creating more unemployed. This political calculation would only diminish in strength as unemployment starts to fall, and those in favourite (high-wage) employment clearly become the majority.

There is visible evidence of government concern about creating too big an unemployed underclass. There is its policy of wage moderation in the public sector (partly shaped by its need to reduce the budget deficit, but plausibly also as an example to private sector labour in terms of Gear); its undertaking to address any unintended consequences of labour legislation (especially at smaller employers); and its willingness to promote trade competition, allowing business to shed labour as it faces both foreign producers and domestic labour demands, and potentially indirectly disciplining such demands.

As our economy proceeds to open up, trade competition will increase further, with business able and willing to meet such a challenge through capital deepening and greater use of technology and more skilled, pay-differentiated labour. This seems to result in a natural restructuring of the labour force, away from older, labour-intensive sectors employing less-skilled labour benefiting most from union representation, towards newer, service-based, higher-skilled, pay-differentiated employment gaining less from such representation. This is of course what happened overseas, too, when economies such as the United States, Britain and Australia were transformed by greater trade specialisation.

At the same time, we should take cognisance of the fact that labour union membership and power in the United States has been rising again, apparently in the wake of globalisation and trade-induced layoffs and real income declines among the less-skilled.

Through natural rebalancing of the labour market over time as demand for skills becomes better balanced with supply, real wage growth should be restrained in line with underlying productivity, in favour of greater labour absorption through new job creation. Such an outcome is still expected, even if most of today's unemployed are largely unemployable in a modern service economy due to a low level of education, when the need is for higher skills. For in a reasonably high growth environment with a realistic real wage progression, labour shortages will come into being that will encourage a greater business willingness to train available labour (the same logic that governs the fixed investment decisions of private sector companies).

Consequently, unless there is a change in the political condition of the country, favouring protection of labour anew, there should be slow but steady erosion of real wage growth and a comparable improvement in labour absorption, with a modest improvement on the 1990s record.

Deregulation

Deregulation is part of the concept of reducing the size of the public sector, even though it does not always reduce the size of the budget *per se*. Making previously regulated public services more closely subject to market forces presumably enhances efficiency and contributes to economic growth, to a greater or lesser degree, depending on the activities deregulated.

The United States economy underwent fundamental deregulation, starting with President Reagan in the 1980s. In many areas the rules governing business practice were simplified, or even abolished (though in other spheres, for example, environmental and consumer protection, the rules have been tightened). Generally, market processes, reliant on price signals rather than bureaucratic regulation, received more scope to direct the economic traffic in the 1980s and 1990s. The same took place in the United Kingdom when the Thatcher years saw many changes in favour of market discipline, particularly regarding privatisation of public assets.

This is in contrast to countries and cultures such as Germany and Japan, where the rulebook remained unreformed and privatisation mostly absent. Hewlett Packard could never have been founded in Germany, as it started as an informal partnership in an old garage. Microsoft would never have been started for similar reasons. In the United States anyone can start a business from home without any formality (other than informing the tax authorities at the appropriate time). In more rigid economies, a person is expected to have one or more business diplomas, aimed at regulating business standards of behaviour, but also having the effect of stifling innovation by keeping competition limited, and burying entrepreneurial business talent in demoralising paperwork.

The drive for greater efficiency and a better-performing economy and society can be observed in South Africa. We have a past that has much in common with the American West, where self-reliance was the norm, but thanks to our English and Dutch forebears we also have a history of rule-making. This was taken much further by subsequent Afrikaans governments, very much in the German fashion. The regulation ship only turned again sometime in the 1970s.

Price controls were an early victim to economic rationality. Next to go were prescribed assets (fiscal policy), followed by credit and interest rate controls of all kinds (monetary policy). Physical planning act 'reform' was undertaken (for example, influx control went). Abolition of job reservation eventually took place. Exchange control relaxation was begun. Trade reform commenced by phasing out import quotas and lowering import tariffs (potentially the biggest change agent after politics, in the way it let global competition in).

Monopolies of all kinds were dismantled. The old South African Broadcasting Corporation (SABC) monopoly made way for M-Net, DSTV, CNN, Sky and BBC. Telkom faced new competition from cellphone operators Vodacom, MTN and Cell-C. Similarly, the position of SAA as sole national carrier was ended as new airlines such as Comair/British Airways and Nationwide made their appearance. Transnet's transport monopoly came to an end as more efficient road hauliers and InterCity buses made their presence felt.

The agricultural boards in the countryside and regulated Sundays in the cities at some point simply withered away. Increasingly, the restrictions on business conduct in all forms were relaxed, such as retail opening hours (especially on Sundays and at night), liquor licences, gambling, zoning generally (for example, informal trading), and even the paperwork still required was simplified (such as registering a closed corporation rather than a limited company).

Labour regulations did tighten up, but in other respects the American model appears to prevail: something is allowed unless a rule specifically disallows it. These many changes have made South African society more open, more individualistic, less restrained and inhibited by restrictive rules. Unfortunately, a dark side (crime) thrives for exactly the same reasons under relaxed societal standards. However, this should not be a reason for going back to regulated Sundays, but rather an incentive to spread opportunity even wider.

There is nothing wrong with rules and regulations if they bring useful order to the market process. This generally requires that such rules and regulations:

- be simple;
- are not arbitrary;
- are not fragmented and diversely controlled by different authorities who may see this as an opportunity to acquire a life of their own;
- are not unnecessarily cost-increasing;
- do not give power to bureaucrats; and
- are easily applied/controlled without arbitrariness and the ability of officialdom to delay endlessly to no purpose (other than raising costs).

Unfortunately, reality remains different in many ways. Seeking permission for certain things can be a highly frustrating, demoralising business. Instead of the emphasis being on control, there can be too much arbitrariness in the regulation system—regarding labour, land rezoning, health regulations, and, most fascinating of all, road signage (where too many diverse authorities can be in play)—giving too much power to bureaucratic whim. This does not strengthen the economic base or work for the good of society. Instead, it increases the cost of doing business and starting a business, the lifeblood of our economy (see Chapter 6), and is especially intimidating for small entrepreneurs, who often do not have the time or resources to successfully navigate the rules and regulations.

Despite lingering rules and regulations, there is today much more experimentation, more success and failure, too. This is a healthy state of affairs and it explains a portion of our productivity gains and apparent reduced proneness to inflation. It is called freedom; it is nearly everywhere and allows each of us to perform more in line with our innate abilities, in comparison with what the artificial constraints of the past sought to impose on us. Lest we forget, and do not understand why there is more ferment than ever out there, it is because there are fewer instances of somebody saying 'you cannot', while at the same time the competition for a person's living and breathing space has increased. There are those who resist all such freedom, but this self-reliance and individualism is to be welcomed if it increases economic efficiency.

A Competitively Organised Economy

The micro-restructuring that has followed years of trade reform (reducing import protection) and political activism (putting demands on businesses to pay more for organised labour and incur higher non-wage costs by adhering to government activist legislation) has had one major desirable result: the economy has steadily shed its acquired inefficiencies from the past and has on balance become more productively organised (despite any new imposts incurred). Along with an undervalued currency that has come into being (see Chapters 3 and 4), such micro-economic restructuring has succeeded in making the economy more efficient and competitive.

Not only have the higher economic returns from existing, rationalised factors of production sustained economic growth of nearly 3% for a decade now, but their implications go much wider. What has effectively come to an end is the earlier import-replacement approach to industrialisation, according to which most new industrial activity did not need to pay its way in terms of exporting, while government opted to waste scarce capital on distorting social separation policies and on a scramble for self-sufficiency in critical industrial areas.

The current account condition that these choices brought into being could only be paid for by a remarkably rich mining endowment and forgiving capital inflows. With both these avenues giving out, at least temporarily, in the 1970s, 1980s and 1990s, the need arose for industry to make a far bigger contribution to exporting and to become more frugal about its importing needs.

This change is well advanced, judging by the change in export composition in recent years, and the greater temperance regarding importing even when the economy was growing at 3% annually for some years. This has been the case since 1999, yet the current account deficit has amounted to at most 0.4% of GDP, in 2002 turning into a small surplus on account of a precious metal boost (and the exceptionally undervalued rand in 2001 having a lagged impact).

Such evidence is highly encouraging for the years ahead, once fixed investment starts to expand faster than seen in years, prompted by domestic final demand. The output from such future investment activity is likely to be efficient enough to be able to supply domestic needs as well as service the export market, in the process further reducing the instability of the current account in the longer-term.

If a current account deficit does again come into being, as it likely will, it will increasingly do so because efficient fixed investment spending has once again started to outpace domestic savings. To the extent that such investments offer high economic returns, they should experience less trouble in the future to attract supplementary capital from abroad.

For a country hobbled for three decades with a severe balance of payments constraint over the current and capital accounts, this proposition is like tempting fate (for is this alleged ending of these constraints for real?). Any return to a current account deficit is therefore only likely to be allowed very gingerly by the policymaker, in order to see whether the structural reforms have indeed made enough progress for such a change in the external accounts to be attempted without running into trouble.

The betting now is that a secular turn in our external condition has already been achieved, that we have left the dependencies of the import-replacement policy and gold anchor mostly behind, and that we are already competitively organised enough to be able to sustain a higher rate of economic growth without destabilising the balance of payments on the current account unduly. The proof will lie in coming years as the present economic upswing intensifies by way of faster growth as well as longevity. The role model is Australia: a non-stop business upswing of twelve years and counting, with its balance of payments yet to turn into the constraint it used to be in a less competitive, more inefficient epoch.

The main engine to deliver these results for us will be an increasingly competitive business sector. Whereas previous generations of South Africans often wondered where the entrepreneurial business spirit and managerial capabilities would be coming from to drive a modern trading economy, and with these qualifications continuing to be heard today, South Africa's transformed business structure, with its rich and diverse mix of ethnic entrepreneurs and established business organisations, gives every impression of being up to the challenge. These provide the structure within which much new business initiative can be originated and driven to maturity, provided it is not periodically laid low by interruptions to growth, as happened too often in the past.

Today, South African business activity is conducted in a hierarchy of organisational structures that compares well with such structures in industrial countries. Some 450 listed companies dominate the business landscape, with relatively high (mature) concentrations in most mining, financial and industrial activities. A greater diffusion of businesses can be observed in the services sectors, especially in its modern high-technology niches. In addition to this sophisticated local core of companies, hundreds more multinational companies have a sizeable local presence, adding their expertise to the economy.

In total, there are over 1 million business enterprises in South Africa. Most of these are small, undercapitalised entities of an informal, survivalist nature. But registered business entities form the backbone of our market system. In early 2003, active company registrations included 6 700 public companies, 320 000 private companies and 793 000 close corporations—the new registrations growing at 7% to 10% annually since the mid-1990s (Cipro 2003).

Change in such a corporate context must be considered healthy, with non-viable enterprises failing at a reasonably rapid rate, and with new ones being born even faster. This enterprise 'churn' indicates efficient commercial market conditions at work, allowing continuous renewal of the business structure. Especially at the lower end of the organisational spectrum, the small formal and informal business enterprises fulfil an important function in developing and extending new commercial applications and markets. A lack of capital, a favourite lament of the undercapitalised, does not seem an impossible hurdle. Even many small informal economic activities tend to have access to supplier credits.

Thus, a vibrant entrepreneurial and managerial structure today houses a much-rationalised and more productive formal labour force responding to local as much as international trading opportunities. The contrast with three decades ago is a fundamental one. Then a largely closed-off and protected domestic economy was mainly dependent on a rich mining sector to earn 80% of the country's foreign exchange needs. Today, that reality lies far behind us, as even many small enterprises have rudimentary global links. South Africa is no longer the mining enclave of yore, with a creaking industrial sector locked up behind impossibly high protection walls. Instead, it is now outward-looking across most of its economic spectrum, trading competitively in a way that an older generation would barely recognise. This, in turn, sets the scene for the growth and balance of payments performances of coming years - quite different from the import-replacement and autarkic apartheid model of the mid-twentieth century.

It is this pivotal industrial change that is central to an improved economic performance in the twenty-first century, and that perhaps too many people continue to underestimate as to its inherent capabilities.

6 A SOCIAL TRANSFORMATION

Thus far we have explored two revolutions at work in South Africa—the political and the economic. There is also a third component—a social revolution which incorporates many different aspects. These include ongoing urbanisation, demographics altered by the HIV/Aids pandemic and migration flows, changing income groupings on account of economic factors, intensified crime, and social values in transition. All of these issues have a bearing on our future political and economic development, some of them favourable, some destructive. The demographic changes related to Aids are the focus of this chapter, with migration as another demographic factor discussed briefly in Chapter 9.

Demographic Interruption

HIV/Aids is one of the most debilitating of modern diseases. After a slow global start in the 1950s, 1960s and 1970s, a more rapid spreading of the virus in humans followed in the course of the 1980s. The disease apparently remained well contained in the industrialised world, but has spread much more virulently in large parts of the emerging world, nowhere more so than on the African continent, where today most of the world's HIV victims can be found, and where most Aids-related deaths have so far occurred.

Human Immunodeficiency Virus (HIV) breaks down the human body's immune system, eventually creating a condition called Acquired Immune Deficiency Syndrome (Aids). This is allegedly a condition in which the body may succumb to many different diseases, called 'opportunistic infections', that under normal circumstances the body would be capable of fighting off quite easily.

Modern medicine had initially succeeded in dramatically reducing early mortality in Africa in the course of the twentieth century, in many countries greatly increasing life expectancy. This inadvertently gave rise to population explosions on the continent, as high fertility was to take much longer in coming down, mainly through the effects of long-term economic and social development. The appearance of HIV/Aids in humans has ended population growth in those parts of the African continent most affected. In many countries in sub-Saharan Africa, life expectancies have been halved—back towards their nineteenth-century values.

At this juncture there is no known cure for HIV/Aids, and some virologists contend that there will not be an effective cure for many years, if ever. On its own, the human body could take up to an estimated 40 generations—some 1 000 years—to adapt to the virus successfully (Hooper 2000).

At present, the most we can do is to suppress the illness by taking an elaborate daily cocktail of expensive medicines. Apart from affordability, a major problem with such a course of medication is apparently 'patient fatigue'. A less than 95% adherence to the prescribed course of medication is apparently enough to cause a major relapse in a patient's condition, as well as making the virus resistant to the medication in question and such resistant strains thereafter spreading rapidly.

The most effective solution appears to be personal precautionary measures, such as long-term changes in behaviour (including much more intensive condom usage), as the virus is apparently mostly transmitted via an exchange of body fluids.

Prior to HIV/Aids taking hold in South Africa, there were firm expectations (as firm as these can ever be in demographics) about South Africa's demographic cycle and the pace of demographic change, and what this would mean in the light of the slow economic growth observed during the past three decades.

With the pandemic having taken hold, the demographic outlook may have changed fundamentally, in turn impacting on the economic and social prospects. There will be emotional pain for victims and their families, economic costs for them as well as society at large, but there may also be other unintended consequences, regarding social values and future economic opportunities for those that do not get infected. Untangling these many conflicting tendencies is a necessary precondition for understanding the viability or otherwise of the economic reforms currently being implemented.

As so much about the pandemic is uncertain (its reach, its amenability to medication, its influence over social mores, its economic costs, and society's eventual response), little can be said with certainty regarding the evolution of this condition. But that the pandemic has introduced yet another fundamental change agent into our midst appears certain.

Demographic Changes before HIV/Aids

Population projections are estimates of the future size of populations based on current trends. They are totally dependent upon the underlying assumptions regarding levels of, and trends in, future fertility, mortality and migration. For this reason, demographers tend to differ, sometimes widely, about what the future holds.

Haldenwang (1999), a demographer at the Institute of Futures Research attached to the University of Stellenbosch, has undertaken various population projections for South Africa with varying assumptions regarding fertility, mortality and migration. In order to understand more fully the population scenario facing South Africa in coming years, it is useful to contrast 'what might have been'—a population projection as if HIV/Aids were not going to be a factor, compared to the reality that HIV/Aids introduces.

HIV/Aids is not the only variable that can exert a major influence over how the size of our population and its ethnic, age, gender and geographic composition and spread will develop. As important will be factors such as human development (gaining insight and control over a person's behaviour); the level of income (and the choices it brings); urbanisation (reduced social control); changing values (whether locally derived or imported); the nature and availability of health care; and many others. All these features are associated with the level of development of a country and the choices its government and its population elect to exercise over time. Given enough time, and a fast pace of economic development, it can be truly surprising to see what different population outcomes could materialise, compared to initial expectations. Furthermore, population pressures elsewhere in the world may interact with our own dynamics to generate changing migration patterns.

Projecting population growth, composition and size is therefore not a simple matter and should be approached with circumspection. Nevertheless, it can assist with developing a 'Big Picture' of the future. Some questions to consider include:

- Relative to where we are today, will the population still double or triple in size, and over what time frame?
- Which parts of the population will be growing fastest, and which

slowest, and will this still give rise to significant changes in composition over time, especially with regard to ethnic diversity, age and geographic spread?

- How will this population change tie in with incomplete transformations such as urbanisation? Will the metropolitan populations still grow vastly bigger, and much faster than the population overall?
- What are the implications for physical and social infrastructure (transportation, telecommunication, electricity generation, housing, education, health care, social welfare)?
- Will the country's financial arrangements (old age provision, dependency ratios) be able to handle the coming changes?

For her 'high' population projection through 2031, Haldenwang (1999) did not incorporate the demographic impact of HIV/Aids. This implied that life expectancy at birth increases throughout the projection period, fertility rates decline steadily, and a high degree of African in-migration (200 000 p.a.) is assumed.

On this basis, a population estimated at just over 43 million people in 2000 can be expected to grow to over 76 million in 30 years time, and still not have peaked. If we increase the assumption regarding in-migration (to, for example, 300 000 or 400 000 p.a.), on the basis of a more successful economic performance coming about during this period (the presumption of this book) and/or bigger migratory pressures internationally, the population could have reached over 85 million during this period.

As to population composition, on the Haldenwang assumptions, the White community would remain essentially unchanged in number at 4.5 million. This, though, does reflect a census undercount of at least 10% in the base year, mainly concentrated in the Western Cape, and consequently remains an influence throughout the projection. For practical purposes, it is probably more realistic to proceed on the basis of a White population of over 5 million, even after the large-scale emigration of recent years.

The Indian and Coloured communities can expect to increase by more than a quarter from 4.8 million to 6.2 million, while the Black community may grow from 33 million to over 65 million. Thus, Blacks would increase from 77% to 86% of the total population, while Whites would halve from 11% to 6%.

These trends would have given rise to important changes in age composition and consequently also in dependency ratios, that is, the 'dependants' (those aged 0 to 14 and 65+) expressed as a ratio of those economically active (including the unemployed), aged 15 to 64.

White youngsters (0 to 14) and White elderly (65+) would have swapped their relative positions in society over this period, the youngsters declining from 21% today to 14% of the total over 30 years, while the elderly would have increased from 10% now to over 20% then. This would have kept the dependency ratio relatively constant over time, though radically impacting on needed goods and services: the demand for education facilities and toys would have dwindled, while that for old-age homes, health care, tourism and investment services would have increased rapidly among this population group.

Black youngsters would have declined in relative importance, from 35% of the total today to 24% in thirty years' time, while Black elderly would have increased their share from only 4% today to 7%. The good news would have been that the economically active would have increased from 60% to nearly 70% of the total, making it easier to carry the dependants. Development priorities for Black communities would continue to differ radically from White ones and Black youth would have remained important in setting the tone in coming years, much more than in White communities, where the greybeards would increasingly have made their wishes known.

The Indian and Coloured communities would mirror these changes in an intermediate way, the ratio of youngsters falling less far than for Whites, but more than for Blacks, and the ratio of the elderly increasing less than for Whites, but much more than for Blacks.

The age group 0 to 14 also appears to suffer from a census undercount, especially among Blacks, but more in the sense that 0 to 5 is undercounted and 6 to 14 is overcounted. This is not seen to affect the reasoning expressed here, and it also does not deflect from the relative rates of change discussed.

What do these numbers imply for social and economic development, the cities and quality of life?

This is where the rate of economic development throws up radically different answers. An economy growing at 2.4% p.a. will double in size over 30 years. When growing at 4.8% p.a., it will increase fourfold in size. A slow-growing economy will not grow jobs fast enough and it will not generate the resources to improve educational skill levels fast enough to prevent a rapid increase in the number of unemployed, when the population is still growing as fast as projected here.

Apart from general prosperity, the more crucial issue concerns the broadening of prosperity as employment creation is the only genuine means of making the redistribution of opportunity, income and wealth possible. In a slow-moving economy, where additional resources for more education will only increase gradually, job growth would essentially be minimal, especially for the less-skilled. The composition of skilled labour would still change radically, favouring the Black community due to sheer numbers, and its altering mix would therefore create the impression of visible progress (see also Chapter 9).

The misery at the bottom end of the job scale would grow exponentially, as most of the increase in the 15 to 64 age group would remain unemployed. Thus, the unemployed as a group would mushroom by a multiple from the 6.5 million of today (projections as recent as the mid-1990s suggesting this could increase up to 15 million in twenty years' time). The unemployed would still be concentrated in rural poverty traps, but as urbanisation spread they would also overwhelm the few large metropolitan cities whose size would more than double, if not triple, primarily with poor, less-skilled migrants desperately trying their luck. The story of increasing social decay and crime is then quickly told, with large city concentrations all over the emerging world the likely role model. It sketches a scenario in which our existing modernity could easily have become overwhelmed.

Only a faster economic growth rate, and consequently increased investment in physical infrastructure and human development, would arrest this fatal drift. Employment growth would be higher, absorbing a larger share of those newly entering the labour market, and the ratio of employed relative to unemployed would deteriorate much more slowly, with every possibility of eventually stabilising, and then turning around. The physical reality of the large cities would still change radically as they more than doubled in size, but now in a more viable way as more infrastructure would presumably be built to accommodate at least a portion of the addition in population in a more effective manner than what would happen in a slow-growth environment.

Either way, the high population projection pointed to a South African landscape radically transformed—socially as well as physically—within a generation.

The Standard Worst-Case of HIV/Aids

When the HIV/Aids pandemic is taken into account, the outlook alters radically, and in a totally different direction. The social and economic distinctions would seem to deepen even more than in a population projection without HIV/Aids, as those not afflicted potentially do better under such circumstances compared to those who fall victim to the pandemic. What can still affect such an outlook (apart from a changed pattern of in-migration) would be a medical cure and its successful introduction, or a radical change in social behaviour taking hold among the population groups most at risk.

A population projection, which incorporates the likely effects of HIV/Aids, poses insurmountable problems. What assumptions are we to make?

- Can we take the sketchy data available to date, collected and disseminated in the manner that it has been, and using historic understanding of demographic relationships in our society, to project population size going forward?
- How does the growing awareness of HIV/Aids change public policy regarding the provision of medicines, and perhaps more importantly the social behaviour of those at risk?
- Will a medical cure be found, and if so, will it be possible to make it available effectively on a wide enough scale? And what would be the timing of such developments?

All these considerations throw doubt on any population projections attempting to incorporate the likely impact of HIV/Aids. But that we are looking at a radically different future as things stand appears to be generally accepted. The focus should therefore not be on the decimal point in these projections. Instead, it is the broad outline of what is being sketched that is most relevant.

Two projections are discussed here, neither of which assumes a medical or behavioural change in years to come. This gives us a standard worst-case scenario (apparently a base case used in many HIV/Aids projections and impact studies) on which to base any alternative scenarios with such assumed changes incorporated. However, we should bear in mind that the truly worst-case scenario may be much worse, and dependent on more adventuresome assumptions about the nature of social behaviour and the consequent spreading potential of the disease.

On a total population size estimated at 45 million in 2000, the Actuarial Society of South Africa (ASSA) projects a population of 47 million by 2005, peaking at 48 million two years thereafter and then effectively stabilising at this level (assuming an initial African in-migration of 190 000 p.a. which subsequently dwindles quite quickly). Haldenwang (1999) shows a slightly bigger population increase to 52 million in 2016 and 55 million in 2031 (after assuming continuing in-migration of 200 000 p.a.).

The main implications of these projections appear to be that:

- The total population will not increase much more in size in the next five to ten years before an effective peaking takes place. Thus, HIV/Aids serves to *stunt* population growth and consequently labour force growth as well.
- The current ethnic composition of the population is no longer going to change that much, largely freezing into place the present relative shares.
- The current age composition will change more noticeably, with the 15 to 64 age group gaining relatively more than before, while the 0 to 14 group will at some point (2004) start to decline in absolute terms across the board for all population groups.

These are dramatic demographic changes, with all kinds of implications for, firstly, the mix of future spending and, secondly, other social side effects such as the additional two million orphans the ASSA model projects by 2010.

There is also the question of the likely development of migration. Apart from immigrants being HIV-infected, too, a much smaller increase in the labour force from domestic sources, at a time of improved economic performance coming about due to the reforms enumerated in earlier chapters, could lead to a much higher rate of in-migration than, for example, assumed by Haldenwang (a steady 200 000 p.a.) or the ASSA (some 190 000 p.a., but steadily dwindling). If such in-migration were to be more heavily skewed in favour of those with skills, the implications for the economy and the country would change even more, and for the better. But the likely developments on this score are subject to incalculable uncertainty, further complicating our understanding of the country's likely prospects in years to come.

The very scale of the projected changes, of course, questions the outcome thereof. On earlier ASSA projections, cumulative premature deaths due to HIV/Aids through 2015 would top 10 million, and through 2025 would top 18 million, and this on a population of less than 50 million at any given time. Roberts (2000) mentions that Russia suffered more than any other country during the Second World War, supposedly losing in a matter of four years over 20 million people out of a population of 120 million. Relative to the size of our population, the HIV/Aids pandemic is going to be worse for South Africa than the Second World War was for Russia, even if we take some four decades to absorb the same absolute effect.

Besides the overall impact as sketched so far, there are many more startling developments at a micro-level. Each age-cohort is apparently going to have a unique experience, as will each gender-cohort (males and females being infected at different rates at different ages). Furthermore this picture will change nearly every year, mostly for the worse during the coming decade, before stabilising. To really develop a sense of the ongoing dynamic, we need to highlight the changes in mortality by age and gender-cohort, every year for the next ten years. In some instances, very high HIV-prevalence subsequently gives way to very high annual Aids mortality. In others, there is barely any change over time (the very old, and the still very young). But every niche in South African society will be affected differently, by age, gender, race, social position, geographic location and family relationships (see the ASSA 2000 demographic pro-jections for greater detail for most of these dimensions).

Generalisation about the impact of HIV/Aids therefore has only very limited usefulness. We may want to know how overall population will change as a result, and by major classification such as age and gender. But if an individual runs different risks in different geographic locations, estimating the probabilities and the ultimate impact becomes very difficult. Possible developments in behaviour and/or medical treatment or a change in migration dynamics injects further complexity into the problem.

The major social impact of these projected population changes will be a very limited rise in the number of economically 'actives' in coming years (short of a migration surprise). As a consequence, even on present economic performance, which appears to have stabilised the overall employment level (see Chapter 5), the number of unemployed will grow only to a limited extent. Increasingly, though, as economic performance speeds up following the successful completion of reform as discussed before, both slightly faster economic growth and a higher rate of labour absorption is likely to occur. At some point (sooner rather than later) such a development is likely to arrest the net increase in the unemployed. From that point in time onward, even a slightly positive rate of employment creation compared to a stagnant labour force will start to effect a reduction in the absolute numbers of unemployed, and more progressively so in the unemployment rate. On a 30-year view, therefore, this could cumulatively make quite a difference to the numbers of unemployed.

The great metropolitan cities are no longer expected to increase in size to any significant extent. Johannesburg, for example, would in the absence of HIV/Aids likely have seen its population increase from three million at present to over ten million in a generation, but with the HIV/Aids pandemic the increase may be limited to four to five million over that same period. Limited population growth and a completion of urbanisation, settling at the 75% to 80% level, suggests at most a 30% to 60% increase in large city populations over the period in question. For the country as a whole this would probably imply that a further eight to ten million Black people would leave the rural areas and become urbanised over a 30-year period, compared to triple or more these numbers under uninterrupted population growth assumptions.

The implications for infrastructure development are obvious. It is far more likely that urban decay will be successfully arrested in time, going purely by these numbers (and on the assumption of an improved economic performance still materialising and giving rise to higher capital spending on city infrastructure over this period).

The Wider Impact of HIV/Aids

The most crucial thing to realise about the HIV/Aids pandemic is that it kills slowly. At the coming peak of the pandemic, five to seven years from now, some 85% of the population will not be HIV-infected at any one time in the standard worst-case scenario. The chances of acquiring HIV/Aids some time during a person's lifetime, however, will be startlingly high for some population groups, thereby dramatically reducing—even halving—their life expectancy compared to a reality without HIV/Aids.

Conservatively, those that become HIV-infected have a life expectancy of six to ten years on average, if not on expensive medication (in which case a person could survive up to ten or more years longer). During two years of this period, sickness will be debilitating enough to interfere with everyday living and to be a problem for the individual concerned and the community within which he/she lives and works.

The economic impact of HIV/Aids is centred on productivity losses and the cost of treatment. The BER (2001) estimates the economic impact as being of the order of 0.3% to 0.6% less annual GDP growth through 2015 (for an assumed average of 0.5% p.a.), compared to what could have been expected in an HIV-free environment. Thus, instead of succeeding in achieving average real GDP growth of 4% p.a. or better in future years (in a HIV-free environment), we may now only achieve an average of 3.5% p.a., once we allow for the likely economic impact of the pandemic on our potential growth performance.

When considering productivity losses we should not overstate their potential extent. If at any time 16% of the population is HIV-infected, with a quarter of these suffering enough ill-effects to interfere with their everyday life (the two-year period), we are talking 4% of the population at any one time in sufficient ill-health to have an economic impact. The share of the labour force showing this impact will be higher (5% plus), as the 15 to 64 age group has a higher HIV-prevalence (over 20%) than the 0 to 14 or 65+ age groups. But the distribution of those infected in the population relative to the composition of the labour force that effectively contributes to GDP suggests that the share of the formal labour force whose health is impaired at any given time should be less (about 3%).

When evaluating the loss of experience and social investment, the greater the presence of useful skills and education, the greater the economic loss implied by an early death. If the dying were to occur equally across the formal labour force, this cost could be considerable. But the impact appears to be skewed, affecting the less-skilled and the less-educated to a proportionally larger extent (see the BER 2001). Of great concern is that the country may—as could happen elsewhere in Africa—lose critical parts of its civil service needed to administer or train the next generation. For example, in Zambia, over 40% of teachers are today apparently HIV-infected. This erodes further an already limited capacity for social investment. And yet education is where our largest effort should be if we are going to uplift the whole population.

The implications for businesses begin with how a company's workforce is going to be affected. The effectiveness of labour will on average drop, and there will be cost-increasing effects, such as absenteeism and retraining, apart from medical expenses for those gaining access to medication. The exposure of every sector of the economy, and of every individual business within those sectors, will be different. This is because no two companies have the same staff profile in terms of skill levels, gender, age and ethnic composition, regional distribution, the type of economic activity, the type of social interaction, and the type of people working in the business (in terms of social behaviour and preferences). Every business is a unique proposition.

Consequently, averages will be almost meaningless. What will be important is a company's profile. It will determine costs and management problems. A few businesses will discover themselves to be completely isolated from the pandemic. At the other extreme, many businesses will find themselves entering the equivalent of a war zone. The majority of businesses will be unevenly distributed between these two extremes.

External exposure is as varied and uniquely profiled. Every business will have to ask: who are my customers, my potential customers, my future customers? Some businesses will find the markets for their products heavily affected by the pandemic, while a select few may discover themselves to be relatively unaffected, and the majority will again find themselves spread out across the spectrum.

From a business point of view, therefore, everything depends on profiling—labour force, suppliers, distributors, retailers, consumers, even regulators—to understand a company's exposure and risk, but also in some instances unique opportunities.

The response of company management to specific profiles, strengths and weaknesses is often that 'two or three years ago we looked at this problem and what it means to us'. This was mostly in the late 1990s when annual deaths from Aids-related illnesses were still relatively limited. What still has to sink in is the full scope of the awful reality. In an average year, in a population of 45 million people, some 360 000 people die from non-Aids causes. Aids-related deaths during 2002 are an estimated 250 000 plus, climbing to over 700 000 annually within a decade. We can look at these statistics, but this does not prepare us for the reality of the untold ways in which daily life, both personal and corporate, will be affected.

The Adventuresome Worst-Case of HIV/Aids

The truly worst-case scenario discussed by Clem Sunter at an in-house Rand Merchant Bank presentation, is one in which the reach of HIV/Aids has been underestimated in terms of assumptions about sexual behaviour. Those sexually adventuresome may be at risk to a degree that has so far not been fully appreciated or documented.

In this scenario, the pandemic turns out to be more disruptive of society than projected in the standard worst-case. HIV-prevalence would keep on rising until well beyond current peak projections before stabilising, and then ultimately falling off once the adventuresome group has been effectively eliminated or converted to behaviour change.

Such a scenario would probably see:

- A higher peak HIV-prevalence than assumed under the standard worst-case (that is, higher than 16% of the overall population).
- All population groups would experience a significant rise in their respective HIV-prevalence.
- Annual mortality in the peaking period would be higher than now projected.
- A population decline may occur from present levels, levelling off at some future date.

In this scenario, a growing economy crucially dependent on skilled labour would at some point find itself no longer able to augment adequately its skilled labour requirements from domestic sources. Either economic development would slacken (from a pace faster than prevailed in the 1990s), or a more active migration reality may come to pass, to the point of becoming actively promoted.

The Potential Impact of HIV Medication in the Absence of Behavioural Change

By mid-2002, three factors had already changed:

- The law courts had directed the South African government to take a more pro-active stance in providing medication to HIV-sufferers.
- Private companies had started to provide free medication to staff not covered by medical aid schemes.
- Major publicity campaigns had been launched, attempting to heighten public awareness about the disease, and the advisability of effecting changes in social behaviour.

How could these developments, and their future effects, influence the demographic changes once again? There are no hard-and-fast answers to this question, but the following reasoning may be taken into account when considering how South Africa's population may continue to evolve in coming decades.

As already discussed, at present there is no medicine that will effectively end the HIV-condition. The only medication currently available is HIV-suppressants, delaying the onset of Aids-related diseases and death (but probably not entirely ending the ongoing transmission of HIV to new victims either).

Changes in social behaviour have apparently been observed on a countrywide basis in other African countries after severe Aids mortality stimulated widespread awareness and large-scale publicity campaigns, leading to dramatic declines in measured HIV-prevalence (with Uganda being the country mentioned most often). Coming years, however, will need to show whether such observed reduction in HIV-prevalence is due to changes in behaviour or due to poor data collection in radically transformed social circumstances following the devastating impact of the pandemic.

At present, South Africa is yet to embark on a large-scale campaign providing (free) medication to all HIV-infected sufferers, and the publicity campaigns encouraging changes in behaviour have still to reach peak intensity to be fully effective. Indeed, Aids-mortality may need to reach peak intensity first, for intense publicity to be effective enough to stimulate crucial changes in social behaviour that succeed in reducing the transmission of the disease.

An initial observation would therefore be that from an estimated five million HIV-sufferers in South Africa in 2001, these numbers will still grow while the medication and awareness campaigns are not at full effectiveness. As peak HIV-prevalence in the standard worst-case has been modelled at some seven million HIV-sufferers by 2007–2010, this number may still be reached, before deflection could become possible.

The eventual size of the group of HIV-sufferers has immediate implications for the effectiveness of the medication option. If medication starts to be provided on any scale, in the initial absence of a concomitant change in behaviour (that is, each person on medication changing behaviour forthwith), unintended consequences could follow. Fewer HIV-sufferers would die, yet with HIV-infecting behaviour continuing mostly uninterrupted, the number of HIV-sufferers would keep growing, increasing the HIV-prevalence level in the larger population beyond its present expected peak of 16%. This in turn would give an open-ended boost to the cost of providing free HIV-suppressant medication as HIV-prevalence kept rising within the population.

Furthermore, if the successful introduction of medication leads to early success in delaying Aids-related mortality, this could undermine the effectiveness of the awareness campaigns, as the 'booster' from horrific numbers of deaths may not quite materialise (as it has elsewhere in Africa).

This is not an argument either for not providing medication or for not attempting saturation awareness campaigns. It merely suggests that taming this pandemic's size and reach may be more complex than realised, as are the cost implications of open-ended, ineffective commitments. It may not be so much a question of trying harder, as trying hard and making very sure there are results. A change in behaviour needs to accompany medication, and preferably ahead of becoming HIV-infected. This makes it sound easy, but given the behaviours involved it will be very hard to achieve.

The Potential Impact of Medication and Effecting Behavioural Change

Next let us relax the assumption about behavioural change. What would be the impact on South Africa's demographics of providing medication *and* successfully effecting changes in behaviour?

Even following an extensive build-up in the provision of HIV-suppressant medication, along with changes in social behaviour, the country would still find itself with a large pool of HIV-sufferers (potentially at best, about seven million).

The provision of medication would ensure that premature mortality is arrested. The change in social behaviour would ensure, firstly, that HIV-prevalence would not keep on rising. Secondly, with new infections dropping off towards zero, the pool of existing HIV-sufferers would stabilise and then may start to decline over time due to natural mortality. Thus, the cost of medication would peak early and thereafter tail off over a generation as the pool of existing HIV-sufferers shrank gradually for natural reasons, though HIV-infected immigrants might continue to augment the remaining pool of HIV-sufferers beyond the current generation.

If because of these developments annual mortality starts to decline once again, an important question remains: what would a change in social behaviour, aimed at preventing HIV-infection, do to the country's fertility? In other words, would the population start growing again (because of falling mortality), or would the population continue to stagnate (because of an accompanying decline in fertility)?

One inescapable conclusion is that in the presence of a behavioural change successfully arresting HIV-infection, fertility will not continue unaffected as if still in a pre-HIV age. For the behaviour that determines HIV-infection also has a high input in maintaining fertility. Reducing the one will presumably not come without affecting the other fundamentally, too. This should be seen as being in addition to the apparent effect of HIV in reducing fertility in the infected population. Consequently, demographics would continue to be transformed.

The likelihood of stunted population growth coming to the fore in future decades is probably higher than the alternative of South Africa returning to the demographics profile of the pre-HIV/Aids age. Either we will fail to address HIV/Aids successfully through a combination of medication and behavioural change and rising mortality will stunt population growth. Or, we will successfully address HIV/Aids, but may find that declining fertility and social changes (in all their complexity) drive population growth.

The implications for business may be similar under either scenario regarding potential market size over time. What may be different are the very specific liabilities that may be generated longer-term under a mortality-driven scenario, compared to a fertility-driven scenario, generating relatively much less business risk of a longer-term liability nature. From a production point of view, the impact on GDP growth may be less negative under a fertility-driven compared to a mortality-driven scenario, as there would be less of an efficiency loss.

In the fertility-driven scenario rather than the mortality-driven scenario, we would probably see a much greater development success as well as greater social maturity, given the experience of the preceding and traumatic HIV/Aids age. Besides higher levels of education, female emancipation, urbanisation, employment and income, we would expect such a future generation generally to have reached a more mature outlook (especially gaining more insight and control over an individual's life, objectives and behaviour). It may bring a change in values currently difficult to contemplate. Today, Italy has the fastest shrinking population in the world, with Japan hot on its heels, a phenomenon that is driven from the fertility side. Similar surprises could be lying in wait for South Africa, given its encounter with HIV/Aids (as well as faster economic and social development).

7 PROGRESS WITH SOCIAL DELIVERY

The social revolution in progress in South Africa has as its most debilitating feature, the present and future impact of HIV/Aids (as explored in Chapter 6). However, there are other more positive aspects to developments in this social transformation.

In his opening of parliament speech in February 2001, President Thabo Mbeki (2001) took special care to enumerate what government critics too often feel free to ignore, namely the extent to which there has been social delivery by the ANC government since April 1994. President Mbeki specifically identified the following achievements:

- cumulative total for houses completed or under construction: 1.1 million units (with 1.3 million subsidies allocated);
- 400 000 electricity grid home connections in 2000;
- during 1995–2000 some 6.5 million people gained access to clean water;
- 412 000 new telephone lines installed in 1999–2000;
- 127 clinics built in 2000;
- during 1994–2000, 37 400 households benefited from land redistribution, with 917 000 hectares handed over to new Black land owners;
- during 1996–1999 total employment increased from 9.3 to 10.4 million, a net gain of 1.1 million; and
- during 1995–2000, the average annual increase in real disposable income was 2.8% for Indians, 2.7% for Blacks, 2.1% for Coloureds and 1.1% for Whites.

We have already qualified the increase in total employment as it likely reflects improved survey and sampling techniques by StatsSA (see Chapter 5). In addition, although the differentiated increase in real incomes between population groups is rightly seen as a narrowing of the unequal income distribution, Chapters 3 and 5 have qualified the manner in which this has come about, and its probable impact on unemployment in the country during this period, negating some of the positive impact on the income distribution.

President Mbeki's speech was followed two weeks later by the national budget in which government spending was projected to grow by a nominal 10% during 2001–2002. With inflation at 7%, the public wage bill not increasing by more than 5%, and interest paid rising by only 3% (two items which represent half the budget spent), there seems to be hope that there will be more social delivery in coming years.

Increasing social delivery was also one of the themes at a post-budget seminar hosted by the BER in Stellenbosch, where Van der Berg (2001) provided a most interesting analysis of government delivery so far, along with a realistic forward view.

Van der Berg's main thrust was that the previous political regime had been bad at service delivery, and specifically did not target the poor. In contrast, the ANC government has been faced with high expectations on this score from the start. Yet as we have seen there has been great emphasis on fiscal discipline since 1994, with wage moderation and personnel cutbacks in recent years contributing to a decline in personnel spending as a share of overall spending.

Many people believe that wages are consuming all resources in the public sector, to the exclusion of most else. In fact, wage moderation and improved delivery seem to be the watchwords now. Personnel spending declined from 47.4% of total non-interest government spending in 1997–1998 to 46.3% in 2000–2001, and is expected to fall further in 2001–2002 (to 44.5%) and in 2003–2004 (to 42.2%). This is quite a shift.

Within this spending picture, the richer (and more efficient) provinces have been allocated relatively less money than the poorer (mainly less efficient provinces). Unfortunately, the overall effect of this is to reduce the efficiency of public spending. On a more positive note, there has been increased focus on services for the poor.

Physical and Social Services Delivery

A useful contrast can be made between physical services delivery and social services delivery. There has generally been an increase in the former, but there has tended to be poor delivery of the latter.

Physical service delivery involves a joint effort between government departments and parastatals.

From 1994–1999, some 3.5 million people have been provided with clean water. At best this has kept pace with population growth, but in 1999 there were still 8 to 12 million people without access to running water.

From 1994–1999, some 750 000 low-cost housing units were built, exceeding the rate at which new households were being formed. However, as of 1998 the urban housing shortage was still put at 2.6 million units.

Between 1991 and 1997, 2.5 million people were provided with electricity (over 400 000 p.a.). In rural areas, those connected rose from 21% of the population in 1995 to 32% of the population in 1997. In urban areas it rose from 77% to 82%, and nationally the improvement was from 51% to 59%.

The improvement of roads and infrastructure is best measured by looking at capital spending as a share of total non-interest government spending. This declined from 8.7% in 1997–1998 to 7.6% in 2000–2001, but it is now budgeted to increase to 8.6% in 2001–2002 and to 10.2% in 2003–2004.

In social services delivery, other dimensions can be distinguished. Social transfers (old-age pensions, child support, disability grants) have seen take-up rates increase, the desperately poor are better covered, and the disbursement of these transfers is less corrupt than it used to be.

In the health sector in the 1990s some 27% more medical doctors were registered, and 21% more nurses, outpacing population growth. Yet infant mortality and poverty-related tuberculosis cases have been increasing (with HIV/Aids especially a growing burden). Large numbers of these personnel have emigrated or are working abroad on contract (while remaining locally registered), with their professional services effectively lost to the country.

When reviewing welfare services (mainly private organisations such as Operation Hunger and Child Welfare), two things stand out:

- More should be done in the rural areas.
- Foreign donations are drying up, as these tasks are considered a governmental responsibility. The state tends to be given a block grant, and from this less flows to such welfare services than used to be the case when they received aid directly.

In education there are various disturbing tendencies given that a growing economy needs more educated people:

- The number of matric passes peaked in 1994 (admittedly a very good year) and has since moved lower, with as yet no indication of a reversal.
- The number of university exemptions also peaked in 1994, but has since fallen by a full quarter (threatening underutilisation of staff and thereby the financial viability of these important institutions as funding becomes restricted). This worrisome trend has only been partially neutralised by increasing enrolments at technikons and other diploma-oriented institutions.

Overall, the standard of education is not improving. A more detailed analysis throws up other worrying aspects:

- Matric pass rates for Mathematics and Science have substantial provincial differences. It may seem a simple solution to throw more resources at the problem, but if the administrative and teaching capacity is not there to apply such funds effectively, the returns will remain poor.
- Literacy and numeracy testing in 1999 showed that at least half of Grade 4 pupils did not pass tests that should have been passed with their level of skill. Again, there were great provincial differences.
- With regard to literacy, the South African experience is similar to other African countries, but in numeracy, the South African experience is much worse. However, enrolment in the rest of Africa may be very selective, and limited to potential high achievers as compared to South Africa where school attendance is higher, but therefore potentially scoring comparatively lower.

On the security front, there has been a reduction in spending on national defence, and much more has been spent on policing. Despite this change in emphasis, the country suffers from more crime and a crisis in the judicial and correctional system.

Improving Services Delivery

In order to improve service delivery, Van der Berg (2001) foresees a need for:

- more management/skill capacity in the public sector (not necessarily more funds);
- more/better measurement of output (in education, health, security); and
- incentives, such as the principle of charging for services rendered, and leaving it up to the services providers to decide how to use these moneys. For example, in health services a hospital could be allowed to retain funds earned by charging user fees, rather than having to return these funds to the province, thereby creating rather than denying incentive. In education it is necessary to create new forms of incentives to maintain standards, as the inspectorate has apparently lost its legitimacy (for political reasons). This may require private

sector involvement, allowing easier measurement and implementation (which is already the case with contractors when, for example, building a house).

According to Van der Berg (2001), there should be a qualified optimism regarding the way forward. It has to be recognised that the government has to date avoided the populist route in the provision of public services (which would have been disastrous, had it been attempted). Nevertheless, the danger of such a detour has not completely passed. Our society needs to progress more before we can be confident that such a potentially expensive mistake will not still occur.

As it is, South Africa suffers from limited finances. However, if the human capacity exists to absorb resources effectively, more money should selectively be applied to the extent that it can be made available. For example, there should be a better targeting of the poor.

Poor service delivery can, in many instances, be improved through relatively small changes. This makes the shift to higher social spending in the budgets for 2002, 2003 and 2004 very promising. What is required most, though, is more and better management. It is the human capacity involved in managing these activities that will decide how successful the government is going to be in increasing its service delivery and eliminating the backlogs that remain. Such improved delivery is not a performance revolution in itself. Instead, it is an outcome of economic policy reform, which should eventually give rise to a better economic performance, generating the resources that make upliftment possible.

Social Limits to Growth

Though the government has made much progress in addressing social inequality, and there is still much left to be done, especially in terms of education and housing, it does not mean that there are no limitations to be taken into account in addressing this legacy.

The obvious limitation is one of means, in terms of budget space. Here the government has been very meticulous over the years: healthy national finances are a first priority. Only within existing means can we seek the resources to address the inequalities and social backlogs from the past and hope to increase the stock of our population's human capital, a major key to faster economic growth in the longer-term.

In defining this limitation, it is still easy to lose track of another reality, namely, the manner in which the government's redistributive measures may be putting a ceiling on economic growth. The government raises revenue and spends it, but to what extent are these activities in support of making the economy grow, compared to favouring some at the expense of others? The manner of taxation and spending may by its very nature prevent a faster economic growth rate from being sustained in the longer-term. The benefits obtainable from a faster rate of economic growth than now envisaged (the difference between 6% and 3.5% GDP growth p.a.) must also be evaluated in terms of the greater number of jobs likely to be created earlier than would otherwise be possible. The speed of transformation of the labour market as a consequence, as the unemployed and the underemployed become more fully employed, and the social goods that can be afforded through the higher national income that would come about and the tax revenues it could generate, are also factors in the benefits equation.

This is the true opportunity cost of delivering a slow social transformation by limiting the economy to a growth ceiling that may not even be able to sustain the 3.5% to 4% GDP growth shortly within reach, not to speak of 6% average GDP growth.

The government's redistribution effort has two legs: taxation and spending. The limitation of these factors on faster economic growth is real. On the tax side, redistribution is actively pursued by heavily skewing tax relief in favour of the lower income groups. In making changes to the tax burden, to what extent is it taken into account who generates savings, which go towards funding a higher rate of investment needed to drive a faster growth rate?

This is not to deny that higher incomes have received tax relief from the exceptional burdens imposed upon them in the past. The question is how such relief for various income groups feeds through into the economy, and what its ultimate impact is: more support for consumption spending, or more saving in support of higher fixed-investment spending, less of an import inclination and more independence from foreign capital? After years of tax relief, there has been little increase in personal savings, which continue to contribute minimally to the overall savings rate. This suggests an excessive zeal in favour of redistribution relative to the needs of an economy capable of growing faster than the stagnation reality of recent decades.

Government's redistributive impact is even bigger via its spending priorities. Here, too, we should want to know what is being obtained in return for setting in motion a major transfer of buying power.

There is, firstly, the large increase in welfare spending favouring the lower-income groups, which may be high on equity, consumption and political approval, but what else does the country buy with these outlays that will enhance economic development and the growth effort? How will these welfare payments translate into more human or physical capital, the building blocks of faster growth and development?

Secondly, there are the large sums of money increasingly allocated to basic health care, education and security. Do these public funds yield us increased safety and more human capital with which to drive our growth process?

There is the determination to promote basic health care, but is there in the process less health care being offered to the working population while increasing its cost, thereby allowing a deterioration in the health of the working population? If so, we could be undermining our future ability to grow the economy.

Education and training are cornerstones of future growth and development. Every year we witness education being granted a greater allocation of government resources, yet what is being done with these moneys to uplift our population? Is the education outcome improving, as measured by the number and quality of matriculants, technikon and university students? Do all children entering school at the age of six have a reasonable chance of reaching matric, and by then having acquired a reasonable standard of education, as they do today in South Korea? Do the budget allocations primarily go to building more schools, providing more books and other study accessories, and training teachers to higher standards of ability, thereby measurably raising the education standards achieved by South African pupils and students? Or do the increased budget allocations mostly get consumed in terms of higher salaries and administrative capabilities, without there being a major improvement in the education outcome, as demanded in the workplace and especially by a faster-paced economy?

These are simple questions. The economy's growth of nearly 3% p.a. this past decade and the government's better tax collection capability over many years, has allowed the budget deficit to be narrowed satisfactorily, and more resources have been voted to spending departments critical to the economy's future development. To the extent that the government raises tax revenue and spends it collectively in an attempt to raise our stock of human capital, we may expect a high return on such investment.

It is the difference between having the tax capacity and the ability to invest in human capital—to the point of making sustained economic growth of 3.5% or even 6% annually possible and sustainable—or taxing such moneys, yet often spending these in a redistributive manner that benefits those who receive, yet does not visibly add to the country's stock of human capital by way of vital social investments. Consequently, we are limited in the short-term to a growth performance averaging not more than 3.5% to 4% p.a. on average, but with its long-term sustainability questionable.

The latter growth rate may for the present not be a 'bad' performance, given where we are coming from and given our generally qualified hopes for the future.

However, while growth acceleration to 3.5% to 4% may be attainable in the short- to medium-term, for it to be sustained in the longer-term there will need to be more delivery of human capital than has been the case so far (see the skilled labour projections in Chapter 9). Instead of having reason to be satisfied with its efforts to date, the government will have to put more effort into reinforcing our human capital for the economy to acquire the means with which to grow reasonably fast for many decades to come.

8 A TECHNOLOGY REVOLUTION

In South Africa there is a fourth companion to the three revolutions—political, economic and social—that we have explored thus far. This is the technological revolution that has been sweeping much of the world in the past two decades.

Major facilitators of this change are micro-economic supply-side enhancements (deregulation, more flexible labour markets, greater financial information flow, global opening up and resulting trade specialisation), whose influence is registered in lower inflation and higher productivity growth (see Chapters 3 and 5). A driver of this broader phenomenon can be traced to new electronic equipment and application software that has allowed for greater efficiency throughout the industrial and services sectors, mostly by using information flow much more efficiently in directing production, distribution and financing decisions.

Apart from anecdotal evidence, the US experience has been studied the most extensively, and is seen to apply globally, where such data is less easily available. There has been much hype surrounding the new technology, but there has also been real innovation with concrete productivity gains.

New Technology as a Source of Growth

How do we measure or otherwise reflect a clear gain when an existing economic activity has been substituted by an electronic message dispatched at the speed of light at virtually nil cost? How do we measure or otherwise reflect the explosive increase in such messaging, much of it having a direct bearing on some part of the economic process, again at virtually nil cost?

Such improvements are currently either not reflected in GDP (except indirectly through the faster, higher production at less cost of the economic activity that this information flow impacts on) and/or they register as a decline in economic activity as those things they substitute are lost.

For example, telephone, fax, mail, courier or hand-delivery, around the office or around the world, have to a large extent been substituted with e-mail. The computer and telecommunication infrastructure might be huge and expensive, but its technological capability to carry electronic information traffic is so large that the marginal cost of one (e-mail) message is virtually nil, in contrast to the cost of telephone, fax, mail, courier, or messenger. As the old-fashioned information delivery activity gets substituted by electronic means, it disappears from GDP, with no gain being registered as the e-mail does not register as economic value. Yet time and cost gains made through various forms of electronic signalling are substantial, considering today's flow of information in a modern economy.

The application of this example to the control of various other activities—management, originating, production, distribution, sale, and financing—in a modern economy confronts us with a huge cost structure that can be infinitesimally reduced while gaining limitless economies of scale for information flow. How do these revolutionary gains register in GDP (output produced as measured by cost expended)? Presumably this happens mostly indirectly, indeed seemingly magically, as output rises with no directly identifiable increases in visible inputs (capital, labour). Such gains are then registered as gains in productivity—a largely unexplained phenomenon and catch-all for doing things more cleverly with the same inputs. The resulting gain is distributed as income to the organising entrepreneurial capital or the labour genius whose skill made it possible. Competition, however, eventually ensures that these gains become socialised through lower prices to final users/consumers.

How do we identify the extent of this 'revolutionary' break with the past, if not in value-added rands and cents? Is it by way of bytes of information dispatched and consumed? Or is it the originality of the innovators utilising the additional access to more data? Apart from measuring the number of computers produced, the rest of the application gain is mostly indirect, showing up as 'noise' in an unexplained step-up in productivity growth. It represents human ingenuity, in one of those innovation spurts that seemingly occur from time to time as technical capability of some kind acquires critical mass and becomes functional enough to transform older technologies still doing most of the work. How do we make such a break visible and understandable?

A New Technology Wave

In the 1980s there was a steadily mounting excitement in the global computer industry, which increasingly impinged on other sectors, such as telecommunication, the media, and entertainment. There was increasing reference to the 'information age', but somehow it stood aloof. No connection was drawn with falling inflation in the US, Europe and the UK, rising growth performance, improving fiscal conditions or the enormous expansion of world trade. Financial markets, equity as much as capital and currency, continued to be mostly associated with the 'Big Picture', even though new computer companies were increasingly star performers. If critical mass was steadily being accumulated, it was not that obvious, at least not to most of those outside the information technology sector.

In previous periods 'modernity' had implied new railroads appearing, or a flood of cars or new mechanical and electronic appliances, which were perceived as progress in that they expanded the range of available goods and services. This time around it was computers, big and small. It was far from obvious to anyone how computers should contribute (if at all) to a speed-up in output not primarily linked to greater units of input. In other words, did computers involve genuine technical progress, allowing greater output per unit of input at a higher rate of change sustainable into the future—something called 'growth in productivity'?

Since the mid-1980s, there have been many economic conferences, where the proponents of radical technology scenarios tended to have a gleam in their eyes. They were generally fun to listen to, but were not taken too seriously. Academic economists were the most scathing of all, though their private sector colleagues were not too far behind, few identifying the technical change underway or correctly assessing its potential impact.

Businessmen and technologists were invariably better placed to identify change processes occurring in their sectors (and among competing industries). This is one explanation for why Federal Reserve Chairman Alan Greenspan always seemed so far ahead of the crowd in correctly assessing these changes—making speeches that at times seemed to draw on science fiction novels, and were considered most unprofessional by some (Bernstein 2001). The time he spent talking to businessmen about their specific experiences inside their companies and industries revealed change processes that others mostly only guessed at.

This pattern played itself out repeatedly during the 1990s, where the stories about technological advances became increasingly daring, with more and more companies, activities and people being affected by the changes underway. Nevertheless, it would be very premature to claim that

IT is fully matured as a phenomenon. The global potential is yet to be fully exploited in untold dimensions, and full maturity of IT capabilities could still be a generation or more into the future.

These were breathless thoughts for equity markets around the world, which themselves started to travel the vertical shaft of the speculative S-curve in 1998–1999. The cyclical shake-out finally arrived in April 2000. For the first time since 1985 the more way-out business concepts that are unlikely to prove viable in the long-term were effectively culled. But we should take care not to confuse a cyclical culling with a secular death—it is far too early for that, given the cost-reducing IT innovations that still lie in the future.

The 'new' technology story continues to deepen all the time. It can be seen in the number of other technologies affected, in the manner that 'old' business concepts find themselves facing transformation (and losing a sizeable part of their cost structures), and the numbers of people who are getting connected. In every direction, structures are being challenged, markets are changing shape, prices are being lowered, and cost layers taken out.

Finally, a productivity connection has been made, although now the tendency has been to go overboard and ascribe all the gains made to computer technology, whereas in fact the supply-side improvements of the 1980s provided crucial organisational flexibility on which much of the new IT can thrive.

Do economists come close to understanding these change processes, and what they do to labour forces, competition and government policies? In the end, we can only note changes in production relative to inputs. When structural change is slow, we can rely on fairly long histories of data to reveal structural relationships that make short-term behaviour predictions at least plausible. But when change picks up speed, the underlying economic relationships change in ways that will only become explicit in time. The 1990s were in this respect a rich period, when few people correctly sensed the nature of the changes enveloping them. And this process is far from finished.

Various lessons can be drawn from this. We are talking about revolutionary breaks in economic performance, and about long-term processes. The latter apparently have much longer to run to reach maturity, and this warns us not to be side-tracked by short-term cyclical volatility. Cyclicality can make it look as if a relapse of some kind has overtaken us, making the preceding progress appear like a chimera. Only the long-term will offer conclusive proof on this score.

As performance fluctuates over the business cycle, only occasionally giving us glimpses of accelerated technical progress (productivity gains), there is denial every step of the way regarding the permanence of any acceleration in productivity growth, because the current circumstances do not fit our experience. And what we do not know, we inherently tend to distrust. Unfortunately, such mindsets also tend to bypass opportunities that only in the fullness of time show their true potential. This human reality makes forecasting a particularly hazardous occupation, for getting the parameters right is one thing, convincing a sceptical audience is quite another.

It is not so much the technical facts of these revolutionary breaks that are interesting in their own right (which they undoubtedly are), as the behavioural reactions from people in all walks of life as they grapple with a faster pace of change than they have been used to for some time.

The New Economy

For some years now, a long debate has been raging, focused on the US economy, about whether technology was boosting its productivity growth. This debate is not irrelevant to the South African experience, for just as the US may have benefited in surprising, hitherto unsuspected, ways from a revolutionary technical development, so may our own economic performance have been influenced.

The methodology for evaluating the impact of technology on economic growth (and inflation) can differ considerably, depending on our assumptions. According to Strydom (2000), the technical progress associated with information technology (IT) has thus far been interpreted in two different ways:

- There are those who emphasise returns to scale (what used to be called 'economies of scale'), gaining greater benefit as scale increases because a large part of (investment) costs is fixed and only a lesser (operational) part is variable. This is in essence the same phenomenon underlying the efficiency gains to be had from free international trade ('globalisation'). According to this school, the more these information and communication (IT) technologies spread throughout an economy, the more their scale benefits trigger cost-reductions, opening up newer applications, creating markets on a greater scale, increasing their impact on the performance of the economy beyond their own narrow confines.

- In contrast, the traditional view of technology relies on 'constant returns to scale'. Such a view argues that technology does not yield additional benefits over and above the labour and capital inputs that go into making it. Presuming IT to be of this nature automatically reduces expectations of any exceptional impact on economic efficiency.

With the US economy having slowed down dramatically as of 2000, especially the IT sector, US productivity growth has also once again taken a step down after the strong and above-average gains since 1995. But the deceleration in productivity growth during the recession of 2001 was not major. Nonetheless it has kept the controversy about IT's contribution to modern productivity growth alive. Returns-to-scale supporters continue to see a more fundamental change in efficiency, which is expected to reassert itself as US recovery takes hold more firmly in coming years, while the constant-returns adherents see this slowing as proof that the cyclical effect predominates.

South Africa does not have a large computer manufacturing industry like the US, but like some other countries, Australia for example, we tend to absorb new technology well. The new information technology is transforming the way we work, play, think, relate and do business. The sense of change, for those who find themselves in the middle of it, is sufficiently drastic to qualify for the superlative 'revolutionary'. Among the converts, it is not an issue: the pace of technical change is simply going through one of its periodic accelerations, translating into faster productivity gains than in previous years.

However, this is still not universally accepted. Professor Robert Solow of MIT observed in 1987, that 'you can see the computer age everywhere except in the productivity statistics' (Davies 2000, 3). During 2000 Solow apparently updated this view, but reportedly did not change it much. In 1996, Professor Paul Krugman, also at that time of MIT, said that he did not support the 'new economy' paradigm 'because I cannot bring myself to support a hypothesis that I know to be clap-trap' (Davies 2000, 3). Krugman was reacting mostly against those New Age believers who seemingly thought that the laws of economics were in the process of being suspended. Another much quoted source is Professor Robert Gordon (2000) of Northwestern University who also challenged the notion of a revolutionary contribution by computers to overall technological change.

Gordon showed that only in the actual manufacturing of computer equipment have there been phenomenal efficiency gains as the volume of activity increased rapidly, even as costs plunged. However, outside this small enclave (contributing less than 2% of US GDP), supposedly not even a ripple was to be seen. Indeed, according to Gordon, computer technology does not come close to the impact of electricity, the internal combustion engine, or even railroads. Instead, he sees IT and the Internet as more modest developments, which should be viewed as part of the normal continuum of technical advancement.

Surely the IT revolution is not as barren as this? During 2000, two studies were released, one by Jorgenson (Harvard) and Stiroh (New York Federal Reserve), and the other by economists at the Federal Reserve. These studies purported to show that while computer manufacturing has experienced explosive productivity growth, there is much more solid evidence of faster gains in the wider US economy. In a revision of his earlier paper, Professor Gordon now also claims to see a more diffused acceleration in US productivity growth, but still much less pronounced than that perceived by his peers.

According to Van der Merwe (2001), the thing to appreciate about the technology base of the so-called 'new economy' is that it is not to be equated simply with the Internet. The 'new economy' refers to business activity driven by information systems—a much broader concept than just the Internet. Similarly, we should not confuse the dot.coms with broader e-commerce, for the dot.coms (many now in demise) contributed less than 10% to the Internet economy in 2000. Indeed, e-commerce in all its variety is now being conducted by many traditional businesses and is expected to constitute 25% of all business transactions by 2003.

Even so, in a 1996 foreign affairs article, Professor Krugman purported to show that all growth in South East Asia's Tiger economies had been 'extensive' (simply adding more resources) rather than 'intensive' (transforming the productivity of existing resources). Subsequent analysis by others, especially from the Asian region, has shown Krugman's analysis to be rather simplistic. As to the 'Information Age' furore, computer equipment manufacturing is certainly the most dynamic growth sector, but very small in the overall context of the national US economy. And despite all the imagined potential, there remain large sections of the labour force that have yet to be drawn into using the new methods productively. Think of older workers, those outside of large cities, and the many mature technologies that are at the core of many large industries.

Taking all these factors into consideration, it may be wise to be sceptical, but not to overdo it. Everything suggests that there has been a step-up in US productivity growth, but that this is more widespread than just computers as office furniture. Indeed, the whole supply-side of the global economy is up for discussion: the manner that work is organised, and markets of all kinds (financial, labour, goods and services) operate, and the fact that information is used in as many ways as there are potentially workers (globally, two billion and counting).

The potential for further productivity gains, in making computing and communication equipment and the use thereof, is much bigger than has so far been realised, especially in the more mature industries, which have not been touched much as yet. An informal conversation between then General Electric (GE) Chairman Jack Welch and Sun CEO Scott McNealy (reported by Schlender 2000) is especially enlightening about the older generation still running large parts of the US economy. Almost everyone outside the IT sector is late in seeing the revolutionary impact.

In contrast, Federal Reserve Chairman Alan Greenspan has for some years been making speeches that are deeply illustrative of the manner in which a number of big changes—organisational changes, deregulation, the way people fear becoming obsolete and are increasingly trying to upgrade their skills through re-education, many (new) technologies—are together impacting on US productivity growth. Greenspan sees the US economy shifting away from a physical basis of production towards a conceptual basis. This transformation appears far from complete, yet huge in its potential impact. Gavyn Davies (2000) has tried to put estimates on how much GDP growth will be enhanced by B2B (business-to-business) changes and he has come up with an initial instalment of an additional 5% growth for the US, spread over a five year period (to 2005).

Perhaps surprisingly, the bulk of technical change is apparently (very) ordinary. Two decades ago, Professor Rostow (1983), observed that much of what we imagine to be bunching concentrations of technological breakthroughs are in fact illusions. It is a well-known psychological phenomenon that people are inclined to generalise from a narrow yet exceptional experience, in the process easily distorting the overall significance of their observation. This is as true of inflation expectations as it is in judging superficially the impact of startling technological developments.

Rostow's main contention was that most technical change consists of small-scale, incremental innovations, not glamorously associated with any 'cutting-edge' fashion, and best observed in the number of patents issued over time. This suggests technical change to have inherently much more stability than a 'revolution' (a discontinuity—break with the past) conjures up in our minds. Besides, in many companies in many industries world-wide (and in untold garages), armies of tinkerers daily discover new ways of doing things better and cheaper throughout the entire technology spectrum. These advances are often not patented, and consequently do not show up on any radar screen (except, of course, in the national productivity data). Knowing the number of such tinkerers operating at any one time would presumably be a better basis for commenting on the instability and discontinuity or otherwise of technical innovation, and evaluating whether the term 'revolution' should really apply.

The US economy, never mind the global economy, is a big ship. To make an impact, something needs to be very pervasive to show up. In contrast, our minds are remarkably open to fashionable impressions. Toys-for-boys are an old concept, starting with the bow-and-arrow and now extending to a range of electronic gadgets. But do they genuinely speed up the rate of change in productivity gains? The level, certainly, but the rate of change?

Until 1995, US productivity data did not show any startling acceleration, although inflation had been falling for fifteen years (from 13.5% in 1980 to as low as 1.6% in 1998 according to IMF data). Yet, as noted earlier, since 1995 there has been a dramatic step-up in US non-farm business productivity growth—a virtual doubling—from 1.4% p.a. on average during 1973–1995 to 2.5% p.a. during 1995–2000. US productivity growth eased to 1.1% during the recession of 2001 (compared to 1.1% during the recession of 1991 and –0.3% in the recession of 1980). It then bounced back to 4.8% in 2002 in the first year of recovery (compared to 3.7% in 1992 and 4.5% in 1981), indicative that the earlier average pace of 2.5% during 1995–2000 was being maintained, and still ahead of the experience during the earlier recessions and early recoveries. Though US productivity should ease somewhat to 2.5% in 2003, this performance indicates that the 1990s step-up in US productivity growth is still very much with us.

A period of recession was always going to be a test between those who ascribe most of the productivity gain to temporary, cyclical strength, and those who believe in a secular productivity story that is supposedly still gaining strength. On this score, the jury appears to have delivered its verdict: productivity growth has held up well through this recession, and has bounced back right as expected. However, 2001 was the weakest recession in decades, so perhaps the genuine test is still to come when a 'real' recession strikes.

One aspect does stand out. Throughout the period of accelerated productivity growth in the US, business spending on equipment was also on an accelerating (non-sustainable) trend. It is not the additional capital inputs that are at issue, but whether it was easier during this period to obtain risk finance, experiment with new techniques on an unprecedented, even carefree, scale, and thus increase the pace of technical gains. But with business spending having abruptly topped out and during 2001–2003 declining towards a more sustainable long-term pace, and much less carefree in its application, could it be that this will slow the pace of innovation?

What exactly constitutes productivity growth? Economic growth can emanate from two sources, namely, addition of more actual inputs (labour and capital), and a residual called 'multi-factor' productivity, through which the same units of input deliver a higher level of output. We cannot identify precisely what constitutes multi-factor productivity, but we know it comes about mostly due to technical improvements and organisational changes (and synergies between them) that allow the same production for less cost. In this way, multi-factor productivity also contributes to containing inflationary pressure.

However, the productivity story also tends to have a cyclical component. Cyclicality focuses on the increase in labour force and capacity utilisation, but given the very size of organisational and technical changes, ascribing all of the increase in productivity growth to these alone sounds simplistic. As Greenspan has stated, the proof will materialise once the US economy experiences a slow-down. If productivity growth collapses anew with the slow-down in output and is thereafter sustained at a lower level, the sceptics will have their proof. However, if the pace of efficiency gains is largely maintained even in the face of a slow-down, the structuralists will have won an important battle. In testimony to Congress, Greenspan has repeatedly made the point that so far there is little evidence to undermine the notion that the US productivity increase of recent years has been structural and that the underlying trend may still be upward. Up to early 2003, this stance was apparently borne out by productivity data for the US, which did not as yet hint at a cyclical collapse in its performance. Indeed, Greenspan (2003) in evidence to Congress in February 2003 noted that 'during the most recent downturn productivity held up comparatively well. Indeed, productivity rose at an average annual rate of nearly 3% over the past two years, faster than the average pace of increase during the late 1990s' (18).

Whereas US productivity growth had slowed down (cyclically) to 1.1% in the recession year of 2001, it had bounced back sharply to 4.8% in 2002, the first year of mild recovery. This compared favourably with previous recessions (1.2% and 3.7% in 1991–1992, and –0.6% and 4.5% in 1982–1983).

Greenspan went on to note that 2002's productivity burst may be due in part to the special circumstances that developed after 9/11. However, this gain was not subsequently reversed, indicating that at least a portion of it is sustainable. In addition, the rapid productivity gains may in part derive from ongoing improvements in the use of the vast amount of capital installed in earlier years, and it may also stem from organisational innovations induced by the weak profit environment.

Baily (2002) provides an intellectual underpinning for Greenspan's practical observations. According to Baily, information technology is one major reason for the productivity acceleration post-1995, but it is not the sole reason. Innovative business practices and a broader flow of productivity-enhancing innovations also contributed heavily.

The key to faster productivity growth, according to Baily, is heightened competition in an increasingly deregulated economy with strong international competition (the effects of globalisation coming through). Such survival pressures pushed the need for innovation, which was revolutionary in information technology, given the price declines that were achievable. These effects were also notable in the 'old economy' traditional industries.

Governmental policies tend to sustain competitive pressure by maintaining open international markets, avoiding protectionist measures and pursuing anti-trust measures (encouraging industry change, consolidations where necessary, and resisting anti-competitive actions by dominant companies that could discourage innovation).

The potential for revolutionary change remains huge in the future. Europe's growth has in recent decades been more capital-intensive due to its rigid labour dispensation. In contrast, the US has tended to use more labour and be less capital-intense. US labour participation is near 75%, the European Union's is approaching 70% (though more generously measured in terms of those who have exited from the labour force than in the US, making a comparable figure nearer 60%). There is scope in the US economy for capital deepening with present technology. Something like 75% of US industries have not fully absorbed the many ways in which existing IT technology can enhance their performance. But with the US labour force fully stretched during the late 1990s, cost of capital low, and profitable investment opportunities widely evident, corporate investment outlays became momentum-driven to capture technical advantages ahead of the (global) competition. The last time capacity expanded this way was in the 1960s. The cyclical slowing of 2000–2002 may temper the pace of business expansion for a while, but when the cycle eventually bounces back, so may US business spending. In turn, this is again likely to favour capital deepening, infused by advanced IT technology. This will assist in sustaining the productivity performance as well.

Moore's Law is a case in point. According to Jorgensen (2000), in 1965 Gordon Moore made the observation that each new memory chip contained roughly twice as many transistors as the previous chip and was released within 18 to 24 months of its predecessor. This led him to predict that the number of transistors capable of being packed on a chip would double every 18 months into the future, a prediction that has successfully tracked chip capacity for 35 years. During 2000 Moore extrapolated his trend for at least another decade, at a time that the Pentium 4 (released in November 2000) packed 42 million transistors. It should be possible to reach 1 to 2 billion transistors per chip during 2010–2015 at substantially lower operational costs. Fully absorbing the potential applications inherent in such a change holds unpredictable implications for productivity.

Of course, the statistics are backward-looking. If we rely on the national productivity data, we get an inadequate snapshot of past performance because the measurement is never precise. We are forever confronted with measuring volume and price changes that inadequately capture quality refinements. In times of relatively slow technical change, this does not matter too much. But at times in which new ideas spread like viruses throughout the established technology spectrum, the rate of change can increase. It is not so much that Moore's Law points to inherent stability. It is the explosive increase in applications and their impact on existing productivity that tends to generate an increase in the rate of productivity growth that takes time to reach its full potential, before slowing down again.

This view flies in the face of Rostow and his steadily growing army of tinkerers, whose perception suggests a far more stable technological transformation process. After all, it is difficult to tease new knowledge into being, and technology necessarily progresses slowly. The long-term variations in observed productivity growth are still to be explained. Are they due to a convergence of diverse trends and conditions, creating periodic potential for 'breakthroughs' (accelerated pace of change)? Rostow's robotic tinkerers would deny this possibility. Yet we can observe many fads, wholesale adoptions of new ideas sweeping the board, widespread connections being made and easy finance becoming available in floods. These are phenomena in modern life, which many of us will have witnessed in the organisations that we work for, or deal with. If this is applied in the service of working more productively, at times on a national scale, we would expect variations in technical gains over long periods. Proving it is the hard part.

The Global 'Tech-Wreck': A Temporary Interruption

The US business recession of 2001 has eventually proved to be a bigger and more drawn-out affair than originally foreseen. For over half a decade, US business capital spending increased steadily as a share of GDP. The share of Information Technology (IT) rose from 20% to 60% of the total during 1995–2000.

From the second half of 2000, this trend suffered an abrupt reversal, preceded by the implosion of the NASDAQ (March 2000) and other hi-tech equity markets around the world. The variable fortunes of hi-tech are at the heart of the US economic adjustment. It was not in the first instance the US consumers who lost confidence and the will to spend, as they classically do at the beginning of any downturn when the Federal Reserve starts to raise interest rates. US consumer spending had intensified under the influence of earlier windfalls (commodity price declines, interest rate cuts, wealth effects) and has since more than halved its rate of advance (from 6% to 2% growth). However, apart from the inventory adjustment this has triggered in old economy companies, it has been nearly incidental to the abrupt and far greater change of direction in business capital spending during 2000–2002.

At the core of the US adjustment is a fundamental questioning of all presumptions underlying business spending. The late 1990s saw one of those frenzies in which judgement in many instances became suspended: the Y2K preparation, the dot.com craze, the response by 'old' economy companies, and, not least, the global telecommunications story. As this mania spread, it absorbed ever more fuel. Its intensity can be measured in the meteoric rise of tech equity prices around the world. Capital became essentially 'free' for nearly anything associated with technology. As this capital was spent, so the equity markets valued tech companies even higher. In the process, much tech capacity was created, some valuable and some worthless.

There is much circumstantial evidence as to what ended the mania. It was over a year after oil prices had started rising, nine months after the Federal Reserve first started to raise interest rates, and three months after Y2K proved a non-event that the magic fizzled. Was that a co-incidence or did these developments finally encourage a more fundamental rethink? Once a measure of common sense finally intruded, there was no stopping the cold-blooded analysis. Too many dot.coms suddenly looked 'strange', and new business concepts/platforms were not viable. Capital was no longer forthcoming and businesses with poor cash flows that were dependent on new capital infusions started to die in growing numbers. As demand for new equipment and software fell off, second-hand equipment was off-loaded in a dying global market, and the IT currency devalued more and more. The unravelling was very wide and deep.

Though the process has the appearance of 'the death of technology as we came to know it', this is probably a mistaken notion. Instead, people are widely engaged in rethinking the path of the technology revolution in the foreseeable future. Nevertheless, this reassessment has created a temporary abstinence best described as a 'vacuum' in spending and commitment. By early 2003, this adjustment in US business spending was some thirty months old, yet only inconclusive evidence of an upturn in tech hardware demand, output and (chip) prices had become noticeable.

Thinking about the new technology, and especially about tech revolutions (periods of rapid change and penetration), helps us to think on three different levels. Firstly there is *knowledge creation*, that is, laboratory research, the frontier of science. The guide to future potential is the distance still to be travelled before being constrained by laws of nature, which are probably immutable. But before we get to such limits, it is likely that enormous technical gains are still possible, in a relatively short period of time. The cost of many of these technical capabilities is falling at over 50% annually. This certainly constitutes a revolution, probably the biggest in our existence, even if we cannot fully comprehend its many ramifications in time.

At the second level, *business concepts* are born, turning the new technical knowledge into applied products. Finally, at the third level, we encounter the *funding constraints* on such business applications.

Essentially, the outlook is still satisfactory at the first level, but on levels two and three things fell apart from late 2000. This served to highlight that although technical knowledge continued to race ahead, the know-how development is quite separate from the process that actually creates useful products and services, and which requires funding.

Application and funding of hi-tech has abruptly all but dried up. This has always been a regular feature of technical progress, but judging by the fall-off in IT equipment demand, the drying up of capital and the loss of enthusiasm, this may not be a two-year interruption. It could well become (much) longer.

There is also the alleged saturation of markets to consider. For example, the view that all the cellphones and personal computers that can be used effectively have already been bought, and the question of why anyone would need more, essentially useless, technical advances and capabilities. This kind of reasoning merely reflects ignorance of future applications still to be conceptualised, while probably hugely underestimating the creative capabilities and needs of future generations of computer-savvy users.

The key is the collapsing costs of many of these capabilities, and this has always been the case.

Nevertheless, there has been a tremendous loss of enthusiasm as the tech-wreck has unfolded. Huge financial losses have been incurred, and demoralisation has set in. Yet there is very little new about any of this, given past economic corrections of a similar kind. As better technical capabilities keep on being born, and the current meltdown and renewed conservatism at company and finance level is sorted out, technology should be back for another bite. And the next bite could well be as promising—if not more viable and sustainable if guided more by common sense—than what we have already experienced.

The New Technology in South Africa

South Africa does not have a major computer manufacturing industry of any consequence (assembling hardly counts), so we do not have the benefit of that particular boost. We are not (as yet) experiencing a fixed investment boom driving modernisation onward, even if fixed investment by early 2003 was already very lively. Our services sectors, where information technology spreads most quickly, produce just over 60% of GDP (compared to nearly 80% in the US). In addition, our economy is not as computer literate as the leading-edge countries globally. Consequently, we have to scale all potential impact downwards, but this does not mean that we have to stand back too much.

South Africa is recognised as a high technology adopter. During 2000 Internet and e-mail users in South Africa reached the 2.5 million mark. On an employed labour force of just over 10 million, that is 25%, compared to 60% in the US and near 50% in Europe and Japan (and rising rapidly).

However, given the high number of television sets (6 million plus), passenger cars (4.5 million plus), and cellphone users (14 million, with a suggested market potential of some 17 to 21 million by 2007), we may eventually top out at over 60% Internet and e-mail users in the formally employed labour force (currently numbering 6.7 million). This would be a highly respectable incidence compared to the US, Europe and Japan today.

As a result, our economic growth performance and our inflation performance should also benefit. We have been absorbing most of the leading-edge innovations developed abroad, and we are likely to continue doing so in the future.

In the US the debate is about what caused a doubling in productivity growth from 1.4% p.a. in the late 1990s. In South Africa we have gone from no productivity growth to over 5% annual growth in a decade. A large part of this improvement can be attributed to other causes (see Chapter 5), but these may not explain all the change in productivity gains. Similarly, our inflation performance has improved greatly this past decade, from near 15% to below 6%. Both these processes have benefited from the efficiency gains obtained through the opening up of our foreign trade. Variously described as increased competition (in Chapter 3), these improvements are of a similar nature to that of the widespread introduction of the new IT technology. Our markets are functioning more efficiently being information-based, and supply has been boosted through economies of scale, lowering costs and increasing the need for more skilled labour by encouraging greater specialisation.

In the process, we have gained in productivity growth, have had costs suppressed, thus lowering inflation directly, and have had the influence of unionised labour eroded through changing supply structures, indirectly lowering inflation pressures. In their own right, each of these gains is major and helps to explain the revolutionary nature of our productivity revival and inflation decline (see also Chapters 3, 4 and 5 where these effects have already been mentioned).

The really interesting news must be that these opportunities have yet to be fully harvested. The benefits from free international trade are still limitless, but it would appear that technical innovation also may have much to contribute to our economic performance and well-being in the years to come. While remaining very much aware of the danger of overstating these potential benefits, we should be careful not to err the other way by remaining too wary.

Keeping a close eye on scientific progress, the capabilities of new technologies and the evolution of their innovative applications should therefore feature prominently in fully understanding our development potential, even if we are mostly dependent on the outside world to supply us with these technologies—a phenomenon which applies in many fields, and does not make the potential gains to be had any less real. A major challenge to South Africa in this regard is to invest in and develop its human capital. The potential benefits from the technological progress associated with the hi-tech sectors can only be realised if people are equipped with the necessary skills and knowledge.

9 FUTURE PROSPECTS

How do the various revolutions we have discussed—political, economic, social and technological—combine to influence the future of South Africa? Will popular perception remain dominated by the apparent continuous social decay as an extrapolation of past trends? Or is there a successful renewal underway, still being neutralised in the mood of some by perceptions of decline (some of it real enough), but which is gradually strengthening the structure of our society and will allow us to improve our economic and social performance significantly over time?

Economic Reforms and their Resulting Achievements

The apparent economic underperformance of the late 1990s was largely self-inflicted, but, as is perhaps not always fully appreciated, corrective action was taken.

Monetary policy was very much on a learning curve as it bid goodbye to the protection of exchange control and started living within the confines of more internationally dominated market processes. This transformation did not proceed smoothly, and the price we paid was two interest rate shocks, in 1996 and 1998, which we can only partially blame on either external events or our traditional balance of payments constraint (specifically the political constraint lingering over the capital account). From 1999 though, the rand has floated much more cleanly, deflecting external pressure rather than storing it up. Interest rate policy and expectations are focused on inflation, and its behaviour is steadily being tamed from within the economic structure, especially through the decline in the budget deficit and the slower increase in unit labour costs.

Instead of periodically incurring large disruptive interest rate shocks, the domestic economy can look forward to a smoother performance on account of more stable interest rates, with a downward bias over time. In this context, the interest rate increases of 2002 must be seen as a temporary interruption following the rand's spectacular free-fall of 2001. As the imported inflation shock passes through, interest rates (like inflation) can be expected to resume their secular downward path.

Fiscal policy has achieved a structural norm by reducing the budget deficit to 2% of GDP. While the budget deficit was being reduced, fiscal policy restricted demand in the economy. This headwind has also apparently come to an end as the deficit has been reduced far enough. Henceforth, higher public capital expenditure, and especially greater social delivery, should provide support to domestic growth, though there is likely to be a real social limit to the growth performance in the longer-term (see Chapter 7), if the needed human capital fails to materialise in sufficient quantity.

The micro-economic restructuring, which has been underway since the mid-1980s, has over time resulted in a more productive, market-based economy, yielding higher economic returns on its deployed resources, as fewer formally employed labour endowed with 20% more capital came to grow the economy at an average annual rate of nearly 3% this past decade. The old dependency on mining as a net foreign exchange generator became steadily eroded, as previously protected industry learned to pay its way externally, ending the peculiarly exposed current account condition of the import-replacement and apartheid era.

The country's private sector continued with real fixed investment during the 1990s (prodded along by the forces described in Chapter 3), slowly increasing the capital stock. In contrast, the social and economic infrastructure has essentially been kept unchanged for most of the 1990s, with limited growth in public fixed investment offset by depreciation. Private net investment is at least back to half the pace prior to 1985, compared to the complete cessation in the public sector after 1990. Limited infrastructure expansion in some areas of the public sector was offset by actual contractions elsewhere. This was partially due to excess capacity in some areas, a very strict budget regime and limited administrative capacity to manage expansion. Public fixed investment did not therefore provide the boost to growth it could have done.

However, by 2002 underlying conditions had changed to the point where greater support for economic growth from public capital expenditure could again be expected. The budget constraint had become less strict as more resources were becoming available within the existing budget norms. Excess infrastructure capacity has steadily been whittled away, and as shortages start to loom in future years they will create new incentive to start adding to infrastructure once again. Unfortunately, adequate administrative capacity to manage such new investments, may remain a concern for some years to come.

In Graphs 5 and 6 on page 206 and 207, the private and public sectors are contrasted in their contribution to real economic growth by way of their fixed investment in new production capacity and infrastructure over

Graph 5: Investment-to-GDP: Private Sector, 1960–2002

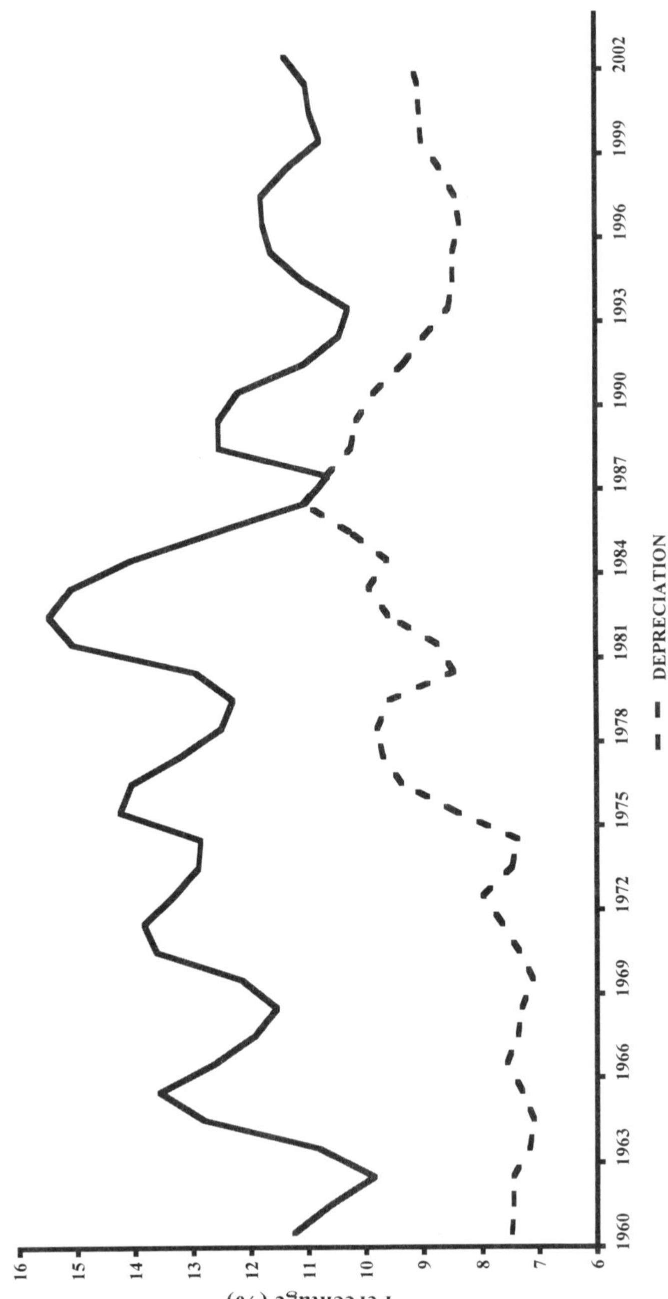

Graph 6: Investment-to-GDP: Public Sector, 1960–2002

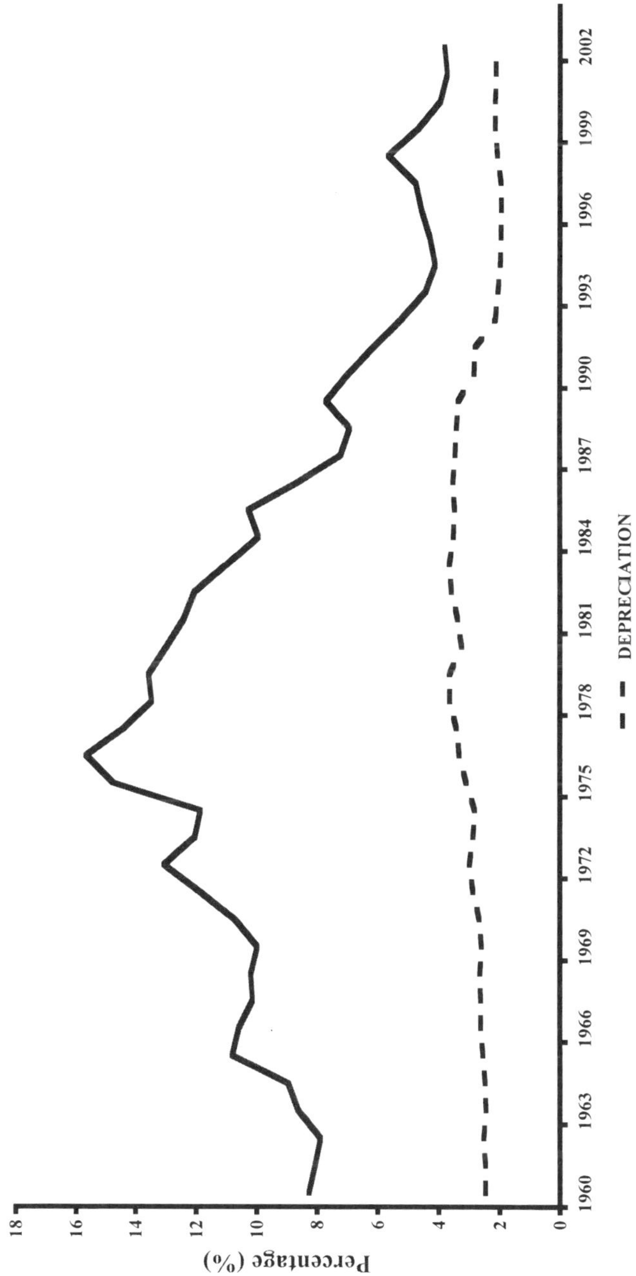

more than four decades. The private sector is shown to have recovered only half its pace of new investment, while the public sector has yet to start making any comeback after playing a very major role in bygone decades. By restoring conditions that will facilitate greater investment commitments by both private and public sectors, the economy's productive capacity should be made to expand faster in coming years, thereby facilitating another step up in the pace of economic growth from the current 3% p.a.

Graph 5 shows private fixed investment as a share of real GDP, highlighting the tendency in gross fixed investment and the depreciation charge. The area between these two lines represents net fixed investment—the actual net increase in private production capacity added each year to the economy, expressed as a share of GDP.

By examining Graph 5, we can see how by 1985 net capacity addition momentarily ceased in the private sector. Thereafter, net capacity addition recovered to about half the pace of the decades before. Although net investment continued in the 1990s, its pace was not yet robust enough to suggest a return to even higher GDP growth rates (in excess of 3%) as had been enjoyed in the 1960s and 1970s. The increasingly productive use of capital post-1990, however, did suggest that higher economic returns were being obtained compared to the larger amounts of capital probably less efficiently deployed during the 1970s and 1980s.

Thus, even with net capacity additions in the private sector increasing only at half the pace of the decades prior to 1985, an average GDP growth rate of nearly 3% was already being sustained in the 1990s, in addition to substituting labour during this period on an unprecedented scale through capital deepening—suggesting that the more efficient deployment of capital, relative to preceding decades, was well advanced.

Graph 6 tells a different story about the public sector. This graph similarly depicts gross fixed investment and the depreciation charge as a share of GDP, while the area between these two lines is the net annual addition to infrastructure. There were huge net capacity additions in the decades through the late 1970s. Thereafter, a steady fall-off in annual net additions occurred, and essentially ceased from the late 1980s.

Although the public sector had made huge net additions to infrastructure in the 1960s and 1970s, much of this increasingly yielded lower economic returns. In the 1980s, infrastructure expansion far outran rapidly slowing economic growth, and public investment finally started to fall off as well, remaining stagnant in the 1990s through to today.

Throughout the past decade, public infrastructure investment has added minimally to economic growth. It thus became an important obstacle to faster fixed investment growth overall (directly, and indirectly through a lack of spillover effects in the private sector), and ultimately to faster GDP growth.

Starting with government capital expenditure intentions as of 2001–2002 and changing parastatal needs as surplus capacities have gradually dwindled, a (much) more active public investment effort can be expected in coming years, bolstering fixed investment and GDP growth anew (as per the original intentions of Gear—see Chapter 3).

One, as yet unknown, twist to events will be the intention to privatise most of the large parastatals. This will presumably cause future investment decisions to be driven by a more commercial point of view, affecting such new investments quantitatively and in terms of timing. This will ensure higher economic returns on such investments than in the past, but may not give as much of a boost to overall fixed investment and economic growth as experienced then.

Further to the economic reforms discussed above, exchange control relaxation has allowed the country to absorb some needed changes. The dual currency regime was ended, the rand became lower valued, and thereby supported manufactured exports to a greater degree. Local investors were allowed to diversify some of their country risk via various legal channels. These gains, as well as the others already mentioned, came to be reflected in an improved country credit rating.

This entire process was attempted from a position of great weakness (limited foreign reserves, and a certain exchange rate management philosophy) that imposed transition costs. Having achieved these benchmarks, though, reform in this area has taken a breather, to await privatisation, faster economic growth and evidence of increased foreign capital inflows, before the remaining controls are lifted, in all likelihood at much less cost than the initial reforms.

Privatisation, long only a distant promise, is now likely to be completed relatively shortly, with 2003–2007 probably seeing the main asset sales. The proceeds realised through privatisation will complete the country's financial restructuring. They will greatly strengthen the external finances, go some considerable way to pay down the national debt and reduce the interest charge on the national budget. In turn, this will create space for stepped up social delivery on a far more ambitious scale than previously seen.

The traditional balance of payments constraint, both on current and capital accounts, reflecting our domestic savings/consumption balance as much as the composition of our exports and imports, is likely to be less of a constraint in future. More efficiently operating factor markets should price our output more competitively, allowing our exports to be less reliant on international commodity demand only, as manufactures keep on gaining market share. Future investments in new productive capacities, a part of whose output is likely to be exported, will also contribute to gains in our market share.

To the extent that fixed investment demand outpaces domestic savings, faster domestic growth will call forth a current account deficit that will be financed through foreign capital inflows. In a post-transition phase, high political risk and low growth prospects should not be the inhibitors to capital inflows that such features (and excessive consumption and limited supply flexibility) were during the distorted decades behind us. That such a structural change has been wrought, and that consequently the balance of payments should be less of a constraint (as happened to Australia in the 1990s) is yet to be fully acknowledged, on the capital account as well. However, we are making progress, as reflected in our steadily improving country credit-risk rating, monetary policy reform and the gradual transformation of our external finances (as yet to be completed). Fully relaxing the balance of payments constraint over our domestic affairs will be the main fruit of our structural reforms.

Even so, the balance of payments, our economic structure and our political risk were only some of the constraints on our growth. The actual quality of our labour force and the manner in which education prepares people for economic participation will be the genuine supply constraint on our performance in future decades.

The economic reforms and their resulting achievements discussed above, along with political stability, and its attendant continuity and predictability, form the crux of the ANC government's structural achievements. From these achievements we now have every right to expect a pay-off (even a major one) in terms of faster economic growth, greater employment creation and an improvement in the distribution of income, human capital and wealth over many years to come.

These achievements are crucial to understanding our future economic growth potential, for risk-taking and new investment commitments do not thrive in a stagnating, frequently interrupted business environment. Instead, the growth 'runs' will lengthen, and the risk of shock interruptions will lessen, together with the risk-aversion, high investment hurdle rates and short payback periods that we have become used to in the past three decades.

The envisioned changeover to a faster economic growth performance will not materialise suddenly, but it will occur. Only in time, looking back, will it stand out that the 2000s decade was different in texture from the reforming 1990s. In this respect, our closest role model, apart from the likes of Malaysia, is probably other OECD commodity-exporting countries, such as Australia, New Zealand and Canada, with whom we have much in common historically, given our resource endowment and industrialisation route. The Australian experience with reform since the 1980s especially comes to mind. The Australians made mistakes just as we have, but eventually they did get their reward during a long period of expansion in the 1990s. In the course of this expansion they managed to average 4.2% annual GDP growth during 1993–1999 (implying high per capita gains for a country with less than 1% population growth). By early 2003, Australia had completed twelve years of non-stop expansion. This offers a tantalising pointer to South Africa as to what may lie ahead, if we persist with and complete our many reforms and perhaps become an 'emerging' Australia.

Our Growth Story Going Forward

Taking the longer view (a decade, a generation), South Africa's domestic prospects look good for a gradual acceleration in growth momentum, given the reforms being implemented (as discussed in Chapters 3, 4 and 5), unless some global financial event intrudes and puts us back badly.

In the late 1980s and very early 1990s, GDP growth had slowed to a crawl (averaging 0.7% p.a. during 1983–1993, which admittedly included two severe recessions). Since then, the pace has been boosted to an annual average of 2.8% during 1994–2002 (including only one growth recession). Now we should contemplate the next boost in average economic growth performance towards 4%, as originally intended by Gear.

Such a boost will primarily come from the demand side of the economy, from the composition of growth, and from the factors of production themselves (mainly management, labour and productivity). The aim should be average annual GDP growth of 4% or better. Even if the HIV/Aids pandemic were to cost an average of 0.5% p.a. in real GDP growth (BER 2001), it would leave as much as 3.5% annual per capita growth on an essentially stabilised South African population, implying a doubling in real national income per capita every twenty years. This would compare with an effective stagnation in real per capita income these past thirty years.

The domestic demand side of the economy could contribute more to our economic growth than most people seem to think. Too often, however, this is not mentioned as the primary engine for our growth performance, and instead we hear a preference expressed for export-led growth. This is not a magic formula as such growth is dependent on foreign demand and is exogenous—and therefore precariously determined. We have no say over how much foreign countries want to consume. Alternatively, we could opt for proactive government micro-intervention, such as investment and labour incentives of all kinds, instead of leaving such allocation decisions to market forces. Each year's budget tends to carry another instalment of such supportive measures, yet their potential for decisively improving economic performance remains dubious.

Of course, strong export demand would be first prize if it were to be continuously available. It is, however, unrealistic to expect the outside world to be such a stable and willing source of demand for our products. Instead, external demand should practically be seen as a secondary source of spending stimulus to the economy (though crucial to paying our way over the balance of payments), with the primary demand source being what we can generate domestically.

What is needed on the demand side of the economy is less financial interruption from outside the country (as mentioned in Chapter 4). The growth 'runs' in our economy have been too short for decades now, making business increasingly risk-averse. Interrupted growth, high financial volatility and political uncertainty have tended to increase the sense of business risk, and have resulted in less willingness to think big (except for finding ways of getting out and going global, preferably from an overseas location). Thus there has been an emphasis on cost-cutting, which hurts employment and restrains fixed investment and inventory demand. If we can succeed in lengthening our growth runs, demand-led growth should overcome a lot of caution, which is currently keeping businesses back. We still suffer too much from a stagnation mentality rather than enjoying an expansion-dynamic in many sectors of our economy. Any step up in their investment commitments would today see a far more balanced development of import needs and export capability, with a more productive, competitive economy and supportively priced currency as background, thereby limiting any current account constraint over our growth prospects.

The country's financial condition has been so precarious these past three decades that we have become overly vulnerable to balance of payments crises driven by the capital account condition and the accompanying interest rate shocks and loss of business confidence. Even a marginal improvement in this condition is likely to lead to longer growth runs, which should reinforce the business case for expansion. Cost-consciousness will still prevail because of intense trade competition and labour demands, but we should regain a greater emphasis on fixed investment and appropriately skilled labour resources.

What will make such longer growth runs possible is a stronger financial structure including:

- low budget deficit;
- privatisation;
- smaller national debt;
- lower debt-servicing burden;
- more social delivery;
- stronger foreign reserves;
- low foreign indebtedness; and
- improved country credit rating.

All these 'good' things should ensure a stronger inflow of foreign capital, less inclined to interruption, and the ability to run a larger current account deficit without every so often having to restrain the economy because the means have run out to pay for imports. In turn, we should be able to afford modestly lower short-term interest rates (real as well as nominal in coming years) without triggering financial instability. Lower interest rates are a key element in reducing risk perceptions and hurdle rates, for both consumers and business.

Easy money alone will not do the trick. Growth can only happen in response to structural reforms already in place and the completion of our financial reforms over the next few years, something we have been waiting for since the mid-1960s. But besides longer growth runs creating more business certainty and appetite for risk, government has the means to reinforce such perceptions by using its very size to provide more stability to the long-term planning horizons of what remain mostly smallish enterprises. Thus long-term contracts for infrastructural improvements are a two-way street. Infrastructural spending strengthens the productive ability of the economy (provided it is of the right kind), as well as raising demand in a predictable manner. It made a major contribution to growth in the 1960s, and could do so again, provided it is well managed. Government seems intent on increasing capital spending considerably in coming years. It will need to make sure, though, that it has the managerial capacity to implement such plans.

On the production side of the economy, we have absorbed an enormous change in composition of output over the past two decades. Gold mining has more than halved in size (a loss of 4% of GDP), and building and construction activity as a share of GDP has also been halved due to stagnation in infrastructure expansion, low maintenance spending, and the impact of interest rate shocks (another loss of 3% of GDP). Agriculture has shrunk further by 1% to 3% of GDP since 1970 as less subsidisation has led to reduced marginal activity.

The biggest change by far has been a gradual one and mostly only experienced as an opportunity loss: the decline in inventory levels throughout the economy. These have fallen from a peak level of 35% of GDP in 1977 to 14% of GDP in 1993, a decline of 21% of GDP spread out over sixteen years. Working off such excess inventories represented a drag on overall demand growth and reduced GDP growth on average by 1.3% annually during 1977–1993, compared to the pace at which final demand was expanding. Most of this opportunity loss came at the expense of manufacturing activity.

The good news must be that all these structural features will not repeat themselves to anywhere near the same extent in the years ahead, thus allowing a higher average GDP growth rate as the increase in final demand drives output growth more fully.

Manufacturing has been especially hard hit during the transition. Heavy manufacturing industry has found demand for its products stagnant and has rationalised its workforce, in part reflecting the experience of slow and interrupted fixed investment spending in the economy.

Unfortunately, we also find key aspects of traditional goods manufacturing and retailing (such as foodstuffs, beverages, packaging, textiles and other household goods) under pressure as consumer tastes, preferences and employment realities have shifted. Most of this structural shift, along with the need to specialise more as import protection has been lifted and imports have gained a greater foothold, has probably already occurred, although there could still be some pressure in these areas.

These problems can be contrasted with the favourable impact from the platinum boom, the revolution in communication services, the strong performance of the chemical industry, assisted by high world prices for oil/coal, and the export success of the motor industry. These four sectors are the high performers of recent years, along with a strong performance by financial services, but other businesses have also repositioned themselves or have come into being, most visibly in Gauteng and the Western Cape.

The sources of growth have changed. Manufacturing needs to specialise as well as to cut its costs in response to import competition, even as important demand sectors such as mining and basic consumer spending have faded. Mining, however, appears selectively to be on the comeback trail, judging by investment commitments made in the precious metal sector in recent years, partly in response to the progressively undervalued rand in the past decade. In addition, manufacturing is the main beneficiary of increased exporting into Africa, a natural geographical hinterland for our basic manufactures and technologies. Its share of our total exports has increased from 6% to 13% in the past decade. The economy's main growth dynamic resides in services, a net creator of employment and new activity ranging from communication to protection services. Future growth drivers will also include infrastructure (such as power and transport), building and construction (on housing) and tourism (still underexploited). Demand growth will be partly from the outside, but primarily from within, that is, demand for new technology applications, infrastructure, fixed investment and expansion of the consumer market. Some of these, especially new technology and infrastructure, have supply aspects as well, by cutting costs and improving efficiency throughout the economy.

The ultimate key to our GDP performance is productivity growth. Economic growth equates to increasing inputs of labour and capital plus technology. We seem to be absorbing new technology well, while also being forced to use our labour more productively. Entrepreneurial talent is indispensable to make this work as the rules have changed. The lifting of external constraints, such as import protection and political ostracism, are the main drivers in allowing us to more fully exploit our domestic resources and economic opportunities.

The biggest bottleneck still lies ahead. We have not yet suffered critically from a shortage of skilled labour as the structural changes of recent decades have freed up a lot of skilled labour that will be reabsorbed first (see Chapters 3 and 5). It will, however, become the key constraint as structural reform progresses and the pace of growth picks up. If 36% of the labour force is currently unemployed and a further 30% are underutilised, it is plain that too many of these people are underskilled for a modern service-oriented economy. This shortcoming, more than anything else, will cap our growth rate and keep unemployment high—even when prosperity will grow more evident for those in formal employment.

The only truly viable answer to this discrepancy in wealth and income is better education all round and a population which is able to absorb it. Such a breakthrough will not come about rapidly, though it should have the highest priority. We would all gain from the political viability this would bring in its wake, and it would be the key to sustaining the next step-up in our growth rate over a longer-term.

Changing Sources of Growth in the Regions

South Africa's major growth poles today are Gauteng and the Western Cape, with the Rustenburg area in North-West and Richards Bay in KwaZulu-Natal as special export beneficiaries, and Port Elizabeth/East London focused on their port facilities and the motor industry.

Gauteng has had to absorb major industrial changes during the past two decades in terms of gold mining cutbacks, as well as the rationalisation of heavy industry, especially in engineering. Furthermore, like the Durban-Pinetown axis, the East and West Rands are still heavily populated with non-durable and semi-durable consumer goods manufacturing such as foodstuffs, beverages, textiles and assorted household goods and industrial materials manufacturing. These types of activities have tended to stagnate during the 1990s as non-durable consumer spending grew by only 1% annually.

In contrast, the main office nodes north of the Witwatersrand watershed (Sandton, Randburg, Fourways, Midrand and Centurion) have benefited from increased financial sector activity, distribution, warehousing and business services, especially related to computer and other IT activity, with Pretoria having a strong presence in car manufacturing, and public services. Clearly, the Gauteng push is in services. It remains the premier head-office location for many national companies and it generates over 40% of South Africa's GDP.

Furthermore, the redeveloped port of Maputo may be outside South Africa's borders, but it is in a pivotal position to win more Gauteng traffic as well as heavy industry based on cheap natural gas, as already evidenced by the aluminium smelter there.

The Western Cape contains a fairly good balance of activities, exploiting natural advantages, led by tourism, agriculture (wine, fruit, grain) and business services (financial, IT). It provides a modern base, and was an early beneficiary of relocations and retirees from Gauteng, to Cape Town, the Boland, as well as the George–Knysna–Plettenberg Bay axis. The 'great' influx from Gauteng, however, ended some time ago. Indeed, there are more returnees today as the economic opportunities of Gauteng have reasserted themselves.

In contrast, the Durban–Pinetown area is a much more mature industrial location, still importantly benefiting from the great natural advantages of major port facilities, and inland transportation, as well being a tourism hub. As a head-office location, it has been losing activity to the other growth metropoles, and while modern service activities are obviously present, Gauteng and the Western Cape appear to enjoy an important edge. Nevertheless, Durban still has great infrastructure, including an international airport (with a huge new one in the planning stage) and major universities. It certainly has the benefit of critical mass in its urban population and skills base.

Rustenburg, located in North-West, and to a lesser degree key towns in the Northern Province, are beneficiaries of the 'new gold' boom in platinum group metals (PMG). During 2000, PMG exports for the first time outstripped gold exports in value (R30 billion versus R27 billion). Even though PMG's dollar prices subsided again during 2001, they have risen anew in 2002, and expansion plans at the various PMG mines suggest that the bonanza will continue into the future, benefiting the immediate major towns.

Richards Bay is the Rustenburg of KwaZulu-Natal, without the platinum. It is dependent on its coal export terminal as well as a few very large industrial plants—aluminium, fertiliser, pulp and paper, titanium, timber and sugar.

The country's regional imbalances are becoming bigger again. Just as distinctions internally within the larger metropolitan areas are sharpening, as the poorer areas lose whatever small business locations they may have had to newer regional shopping and office developments, so a few city and port locations succeed in gaining most of the new business activities that are to be had, with the greater part of the country losing out, despite retaining large populations.

In nearly every province there are also what may be called second-tier cities (to distinguish them from the first-tier metropolitan cities). These remain vibrant locations, and quite a few of them enjoy steady growth and development momentum, but they are not in the same league as the main growth metropolitan cities. Some of them could become more significant locations in the future, once the country's growth rate has picked up more than it has done so far, for instance for specialised high-tech companies.

Which city/region will become our own Silicon Valley? In debating this, we look for proximity to the first-tier metropolitan cities to offer life-style, excellent communications including a major airport, and probably a university or two, already ensuring a certain physical and skill infrastructure. Potential candidates include the Boland and Stellenbosch, the Natal Midlands and Pietermaritzburg, and to a lesser degree Port Elizabeth, Bloemfontein, Potchefstroom and Klerksdorp, and even Oudtshoorn and George (with Pretoria and Westville and their universities respectively counted as part of Gauteng and Durban rather than viewed separately).

We can identify many more second-tier locations. In no particular order, and at the risk of overlooking an obvious name, they are Paarl/Wellington, Worcester, George, Nelspruit, Newcastle, Pietersburg, Witbank/Middelburg, Kimberley and Upington.

Growth Drivers for the Future

On balance, South Africa is growing and moving forward. The few very strong growth drivers are steadily outperforming the many retreating or stagnating sectors and regions in our economy, in the process shifting the structural centre of economic gravity. Over a period of 150 years, agriculture had to give way to mining, which had to give way to manufacturing, which had to give way to services. Today, certain types of mining such as platinum group metals are in the ascendancy, and selected manufacturing activities—motor industry and chemicals, including paper—are maintaining a reasonable presence.

The real driving force of the economy and of new employment opportunities is the services sector, which is technology-based and focuses on IT, banking, investment, entertainment and communication. This is increasingly a new 'industrial complex' that is very different from the self-sufficiency orientation of heavy industry that preceded it.

Despite concerns that are often expressed, this is a credible basis for a viable future as it is based on natural advantages (mining, tourism), specialisation (manufacturing), and technology-driven innovation (services). South Africa's modernisation is now very much services-driven, copying experiences in North America, Europe and Australasia, and in common with many emerging countries in Asia, Latin America and Central Europe.

One sector that could return strongly in the future on the back of generally faster economic growth is building and construction. South Africa has enormous social backlogs and building is probably the easiest way to promote some redistribution in a noticeable physical sense, apart from infrastructure needs. This rebound also promises an increase in related employment opportunities, a critical linchpin sector in creating less high-skilled jobs, compared to the future high-skill demands of the manufacturing and services sectors.

As to the African and tourism markets, we should not overstate the benefits to be had in the short-term, but there is untapped potential that is likely to be reaped over time. The same can be said about the mining and industry potential of natural gas (West and East Coast).

As already discussed, the relative regional disparities can be expected to worsen over time. Nevertheless, a large part of the forced rationalisations, by industry and region, has probably already been absorbed. In their new make-up, these sectors and regions should over time experience absolute gains, rather than keep on backsliding. Such gains, even if often meagre, will constitute progress for the people experiencing them. That it will not be quite at the rate and level of a Gauteng or Western Cape, Richards Bay or Rustenburg is nothing new, but a reality of local—and global—economic history and its evolving line-up of relative winners and losers.

The Prospects for Skilled Labour

The biggest myth about skilled labour in South Africa at present must be that there is a shortage. In fact there is not. The quarterly BER manufacturing survey for the fourth quarter of 2000, showed the availability of skilled labour as the constraint least worrying to business executives (see Table 10). This condition has continued mostly unchanged as borne out by subsequent BER business surveys.

Table 10: Business Ranking of Main Constraints, Fourth Quarter 2000

Factors	% of all responses
Domestic demand	22.6
Crime and violence	13.2
Political climate in South Africa	12.7
Labour costs	10.0
Exchange rate fluctuations	9.1
Labour relations	7.6
Regulatory framework, governance	5.5
Political climate in rest of Africa	5.3
International demand	5.1
Short-term interest rates	4.6
Taxation	2.3
Availability of skilled labour	2.1

Source: BER (2000).

Admittedly, manufacturing is not necessarily reflective of the whole economy, today contributing 21% of GDP. But it is still a large employer of formal labour (core employment of just over 1.2 million or 27% of the economy's formal core in 2001). This ranking of skilled labour as the least of worries, at a point in time well into cyclical economic recovery, is remarkable. It is particularly remarkable when we consider that South Africa has lost an estimated half a million people to emigration in the past two decades. A good portion of these were dependants, but those of working age were mostly skilled workers. It has been twenty years since the country had a non-sustainable gold boom (1979–1980) and thirty years since it could ride the coat-tails of a prolonged global expansion (1948–1973). Well over half our current managers and professionals do not know what an economic boom feels like (those in the cellphone industry and platinum mining excepted).

Consequently, the combination of two decades of economic stagnation followed by a decade of deep employment rationalisation depressed demand for skilled labour. Added to this, a vastly increased high school, technikon and university enrolment has boosted the supply of skilled labour, while increased trade competition and affirmative action has released skilled labour, and technological change absorbed skilled labour. On balance, these many cross-currents have created a large, if temporary, surplus of skilled labour.

The surplus, boosted by the immigration of skilled labour, became so big during the 1990s that the country did not appear to be registering the emigration brain drain at all (except to the extent that really good staff are always in short supply—a reality nearly everywhere in the world). This was not the popular perception that was reflected in the media (see, for example, *Business Day* 2001).

However, this situation will assuredly change before long as our main social and economic trends change tack once again, while the principal technological trends are still likely to deepen immeasurably. South Africans, especially the skilled cadre, therefore find themselves at an important crossroads that will make this aspect of our resource base the main driver of future economic performance.

The total number of skilled workers in South Africa in 1995 was an estimated 1.2 to 1.7 million people (see Table 11 below). For the period 1995–2000, some 500 000 of such skilled potentials will have entered the labour market. Emigration during this period probably absorbed 200 000 of these, but immigration may have yielded 100 000, with retirement withdrawing 200 000 from the pool. This suggests a net addition of up to 200 000 skilled personnel, for a total of skilled labour ranging from 1.4 million to just short of 2 million by 2000.

Some 25% of skilled labour consists of executive, managerial and administrative workers and 75% of professional and technical workers. There were about 1.2 million people with a higher education (over and above matric) in the country in 1995 (as many as 24% of adult White South Africans being so qualified as opposed to only 3% of adult Blacks). In addition, there were 3.5 million people with at least a matriculation certificate, some 40% in the case of adult Whites and 12% of adult Blacks. For 1999, StatsSA (2001) has further updated its estimates (see Table 11). The numbers give a good idea of the education profile of most skilled workers. It is a relatively small group out of a labour force of 19 million and a population of 45 million people.

Table 11: Education Profile and Skilled Labour, 1970–1999			
Million	**1970**	**1995**	**1999**
Those with a post-matric qualification (university degree, technikon diploma)	0.2	1.2	1.9
Those with matric as highest certificate	0.7	3.5	4.7
Estimated pool of 'skilled labour	0.4–0.7	1.2–1.7	1.4–2.0
Sources: Bhorat and Hodge (1999), StatsSA (2001).			

In themselves, these numbers indicate that although there is currently no shortage of skilled labour as a constraint on growing existing GDP, the structural reality is quite different. To uplift the two-thirds of the labour force that is currently still unemployed or informally employed will require a great increase in the amount of available skilled labour. This is the stark development challenge facing South Africa's next generation.

A 1999 study by two UCT academics (Bhorat and Hodge), using Statistics South Africa data for 1970–1995, shows a 15% increase in the workforce from 7.5 million to 8.6 million (a period during which real GDP expanded by 72%). Within this workforce, skilled labour jobs increased from 0.4 million (a 6% share) in 1970 to 1.7 million (a 20% share) in 1995. Lewis (2001) quotes Edwards, on a narrower definition, identifying for 1984 some 0.7 million skilled workers (10% of the 6.7 million formally employed), rising to 1.1 million (18%) in 1997. In other words, there was a substantial increase in skilled workers employed over time, tripling their share to about 20% of the labour force today, in spite of net emigration.

The main reasons behind such trends are that, firstly, the population increased during these three decades, but it was a bare doubling, compared to the explosive increase in the numbers of people enjoying higher education. Secondly, the pool of higher educated workers holding a post-matric qualification (for example, university degree, technikon, teaching or nursing diploma) increased from as little as 0.2 million in 1970 to 1.2 million people in 1995, and then to an estimated 1.9 million by 1999. This was the main group from which the country drew its skilled workers. Those with matric as their highest education increased from 0.7

million to 4.7 million people over the same period, supplying a lesser number of our highly skilled labour. Thirdly, while South Africa may have lost skilled labour through emigration, it also gained through immigration, including:

- Eastern Europeans (since 1985, before the Wall came down and especially afterwards);
- Chinese, Indians and Pakistanis (from Asia and Africa);
- Cubans; and
- Africans (from Zimbabwe, Zambia, Malawi, Namibia, Botswana, Mozambique, Ghana, Congo, Kenya, Cameroon, Nigeria).

The primary reason for the increased deployment of skilled workers within industries was due to changes in production techniques—mostly using more, increasingly sophisticated, machines. A lesser reason was the shift between sectors, with all kinds of services expanding rapidly, especially those with a computer, other IT or financial services connection. Both these features reflect global trends, and merely confirm that we are not moving out of step with the world economy.

The greater use of machines, and the relatively faster expansion of the services sector, produced a lot of surplus labour lower down the skills ladder. Edwards, quoted by Lewis (2001), estimates that in the skill category immediately below skilled, in what he terms 'semi-skilled', some 300 000 jobs were lost (net) between 1984 and 1997. Various horror stories abound about employers not being interested in training people, but it is unlikely that all 300 000 of these surplus workers became permanently unemployed.

A portion became self-employed, and were probably sophisticated enough not to be counted as informal sector, and should thus now be counted as formally skilled. They upgraded themselves by becoming successful entrepreneurs—the car mechanic who starts his own garage is a process that continues today, only that person is more likely to end up running an IT business.

Some of the remainder probably received promotion, as more work was allocated to them. Their jobs were regraded, becoming more skilled and being recognised as such. There may have been a measure of 'title inflation' in some instances (a phenomenon not unknown in New York or London where 'managing directors' abound); while in others there may have been increases in employment linked to affirmative action that did not always immediately displace an incumbent.

For these varied reasons, the ranks of our skilled workers may have been joined by those who not so long ago would have been defined as semi-skilled.

Lewis, still following Edwards (2001), identifies for 1984–1997 three causes that help to explain the creation and destruction of skilled jobs: final demand, net foreign trade (exports and import substitution) and technology. Despite popular impressions to the contrary, trade liberalisation has not been a net destroyer of jobs. Although import penetration has risen, the associated job destruction has been offset by rising employment linked to exports (especially for skilled work, less so for less-skilled work). The really big change agents have been technology and changes in final demand. With regard to skilled labour, Edwards estimates that during 1993–1997, the pace of net skilled job creation (over 3%) was double the pace of 1984–1993 (but then economic growth was faster, too). While trade had a neutral impact, and final demand has only started adding jobs seriously since 1993, technology has been a great engine of skilled job creation throughout. This should not come as a surprise, given capital deepening, greater specialisation, increased machine sophistication and the shift towards services with the IT, computer and financial expansion being most dynamic.

There have also been major ethnic and gender changes in the ranks of skilled labour, as summarised in Table 12. These changes, obtained using well-structured surveys, paint a picture that suggests much greater progress in this regard than perhaps is generally portrayed in the popular press, and popular perceptions may therefore lag behind reality by a considerable margin.

Between 1970 and 1995, according to Bhorat and Hodge (1999), the number of skilled jobs increased four-fold from just over 0.4 million to 1.7 million. In 1970, Whites held over 90% of the executive and administrative jobs, and two-thirds of all professional and technical jobs. Since then there have been huge changes. By 1995 the numbers of Whites holding managerial positions had tripled to 0.3 million, but this now represented 70% of such jobs. White professional jobs had also tripled in number, but now represented only a third of their total. In contrast, the Black share of professional jobs doubled to 50% (a seven-fold increase to 660 000) and their share of managerial jobs increased from 3% to 20% (from 3 000 to over 80 000 managers). Indians gained in both areas, from 3% to 4.5% of professional jobs and from 2.6% to over 7% of managerial jobs. Coloureds gained from 2% to over 4% of managerial jobs, but stayed the same at 7% of professional jobs. Women increased their share of professional jobs from 43% to 50% and from 8% to near 20% of managerial jobs. None of these changes can be considered insignificant in a society as sensitive as South Africa during this transition period.

Table 12: Estimated Changes in the Composition of Skilled Labour, 1970–1995

	Managerial		Professional	
'000	**1970**	**1995**	**1970**	**1995**
Whites	106	300	230	490
Indians	3	30	10	60
Coloureds	3	20	25	90
Blacks	3	80	90	660
Total	115	430	355	1 300
Women	9	85	155	650
Men	106	345	200	650

Source: Based on Bhorat and Hodge (1999), data rounded.

The White share of skilled jobs fell mostly because White population and labour force growth was much lower than for the other population groups. Thus, economic growth as well as technical and sectoral changes opened up opportunities for these other groups, mostly, though not entirely, without large society-wide dislocations. This should continue to be the case going forward, with three additional features:

- We have probably upgraded all those existing semi-skilled workers that had the potential to be so promoted, depleting this particular pool.
- As stated previously, economic growth should be faster in coming decades compared to the very slow growth since 1970.
- Unless something changes the current trend, HIV/Aids will ensure a topping out of the population and labour force size within a few years.

With technical and sectoral change far from being at an end, the two remaining great unknowns are: how will education and training change the supply of matric and higher educated youngsters; and what will the net migration trend be?

An increase in average economic growth towards 4% annually from 2.8% since 1993, along with technical and sectoral changes continuing for a long time, suggests at least another doubling or tripling in the demand for skilled labour towards a level of 4 million to 5 million such jobs in 30 years' time as compared to 1.4 million to 2 million today. The Actuarial Society of South Africa, for example, projects skilled labour to rise to 26% of the work force by 2015 compared to 6% in 1970, 10% in 1985 and 20% today (Bhorat and Hodge 1999, World Bank, ASSA). If this ratio were to increase further to 30% in 2030 on a total employed by then of 16 million (some 10 million formally employed and the remainder informally), it would yield an estimated skilled labour component of 4.8 million by that year.

If we express today's skilled labour as a ratio of formal employed only (6.7 million), its share is already 30%. For confirmation of this trend, we only need to look overseas. Some 45% of new employment in the US since 1995 has been highly skilled. Many emerging countries are likewise structurally upgrading, though some, such as Korea, far more aggressively than others, for example, the Philippines. As our labour force growth should peak within a few years, and thereafter effectively stagnate, it will be up to our education effort and net migration to close the gap between the demand for and supply of skilled workers. The number of pupils matriculating peaked in 1994 and has since fallen, and the number gaining a university exemption has decreased by a quarter as a proportion of those matriculating since 1994, as mentioned earlier in Chapter 7.

In the coming years, the pool of quality youngsters will grow slowly, potentially very slowly, given the low quality of education in too many locations, the small numbers learning the maths and science needed by the new technology base of the future economy, in addition to the impact of emigration and Aids. The universities and technikons currently deliver some 70 000 newly minted graduates annually, but these institutions will probably only partially supply our overall future need for skilled labour. Not everyone with such degrees will succeed in becoming genuinely skilled in line with the economy's needs. Furthermore, increasing numbers of youngsters may feel that such studies do not prepare them adequately for their chosen working lives or may not continue their studies because of financial constraints.

We also need to consider that the age group 0 to 14 is expected to decline by as much as a quarter over the next 30 years, partially on account of HIV/Aids. The school population can be expected to shrink in absolute numbers, reducing the base from which a bigger proportion of youngsters will need to progress to university and technikon level, if we are going to meet the future demand for skilled labour from domestic sources.

The current gross enrolment for tertiary education as a percentage of the relevant age group is just over 15%, on a par with Brazil and Mexico. The government would like to see this rise to 20%, but several of our education authorities remain sceptical. Some other countries are far ahead of us in this respect: Turkey at 20%, Czech Republic, Hungary and Poland at 25%, Chile at 30%, Argentina at 40%, and Korea at nearly 70%. If we want more modernisation, the writing is on the wall: either we produce more higher education graduates or we encourage vastly more immigration. Failing these two options, we will have to accept slow economic growth. It remains a relatively simple choice.

Over the next 30 years, our institutions of higher learning on present trends may at best supply some two million graduates of all kinds, some of whom will join the ranks of skilled labour. In addition, some of those achieving matriculation as their highest education level will, as in the past, follow more adventuresome paths to become highly skilled. However, allowance still has to be made for the retirement of existing skilled workers (at least 1 million over this period).

The numbers overall do not quite add up, suggesting a new and widening skills gap. This gap could still be partially met from, firstly, the increased pool of those only holding a matric, and, secondly, from much greater capital deepening as skills are embedded into machines (Sadie 1983). Thirdly, the younger age cohorts are better educated than their predecessors (see Table 13 on page 228 for the age distribution of those having achieved at least a matric), and offer some hope for more success with adult education in future years.

There is obviously a case to be made for skilled immigration, which will rise as the economy's performance improves. There appears to be movement of some sort in the country's labour, education and immigration policies. Apparently, it is now the government's intention to recruit foreign skills for at least the next twenty years, using foreign affairs offices abroad to do so, while making an effort at home to educate enough young people in the areas of critical need. While these sentiments are to be welcomed as a healthy recognition of likely future needs, such efforts will probably in time come to represent the tip of an iceberg. If the experience of other countries is anything to go by, many immigrants will come by foot, against all odds and find a niche for themselves, if needs be, illegally. The real potential of immigration will therefore unfold only slowly, as our own economic performance improves and as global conditions governing people's movements continue to evolve. The potential for surprise on this score may be huge, judging by modern experiences in North America and Western Europe.

Table 13: Age Distribution of Those Holding a Matric as Highest Level of Education

Age group	% holding at least matric
20–24	35.9
25–29	40.5
30–34	33.8
35–39	27.8
40–44	22.5
45–49	20.6
50–54	20.1
55–59	17.0
60–64	13.7
65–69	13.7
70+	13.1

Source: StatsSA, OHS (1999).

With regard to emigration, the biggest part of the current wave is probably behind us, linked as it was to restructuring, though we can expect to lose educated youngsters for a long time to come, as is experienced elsewhere in the world (see the next section). Adding all these supply and demand trends together suggests a genuine shortage of skilled labour ahead. It will create more traditional avenues of advancement as promising early school-leavers get another chance after their first job, eventually going back to (evening or other) school or correspondence college, increasingly employer-assisted. For such youngsters the long drought is about to end. But even this will only go part of the way. So either education gears up more impressively than it has done so far, or our economic growth will get capped, indeed non-sustainable at higher rates in the longer-term.

Revolving Doors: Migration and Aids

The popular impression is that emigration is rapidly depleting our stock of highly skilled labour, but the reality is more complex. Emigration has certainly not augmented our stock of medical, engineering, academic, accounting, managerial and other professionals. Nevertheless, South Africa has also visibly enriched its cosmopolitan mix in recent years with returning political exiles, an influx of African immigrants, and incoming Asians (especially Chinese) and Eastern Europeans of all nationalities, as well as Cubans.

If the country has lost skill in depth, it certainly has not been noticeable in our political arena. There the impression is easily formed that, given so much virtuosity, the country has only gained skill in recent years. But in nearly all other categories of labour skills, stepped up emigration appears to have sapped our national vitality, not necessarily in a quantitative sense of late, as there remains a reservoir of surplus skilled labour at present, as mentioned before, but certainly in a qualitative sense.

South Africans like to think that because of our political change, crime, stagnant economic development and affirmative action, they are going through some historically unique process of catastrophically losing key people, on a par with Yugoslavia in the 1990s, Zimbabwe in the 1980s, Vietnam in the 1970s, Algeria in the 1960s, East Germany in the 1950s, Western colonists in Asia in the 1940s, German Jews in the 1930s, and so on into ancient history. But such comparisons are not always appropriate. Our changes are in the main not forced, while regionalisation of labour forces is in full swing around the world, and has been going on for many years prior to our latest national experience. It is the ultimate confirmation of an integrating, globalising world civilisation where the really promising opportunities are concentrated in the leading metropolises.

This even applies to such desirable emigration destinations such as Canada, Australia and New Zealand. Canada loses its top achievers to the USA, as do Mexico, Britain and India. Australia loses them to the US, to London, and to leading Asian cities. New Zealand loses over 30 000 promising youngsters annually to Australia, on a population of 4 million. That comes close to South Africa's unofficial estimated (White) loss of 30 000 emigrants annually (though that is probably an underestimate), many of them to Australasia.

There is no reason why an economy cannot survive being marginalised like this, within reason of course. Obviously, we do want to retain some intelligence in our labour force, but, just as not everyone becomes HIV-positive, neither do all a country's people emigrate, not even its skilled people, unless truly catastrophic conditions come about. In the modern world, voluntary emigration is only for the favoured few, based on family links, educational or skill level, wealth, or for the hardiest survivors. Most of us do not fall into these camps, and there are certainly enough of us to keep the South African economy humming, even if specialised services can only be obtained at a cost from richer parts of the world.

The Aids Pandemic and the Skills Drain

While emigration has so far demonstrably not been the problem it has often been perceived to be, the impact of Aids on South Africa's limited pool of skilled labour requires careful consideration. As emigration implies at present mainly a loss of highly skilled labour, what is the likely comparative impact of HIV/Aids going to be on the higher-skilled component of the labour force? Which has been the more important source of loss, and what is it most likely to be in coming years? Most importantly, will these losses cripple our economic development or will the social system respond appropriately to the situation?

As a standard worst-case scenario, HIV-prevalence among Whites, Coloureds and Indians is estimated to peak at some 4% by 2010 (BER 2001). This would imply, for example, that about 0.4% of Whites might annually be dying of Aids in a decade's time. This amounts to 20 000 people, of which roughly half would be dependants and half labour force participants. The annual loss of skilled White labour alone may therefore already be 4 000 to 5 000 by the end of the 2000s decade.

But as data by Bhorat and Hodge (1999) illustrate, the days are long gone that our skilled labour originated exclusively from among White South Africans. The ethnic make-up of the skilled labour force has already changed significantly, and is projected to change further in coming years. Although various ethnic groups apparently have different HIV-prevalence rates, practical experience has been encouraging some observers to assume that a convergence in HIV-prevalence towards lower levels apparently takes place as a person acquires higher skills and incomes (see BER 2001). According to this line of reasoning, it would appear that despite the changing ethnic composition of our skilled labour force over time, eventual mortality among our skilled labour will stabilise at lower levels than for those that are less-skilled. This is in contrast with the HIV-prevalence in the total population, which is estimated at 12% in 2002 and is predicted to rise—in the standard worst-case scenario—to an estimated peak of 16% within the 2000s decade.

An estimate for Aids-linked mortality among our skilled labour may be obtained by projecting the expected size of our skilled labour force over time. Using Bhorat and Hodge's data again, the 1.7 million skilled workers in 1995 were 47% White, 42% Black, 6% Coloured and 5% Indian. This pool is estimated to have grown to some 2 million in 2002. Assuming an HIV-prevalence among all skilled labour of some 4% at its peak intensity (implying some 80 000 HIV sufferers), we arrive at a mortality due to Aids among all skilled labour gradually building up towards some 10 000 annually by the end of the 2000s decade.

Obviously, all deaths from Aids are to be deplored. Though there is no firm data as to the skill profile of our emigrants, for comparison's sake it may be useful to assume them all to be skilled. It would then seem that mortality losses due to Aids remain a secondary drain on our national stock of skilled labour compared to the loss via emigration of some 30 000 plus annually, at least in the 1990s and probably still so in the early 2000s. Global regionalisation (should we call it marginalisation?) thus appears to have a greater impact on the economy than the draining of the more highly skilled pool of labour via Aids in the 1990s or even early in the 2000s.

Over time, two developments may occur. The first concerns emigration. How many of the 1990s emigrants have settled in well overseas? Could any of them be enticed back if a genuine skill shortage were to develop along the lines envisaged, with remaining South Africans also becoming less inclined to leave? By 2002 anecdotal evidence suggested that such a shift might already be underway (in part due to less favourable circumstances developing internationally—as much economically and financially as geopolitically).

Secondly, if a differentiation in HIV-prevalence remains among social strata and as the composition of the labour force continues to change (especially in favour of higher skills), could Aids become a much bigger factor in the loss of critically skilled labour? Such a development could coincide with emigration slowing down as faster economic growth and a budding skills-shortage improves the employment chances for remaining South Africans and new immigrants. On such assumptions HIV/Aids could become more important than net emigration with respect to a loss of skilled labour over time. Over a 30-year period, HIV-prevalence may still be in the region of 4% among skilled labour, unless deflected through behavioural change and/or medication. Applying this figure to a skilled labour force of 4 million in 30 years' time, we get a steady build-up in the intervening years of annual Aids mortality, approaching 20 000 by 2030.

However, this number should be approached with care, as skilled labour in South Africa tends to be well covered by medical aid, with many in this category working for large businesses. Infected skilled labour may therefore more easily gain access to medication, and with the necessary personal discipline in taking their medication, succeed in prolonging their useful life, cutting the theoretical Aids mortality at least by half (to 10 000 annually by 2030, possibly even less).

On these same assumptions, given their status as skilled labour, this group of South Africans is probably best placed to learn how to change their social behaviour in order to minimise HIV-infection. If so, an even more dramatic fall-off in the projected Aids mortality among skilled labour over the next 30 years should present itself, rivalling the annual emigration loss for being a less important source of skilled labour loss.

In this way, either loss could become minimal compared to the present experience, which would be heartening news.

Aids will, of course, also impact among people other than skilled labour. However, that impact on the economy should apparently also be differentiated according to education, skill and income levels and the consequent individual contributions to GDP. Here the outstanding feature of the South African economy remains one of labour surpluses rather than shortages, something that will still characterise our condition for some years to come.

Unfortunately, the picture changes for the worse if some of the assumptions inherent in the standard worst-case scenario are relaxed, ending with an adventuresome worst-case scenario. For example, it may materialise that:

- HIV-infection does not stabilise at low levels of prevalence among skilled labour.
- Medication may only be effectively available for some, not all, skilled labour (depending on medical aid coverage, willingness to be tested, willingness to take medication, and the ability to persevere with a very disciplined approach to the taking of medication).
- Behaviour change limiting new infection may not be as easy to achieve as is perhaps generally assumed.

If, for instance, HIV-prevalence among all skilled labour were to rise towards 10% peak levels, dramatically different labour market conditions would come to prevail. On a 30-year view, a 10% HIV-prevalence peak among skilled labour would imply 400 000 HIV sufferers and annual deaths of up to 50 000, if medication and behaviour changes are not effective.

Even if such mortality were to eventually fall off, its impact on economic development would potentially be much more severe than in the standard worst-case. However, it remains to be seen whether economic development would cease or whether social change would transform the situation.

A Generation of Newcomers

The story of South Africa's migration experience and prospects would not be complete without a closer look at immigration. In recent years, judging from various newspaper reports, South African society has been characterised by rising xenophobia. This fear of foreigners is expressed in various ways, mostly focusing on the 'unfair' competition for limited jobs and social benefits. Two types of argument prevail, the one focusing on mass unskilled labour, the other more narrowly on skilled labour.

According to negative sentiments, there are allegedly millions of poor neighbours (Mozambicans, Zimbabweans and Malawians in particular) already settled in South Africa, and many more that potentially can still come, as conditions deteriorate further in their home countries. This human flood is portrayed as a burden that will weigh on us without benefit, undoing whatever we succeed in putting together. Furthermore, educated immigrants are seen as capitalising on our political revolution, with too many poor South Africans not yet getting a fair deal.

Such opinions do exist and from time to time they break the surface. Fortunately, the friction appears to remain very limited, and the country's improved performance and consequent more abundant opportunities should greatly assist in keeping such sentiments manageable.

More realistically, Professor Sadie (2002) of Stellenbosch doubts that more than 1.2 million near-African neighbours have entered South Africa since 1990. Haldenwang (1999), in her 30-year population projection, assumes in-migration of 200 000 annually, presumably mostly from Africa (see Chapter 6). But we have no sure way of knowing how many of working age and some of their dependants will eventually make this new inward 'Great Trek' as the South African economy steadily performs better in coming years and decades. Perhaps we have to start with the current total employment base of 10 million and project from there (see Chapter 5). This could well suggest, and support, an annual influx of up to 200 000 new arrivals (a portion of them dependants), creating real competition for some of South Africa's unemployed and new labour entrants. As time goes by, though, and our employment base expands even as our pool of unemployed shrinks gradually, a steady increase in the number of new arrivals could easily be accommodated in a growing economy.

Based on other countries' projections for the next 30 years (for example, immigration to Germany from Eastern Europe following the expansion of the European Union), South Africa can estimate an immigration of 200 000 annually in the first decade, 300 000 annually in the second decade and 400 000 annually in the third decade. This would add as many as 9 to 10 million people of foreign extraction to a population numbering at most 60 million overall in 30 years' time. The implication is that by then 15% of the South African population could be 'newly' foreign born (probably 80% to 90% of them African). This would constitute an enormous infusion of new talent, on a par with periods in America's past when it was essentially shaped by large inflows of immigrants. Indeed, according to the Economic Policy Institute, as quoted by the *Economist* (March 2001), the immigrant share of the US labour force is currently rising rapidly, from 7% in 1979 to 10% in 1988, and is expected to be nearly 15% by 2005. We would find ourselves in good company if a similar development were to occur here.

What will matter more than raw numbers will be the human capital profile of such immigrants. Will they be mostly uneducated or will we succeed in attracting the above-average citizens—in terms of years of completed education and entrepreneurial talent—of other African countries? People often assume that only the destitute without any hope will migrate. On the contrary, it is often those who have something to contribute, but have no outlet in their underperforming home countries that are driven to migrate to where opportunity for their talent is greater.

So far we have looked at immigration in an old-fashioned way, as people augmenting the local labour force. There are two other groups, though, which in future years are likely to grow and from which South Africa stands to benefit: snowbird retirees and footloose global professionals. The former like to divide their time between northern and southern climes. The latter are highly-skilled professionals whose business dealings are global and quite independent of their actual location. Both of these types of people originate in the northern hemisphere, but are increasingly seeking a southern hemisphere presence, for at least part of the year, or even as a permanent base—purely for lifestyle and climatic reasons. As South Africa's reputation improves once again, along with its economic performance and social conditions, such high net-worth migrants can be increasingly expected to make an appearance. They would not in their own right add to the local labour pool, but their global business dealings would nonetheless have important spillover effects for the local economy. Such 'immigrants' should be accommodated in every way possible, as they will bring only benefits, as well as being good ambassadors abroad (word of mouth being the ultimate recommendation).

Changing Income Distribution

The aim of the ANC government is to obtain a fairer reflection of South Africa's population structure, not only in its politics (as has been achieved), but also in the country's economic and social life. This means an eventual distribution of jobs, income and wealth that will be quite different from the present situation.

According to the LFS 2000 (mentioned in Chapter 5), there are presently 12 million South Africans at work, of which about 1.9 million are White, a further 1.6 million are Coloured and Indian, and about 8.4 million are Black. These proportions are roughly in line with the country's population structure (that is, 77% Black, 11% White and 12% Indian and Coloured).

The division of jobs, though, remains very unequal, with most of the 5.2 million informal jobs filled by Blacks. In contrast, Whites, Indians and Coloureds continue to occupy nearly half of all the formal jobs in the economy (twice their share in the population), though already much less so in the public sector.

As the earlier section on skilled labour has shown, the shifts in favour of Black South Africans in particular have been very pronounced over the past three decades. It may take another generation, though, for a more representative distribution of jobs to come fully into being. If this is to occur along market lines, it will depend critically on an improvement in public education. To the extent that this effort disappoints, and depending on migratory flows, some inequality in the higher reaches of skilled labour is likely to persist for longer. Alternatively, the issue could be addressed by quota requirements, but this would run the real risk, from an economic point of view, of encouraging further emigration and endangering the future pace of development.

The change in the distribution of income is less advanced than the physical change in job distribution. This highlights the remaining disparities in education levels and consequent job opportunities in terms of skill and earnings capacity. Nevertheless, the income picture has not been static during the stagnation and restructuring decades since 1970, as Table 14 sets out.

Table 14: Share of Total Income per Population Group

	Share of total income (%)		
	1970	**1991**	**1996**
Black	19.8	29.9	35.7
White	71.1	59.5	51.9
Coloured	6.7	6.8	7.9
Indian	2.4	3.8	4.5
Total	100.0	100.0	100.0

Source: Whiteford and Van Seventer (2000).

Table 14 shows how Black South Africans have nearly doubled their share of total income during 1970–1996, while the proportion accruing to Whites has been reduced by nearly a third, with Indians the biggest relative winners (doubling their share). As can be seen from this data, two-thirds of the observed shifts occurred prior to 1991.

It is surmised that 1997–2001 has seen further changes in the general direction of the 1970–1996 tendencies, due to continuing emigration of Whites and affirmative action appointments, mainly Black people, in the public and private sectors.

The ongoing shedding of formal employment and the growing share of skilled work has possibly worked against this general trend in the short-term, while there is still a reservoir of skills in evidence.

The Population Distribution by Income Category

Details of income distribution and the way in which it has been evolving since 1970 are shown in Tables 15, 16 and 17 on page 238 and 239. In these tables the population composition of ten income categories is reflected, ranked from 'low income' (decile 1) to 'high income' (decile 10), for the years 1975, 1991 and 1996. The data have been rounded to bring the total to 100.

The three tables show the absolute inequality between the population groups in each of these years. It is also possible to detect distinct shifts in relative position over time for each population group, either larger numbers moving higher up the income scale (ascending) or larger numbers being seen lower down the income scale (descending).

Tables 15, 16 and 17 show that low-income Coloureds were the great winners of the 1980s. Many of them moved a few deciles higher during 1975–1991 as the last decade of White nationalist rule favoured their upliftment. The Black share of the top 10% of income increased from 2% in 1975 to 9% in 1991 to 22% in 1996. The White share of this income category declined from 95% to 84% and then to 66% respectively. These tables also show, though, that by 1996 Blacks still represented over 90% of people in the lowest 40% of income categories, a share slightly higher than it had been in 1975 (partly due to fewer Whites descending as Coloureds ascended in relative position).

Table 15: Racial Composition of Income Categories, 1975

Income decile	African %	Coloured %	Indian %	White %	Total %
(low) 1	86	10	2	2	100
2	86	10	2	2	100
3	86	10	2	2	100
4	85	11	2	2	100
5	90	6	2	2	100
6	86	7	4	3	100
7	74	12	6	8	100
8	50	16	8	26	100
9	7	7	3	83	100
10 (high)	2	2	1	95	100

Source: Whiteford and Van Seventer (2000).

Table 16: Racial Composition of Income Categories, 1991

Income decile	African %	Coloured %	Indian %	White %	Total %
(low) 1	92	4	1	3	100
2	92	4	1	3	100
3	90	6	1	3	100
4	86	8	1	5	100
5	84	10	1	5	100
6	78	11	3	8	100
7	69	13	4	14	100
8	48	15	7	30	100
9	22	11	6	61	100
10 (high)	9	4	3	84	100

Source: Whiteford and Van Seventer (2000).

Table 17: Racial Composition of Income Categories, 1996					
Income decile	**African %**	**Coloured %**	**Indian %**	**White %**	**Total %**
(low) 1	91	4	1	5	100
2	93	3	1	3	100
3	91	5	1	3	100
4	90	6	1	4	100
5	86	8	1	5	100
6	81	10	2	7	100
7	72	12	4	12	100
8	60	14	5	21	100
9	39	12	7	42	100
10 (high)	22	7	5	66	100

Source: Whiteford and Van Seventer (2000).

The Income Distribution by Population Group

Statistics South Africa published income distribution data per population group for 1990–1995 in which some clear shifts can be noted. Table 18 on page 240 shows that among Blacks, those with income in the top 20% (Q5) increased from 2% of all Blacks in 1990 to 6% in 1995. Those in the lowest 20% (Q1) also increased, from 34% to 38% of the total. Thus Blacks experienced upward as well as downward mobility. This reflects the attainment of political power, affirmative action, especially in the public sector, greater participation in the private sector in the senior and middle positions as well as the labour shedding for trade, wage demands, legislative, technology and slow growth-related reasons (as discussed in Chapter 3).

Table 18: The Composition of Income Quintiles by Race						
	Q5 %	Q4 %	Q3 %	Q2 %	Q1 %	Total %
	(high)				(low)	
Black						
1990	2	10	23	31	34	100
1995	6	9	18	29	38	100
Coloured						
1990	8	28	32	20	12	100
1995	9	26	17	35	13	100
Indian						
1990	17	36	27	12	8	100
1995	27	22	25	12	14	100
White						
1990	50	30	12	5	3	100
1995	33	29	22	10	6	100
Source: StatsSA (note data rounded to total = 100).						

Table 18 also shows the relative differences between the various population groups. In 1995, two-thirds of Blacks still found themselves in Q1 and Q2; over three-quarters of Coloureds were in Q2, Q3 and Q4; three-quarters of Indians were in Q3, Q4 and Q5, and two-thirds of Whites were still in Q4 and Q5.

Whites showed relatively the greatest decline overall since 1990 and Indians the greatest gain in Q5. Interestingly, Blacks, Coloureds and Indians all found their distributions changing in favour of the extremes (that is, becoming less equal), both the lowest and highest income quintiles gaining at the expense of the middle ones.

Whites still had 50% of their population in Q5 in 1990, but their relative position had shifted dramatically by 1995. Other population groups (especially Indians) increased their incomes, with only 33% of Whites still in Q5 by 1995, and White numbers doubling in Q1, Q2 and Q3 (if from very low levels).

It would appear from this data, especially when extrapolated through

2001, that there probably remains little difference between the income profiles of Whites and Indians. This is a startlingly rapid transformation, but understandable given the depth of expertise in the Indian community, the change in political fortunes, and emigration among especially highly skilled Whites (apart from possible White underrepresentation in the 1995 data due to any census undercounting).

There are various income and wealth distribution options going forward and we should take care to consider them all with an open mind. While the pessimistic conclusion may be that these lingering inequalities are reason for expecting social strife and disruption, the potential for alternative outcomes has not been closed off.

The state is not neutral in its influence over the future income and wealth distribution. Its income taxation is progressive and, together with its wealth taxation by way of capital gains, is very much aimed at higher incomes. At the same time, its spending tends to favour lower incomes, especially in respect of education, healthcare, housing and welfare (as mentioned in Chapter 7). The government's own employment policy tends to favour previously less-advantaged people, and there are legislative initiatives aimed to secure less one-sided employment practices in the private sector than in the past.

When considering the future evolution of the distribution of income and wealth, it needs to be considered which influences are going to be the primary ones. Great concern lingers among large parts of minority communities (mainly Whites, but judging by voting patterns in general elections also present among Coloureds and Indians) about the potential for damaging social engineering of various kinds at their expense:

- Could a future shift in the political balance among the majority population group lead to a policy reorientation more unfavourable than at present?
- Could taxation become heavier and more differentiated against minorities and higher incomes?
- Could state spending become heavier and more differentiated against minorities and higher incomes?
- Could employment become discriminated more heavily, at worst parallel to the old apartheid regime, only now in reverse?
- Could parts of the private sector become nationalised?
- Could minorities be driven out, as has been happening in Zimbabwe?

The reality to date is one of a social-democratic dispensation organised along capitalist free-enterprise lines, with affirmative action as a (lengthy) transition phenomenon. The real test is possibly a relatively simple one: success in fostering faster economic growth and general social development should lead to an absolute improvement in living standards among the broader population and a less unequal income and wealth distribution. Such an achievement would presumably lessen pressure for political activism along the lines that initiated the current débâcle in Zimbabwe.

The Latin American Option in Perspective

The question is frequently posed whether South Africa will eventually start to experience the problems endemic to Latin America. In recent years key parts of Latin America have found themselves in deep trouble, especially the southern cone of Argentina and Uruguay (with the jury out on Brazil), and Colombia and Venezuela in the north. Theirs is a very special kind of trouble, bordering on national bankruptcy.

At the core of the South American troubles is government financial mismanagement. Many of these governments spend with remarkable abandon and have great difficulty in collecting taxes. Then they exacerbate their problems by wanting to borrow the difference, most of the time short-sightedly. By mid-2002, Argentina owed over $150 billion and Brazil over $260 billion to the world. In addition, many of these governments have fallen into the habit of linking their domestic debt to the dollar (as otherwise their own citizens will not lend to them). Currency depreciation can then very quickly put them in over their heads (as happened in Argentina in 2001, and through contagion in Uruguay, with Brazil so far having escaped this fate in recent years). Over time, Latin America has shown long cycles of periodically defaulting on its debt in this way, as the country debt servicing eventually becomes impossible to sustain.

The reason for this apparent inability of many Latin American countries to manage their affairs responsibly must apparently be sought in their political inheritance from the Old World. Ever since the Spanish and Portuguese landed in South America over 500 years ago, the structure of these societies has been a major problem. The Iberian aristocracy transplanted itself lock, stock and barrel, along with the church hierarchy, to the New World. This meant that land ownership was settled early on in a few hands only, and when industrialisation came it was similarly dominated by a narrow capitalist class. Income and wealth have from the very beginning been very unevenly divided in most of Latin America, in a manner reminiscent of early feudal societies as yet untouched by modern structural reform. There are a very few, very rich families at the top, not a very large middle class, and below them an enormous poor underclass.

Independence came early, and with it democracy. Like North America, most of South America has been free and independent from Europe for two centuries now. Unlike North America, the various parts of the south have never developed strong institutions that could manage these countries along genuinely democratic lines.

When independence came, the colonial social inequalities continued to linger, with vested interests trying to protect themselves, while democratic elements from below were trying to reform. The end result has essentially been a social civil war with no end, where civilian governments have alternated with military ones, each more irresponsible than the last, trying to rewrite the constitutional rules but being thwarted at every turn. This internal weak and divisive condition was then exploited by Cold War superpower rivalry during the twentieth century, which injected often very damaging socialist experiments into many Latin American countries.

In Argentina and Brazil we find 500 years of structural oddities, in which people have either found niches or are attacking them. The playing field is an uneven one that does not encourage stability. This has nothing to do with the southern or Latin character. It is simply an unresolved leftover from ancient Europe, in which aristocratic elements have not been fully subordinated by democracy and where the rules of the game as a consequence remain chaotic.

This has encouraged a lack of focus and rampant irresponsibility. It is a social dispensation in which many 'rights' have been won and entrenched, often in the constitution, often corruptly, without the means to pay for them. A continuous condition of financial civil war can be said to exist. This is arguably true of nearly all democracies, but generally in a much milder form, where excesses need not get completely out of hand before being addressed effectively.

This picture of Latin America (Mexico and Chile excepted) has important implications for South Africa, which ultimately is a Latino hybrid in transition, and engaged in a race against time. In our case, too, land ownership early on became concentrated in relatively few hands that went on to create great social and economic exclusivity during the industrialisation phase of the past 135 years. But unlike most of Latin America, South Africa has been a latecomer to democracy. We have never experienced truly Latino conditions, for the country has known long periods of political domination by one group or another, preserving social and economic stability, if through deepening repression. We have never known military coups, we have never wiped out a middle class through hyperinflation, and we have never genuinely bankrupted ourselves through overborrowing abroad (the mid-1980s debt standstill being more in the nature of a pulling of the plug by foreign banks on our politically bankrupt dispensation).

Today we are a fully inclusive democracy, with the most enormous inequalities needing redress, but we are also a successfully reforming society. There may not be deep solidarity within the population, and historic discrepancies are very much on view. Nevertheless, there is a serious responsibility intent on reforming the worst structural inequalities created by our past. In addition, and unlike most Latin American countries, we are already a very open economy. So even when we experience financial volatility and a weakening rand, at least a considerable part of the economy benefits (that is, exporters and import-competing businesses). This has never been the case in Latin America where relatively closed economies tend to get financially devastated by currency weakness while gaining little by way of trade and economic benefits. We therefore have a structural shock absorber in place that most of these other countries have never had.

The key question remains whether the social peace will hold while we reform. If, like in many parts of Latin America, there were to be successful resistance to fundamental change, aimed at keeping income and wealth exclusive, and shutting off most of the poor, we could bet good odds that we would then drift towards Latin American conditions over time. As it is, South Africa may have a few years, possibly a decade or two, to put into place a serious down payment towards fundamental structural change. At the moment, only a third of society can be classified as 'middle class' (having the benefit of relatively high incomes in the formal sector of the economy). Three-quarters of the Black population do not as yet enjoy this benefit, while nearly all Whites and Indians and most Coloureds do.

For South Africa to remain a stable, prosperous concern, at least half the Black population needs to cross the dividing line, and preferably at least two-thirds or three-quarters of Black South Africans need to be participating in the formal sector, before the inherent threat of political instability starts to recede permanently.

So far only a quarter of Blacks have achieved this condition. Another quarter is informally employed or active, and just short of half the Black population is essentially unemployed. The challenge, simply put, is to halve the number of unemployed. This will require:

- educational and working skills; and
- a growing economy steadily absorbing such numbers over time.

Can we succeed? Will there be time?

Reform is advanced enough to allow faster economic growth in coming years. Population growth has effectively ended, thereby not posing an insurmountable development burden over time. The remaining challenge in the future is to modernise the labour force enough so that it can be gradually absorbed into gainful formal employment, without the country being deflected into a Latino detour.

Politically, South Africa has the benefit of a remarkably focused leadership that is effecting a transition to a generally improved economic performance. This is true, even if the ways and means of economic and social modernisation are not always easily implemented, and certainly not rapidly—especially when the backlogs are like ours. We need time to complete our national development, and the politicians will need to create enough space for it to be successfully accomplished. This is perhaps not as simple as it sounds, and is therefore subject to (sometimes costly) trade-offs.

Ultimately, what counts is whether our overall transformation as a society is proceeding steadily on course, or whether it is starting to fall behind. Thus far, the reforms and financial discipline have been impressive. What now needs to follow through more impressively is the pay-off, in terms of faster economic growth, renewed labour absorption and a mounting emphasis on adding to our national store of human capital.

The signs here are more encouraging than too many people appear to believe, encountering as they do a daily litany of painful social and economic restructuring. However, we should perhaps not rely overly much on anecdotal impressions and ordinary media coverage. Consumer confidence surveys talk their own comprehensive language, and their signalling is mostly a positive one. Let us take this to heart when contemplating likely developments in coming years.

10 CONCLUSION

Future generations will evaluate our reform efforts by their success or otherwise in improving the country's performance. In other words, their inheritance will shape their verdict. Though there remain many important development constraints, improved performance is on the horizon due to planned reforms as well as unexpected developments of a political, economic, social and technological nature as discussed in this book. On balance, a future assessment of these 'revolutionary' years is expected to be a favourable one, for future generations will benefit most from the sacrifices made by the transition generation in shaping their inheritance.

The Role of Economic Policy

Economic policy can be evaluated in terms of both its active and passive roles. In a passive sense, the South African government has been willing to yield control in certain respects. It has reduced trade protection, has deregulated, has relaxed exchange control and is proposing to privatise. While all these reforms are yet to reach completion, they have allowed a more efficient working of markets to develop, and will continue to do so in coming years.

Many of the changes, though, have come about because of what private market participants have done of their own accord in the last decade. Global market competitors put our domestic producers under pressure from the outside, while organised labour demands and political actions did so from the inside. Our producers responded defensively by becoming more efficient. They did this by shedding labour, investing in new technology and organising themselves more efficiently. The result was higher productivity per capital and labour inputs being deployed—in what appears to have been a genuinely revolutionary break with the past, considering the decades that preceded this change.

In an active sense, the government had, and will have, three economic policy instruments at its disposal with which to attain desired aims. These are fiscal policy, monetary policy, and political activism. The manner in which the government has deployed these instruments since 1994 has had mixed results:

- Fiscal policy focused on reducing the budget deficit, with lower inflation in mind.
- Monetary policy lost its footing with the rand, invoking a significant

interest rate defence, which choked off growth for a while in the late 1990s.

- Political activism sought to affect the income distribution through a policy stance favouring labour, as well as working through the areas of spending and tax of fiscal policy.

All three of these phenomena were anti-growth, though the first two, along with the will to survive among private agents and government's political acquiescence thereto, did succeed in lowering inflation and creating a productivity revolution. More importantly, what should these policy instruments attempt to achieve in the future?

- Fiscal policy should aim to support growth, through maintaining a low tax burden, developing infrastructure and providing social goods not effectively supplied by the market (for example, overall security, mass education, basic health care) and, through the subsequent employment growth, achieve a better distribution of income.
- Monetary policy should aim at price and financial stability, which are conditions in which private agents can promote growth.
- Political activism should address inefficiencies in the operation of markets brought about by entrenched special interests, but otherwise stand aside.

By freeing up the economy, a more productive allocation of resources is being achieved. Not only does this promise better economic returns (the foundation of economic growth), but it should also keep the current account over the balance of payments more manageable and thus sustainable. In this crucial respect, we will have completed the transformation away from a closed-off, import-substituting, self-sufficient economy heavily dependent on a fortuitous single-anchor export, to a free-trading economy far more balanced in its development.

Furthermore, by politically transforming (firstly) and addressing our legacy of weakened finances (secondly), we should succeed in more clearly easing our capital account constraint. Faster economic growth in future years should assist in enhancing our attractiveness to foreigners, while their increasing participation in our economy should help to ease the capital account constraint even further.

By easing these restrictions through fundamental reforms (politically, economically, financially), we should once again become capable of higher economic growth performances within our present social dispensation.

What should be obvious about the past decade is that we suffered considerable underperformance in order to get into a sub-optimal position. Now that we are there, and with the imminent benefit of finally finishing various reforms (foremost among these being privatisation, with exchange control abolition a future consideration), a better growth performance should be possible.

It will not be quite the performance which would have been feasible if we had focused the available policy instruments more single-mindedly in the areas in which they best operate, and kept the political activism for where it does most good (delivering privatisation and its needed foreign exchange proceeds). In this respect, the 2000s may shape better than the 1990s.

If Gear failed to deliver higher growth as intended, the interim brought us other building blocks, which should now belatedly allow the moderate growth of 4% p.a. to which Gear aspired. The degree to which growth will be jobless, and the degree to which it will change the income distribution, will depend on the interaction of the commercial survival instincts of private agents and government's political activism. On balance, it suggests we will only get half the net employment gains that we are capable of achieving. This will partly reflect the poor education profile of our labour force, and partly the persistence of high real-wage growth pricing out still marginal labour. The manner in which we will be proceeding will allow the falling unemployment rate to record progress, but it is unlikely to make more transparent the opportunity loss in progress foregone.

An economic revival is underway and it will surprise a population that has become used to stagnation and decay. But it is unlikely to be an Asian Tiger (or an African Cheetah) performance, unless we focus our policies more sharply. This remains a choice that South Africa has to make, and it is something that future generations may want to question us about. Foreign investors are also likely to do so continuously, inspired as they are by best-practice policies and better economic returns.

Exogenous Surprises: Technology and Demographics

HIV/Aids will cost South Africa, directly, in terms of costs incurred, and indirectly through increased inefficiency, in both instances lowering the standard of living compared to what otherwise could have been attained. But the pandemic is impacting in a differentiating way, maximising its social costs (millions of premature deaths over decades unless early evasive action is taken), without necessarily slowing the economy down much, or significantly undermining its growth potential, at least still for some years. Further into the future, how the development impact will play out, will depend on the specific nature of the pandemic, and society's response, in terms of medication, behavioural change and migration (see Chapters 6 and 9).

Under standard worst-case assumptions, as used in many studies and followed in this book, the main demographic impact is to stunt population and labour force growth, capping the level of unemployment slightly higher than the present level of 6.5 million rather than doubling or tripling this number.

Such an outcome would limit the development burden to that of uplifting the present population, rather than a much bigger population that would have come into being in the absence of HIV/Aids. Such a limited population size should also offer greater opportunities for the generation that survives the impact of HIV/Aids (though some observers see a much more adverse effect taking hold). Furthermore, there are still surplus skills available at present, and beyond that a surplus labour pool that is gradually becoming better educated.

Immigration is likely to be a major feature in regulating our skilled labour supply in future decades, importantly augmenting our domestic education and training efforts. Resource deployment will be more efficient than in the past, there will be more capital deepening and growth-enhancing technology to be had. Faster economic growth therefore will remain possible, as discussed throughout. As a consequence, the higher economic growth will accrue to fewer people than otherwise would have taken place, per capita income rising anew after decades of stagnation.

Real GDP growth of over 6% annually will for many reasons—including the impact of HIV/Aids on the labour force—not be attainable by South Africa. However, we are likely to achieve 3.5% to 4% annually, and not much less in per capita terms before long. Anything faster would increasingly become dependent on a major education effort and the presence of effective government delivery capacity—neither of which should simply be assumed.

Another 'surprise' is the steady arrival of a set of technologies that appear to greatly enhance productivity growth, and may continue to do so in the future. There is no agreement on this subject internationally, so here too we will have to await the reality as it plays out. However, going by what we have seen over the past decade, it would appear that we are in the midst of something very promising, the reach of which will go much further than the present, and the benefits of which are also being bequeathed to us by science. As we succeed in efficiently mastering these technologies, our growth-enhancement and inflation-suppressing ability will be further strengthened, as will our globalisation drive—probably the biggest benefit of all in the efficiencies it generates.

Main Risks and Development Constraints

Domestically, the very unequal distribution of income and wealth carries the seeds of social discontent and political upheaval. A state can arm itself against such eventualities, but that is not very efficient. It is better to address the reasons behind this problem:

- high unemployment today; and
- a poor education effort going forward.

Externally, future current account deficits will continue to keep us a ward of the world. South Africa is as yet not a diversified, wealthy country with deeply specialised labour skills. Our growth remains too much affected by global developments, which impact on our type of exports, and by the fact that we choose to save little and look to the outside world for supplementary capital (see Chapters 2, 3 and 4). These are weaknesses which, in times of global strain, tend to make us much more vulnerable than a more diversely structured economy would be. Consequently, the faster we can develop into a stronger economy, the less exposed we will become to the inevitable periodic global crises.

This book has identified a number of critical constraints on South Africa's development process going forward. These are:

- a low level of national saving;
- the uncertain supply of skilled labour; and
- inequality in employment, income and wealth.

A low level of national savings increases the dependence on foreign capital inflows as the rate of economic growth speeds up and with it the pace of capital formation and the consumption of credit-dependent durable goods. There is nothing inherently non-sustainable in this condition, provided sound financial policies are at all times adhered to, in order to maintain the country's impeccable credit rating and assuring continuous access to foreign capital.

The risk in this approach is twofold. Firstly, over time there may be a lapse in domestic financial rectitude, which even if of a temporary nature, may bring the wrath of foreign investors down on the country. Secondly, events may take place globally that interrupt access to such capital markets, in the process showing up the country's dependence.

Either way, we would have little defence, compared to a condition in which we elect to be more self-sufficient, financing our development needs from internal sources. It has been the government's intention to end its own dissaving and lower the national budget deficit so that the national savings rate can rise again from the present 15% to 16% of GDP back towards over 20%. While the government has succeeded in improving its own financial situation and contribution to the national savings pool over the past decade, it appears to have done so largely at the expense of private individuals, who carry a larger tax burden than before and who are observed to be saving less. A decline in personal income tax rates since the late 1990s has been aimed at boosting work and business incentives, and will hopefully lead to higher saving (of which there has so far been no sign, in part due to the strong redistributive nature of the government's many policy reform initiatives), but a general improvement in the economy and renewed growth in formal employment is likely to be as important. This may only materialise over time. Even so, South Africa's growth ambitions of average annual GDP growth of 4% or better will probably require an investment-to-GDP ratio of some 25% (once current surplus infrastructure has become more fully deployed), indicating that faster growth will probably still have to rely heavily on supplementary inflows of foreign capital on a sustained basis. This will constitute an important ongoing underlying structural weakness to the development process, and should at all times be acknowledged as such.

The supply and demand for skilled labour was analysed at some length in Chapter 9. We concluded that the education and training effort, along with work requirements that are increasingly skewed towards higher standards, constitute the main constraints on the pace of sustainable growth once the current reservoir of skills has become fully utilised.

For South Africa to optimise its available resources in terms of capital, labour and talent, more effort needs to be invested in public education and training by employers, while government policy should favour market forces that lead to a more balanced use of available labour.

On this score, training by employers probably has the greatest potential for improvement, as genuine incentive (that is, scarcity) is likely to encourage much greater effort. As skill scarcity reasserts itself, both immigration and company training will prove viable sources of additional skills.

Inevitably, these sources of additional labour skills cannot adequately lift overall supply, compared to likely demand in a growth scenario of 4% annually. A better public education effort is therefore required. Whether this will be forthcoming soon enough to meet the demands of a growing economy, and compensate for the impact of HIV/Aids (especially where it concerns the number of available educators), only time can tell. On present trends, the country will have to limit its development ambitions for educational reasons alone. A country like Korea can aim for 8% sustained GDP growth, as nearly all its children go to school, most of them to matriculation level, and 70% of matriculants go on to higher education.

Short of an education revolution (which should never be considered beyond us, but which should not simply be assumed on present trends), the government could still do much in influencing the demand for labour so that it could sustain the higher rate of growth in the presence of the HIV/Aids pandemic and stunted labour force growth.

In some instances, government policy has been inclined to favour forced solutions rather than market processes. While gains have undoubtedly been made, these were relatively easy gains once political power was attained: taking over the public sector, legislating increased benefits overall, and allowing strong unions to sustain high real wage growth. These last two developments, in particular, have contributed to jobless growth (see Chapters 3 and 5). This has tended to increase the need for skilled labour, which will be in short supply longer-term, and has encouraged capital deepening, thus also increasing the reliance on foreign supplementary inflows of capital. In addition, it has kept the income distribution more unequal than necessary, now not so much between the various population groups, as between 'insiders' and 'outsiders' within population groups. This will remain an area of long-term concern to foreign and local investors alike, as it throws a shadow over the social peace and political continuity.

Public sector wage moderation, further trade reform, and moderation in non-wage cost-enhancing labour legislation would go far in keeping labour costs more closely in line with productivity. These policies would in time allow greater labour absorption and would clearly be to South Africa's benefit in terms of reinforcing social and political stability. In turn, this would make a favourable impression on investors, thereby bolstering the investment decisions driving the growth process.

Survivors' Inheritance

Historically, modern South Africa is best known to the outside world for—in chronological order—diamonds, gold, the Anglo-Boer War, Jan Smuts, apartheid and Nelson Mandela. But while these words capture short historical epochs, they only partly prepare us for what is coming into view. What *will* have been the definitive feature of the present generation, once its first hesitant history is attempted 50 years from now?

We can try to transcend any narrow winners/losers designation by claiming to be in the midst of many revolutions—political, economic, social and technological (as have been explored throughout this book). Instead of any one group being able to claim sole heritable rights to any of these, all South Africans may be making a contribution to shaping these fundamental breaks with the past as they unfold.

In the process of manifesting themselves in a matter of one generation, these four revolutions potentially hold the power to change the South African landscape, and make it unrecognisable. A stronger economic performance, and the resultant prosperity, would safeguard and ultimately enrich the political order, while the social order could transform itself in generally unexpected ways, through outward and inward migration, and a period of extensive premature mortality among large parts of the population.

The resulting population in twenty to thirty years' time should not only be better off, but also be more cosmopolitan. It could be more broadly developed and urbanised, with a new overlay of heritage. It will be globally integrated, and be a major influence in the southern part of Africa.

Much of this sounds new, but in many ways it is a story that has been repeated again and again, in this part of the world and elsewhere. The past few hundred years have seen a number of transformations in South

Africa, but this one could be the biggest of them all, in the shortest time span. Will this great transformation happen? Will it be allowed to happen? The politics of the moment seem firmly democratic, and the economics appear thoroughly pragmatic. But the real test, globally as well as in our own backyard, is going to be social. Is there a political will to arrest Aids? Is there an attitude, as has on occasion prevailed here and in other parts of the world, to seal off the country from within to prevent the arrival of enriching immigrants?

The human will is an important determinant of the outcomes under discussion here. Understanding what will shape such choices should be the best guide as to what the most likely history of this period will look like. It is to be hoped that we will stay sensible throughout—sensible about what brings out the best economic performance, and tolerant of our fellow citizens. This will ultimately be the best way to guarantee national strength, which we will need when the global order experiences one of its periodic breakdowns.

Profiling the Next 30 Years

When considering how the structure of things will change over the next three decades compared to the last three, there are considerable reasons for confidence.

Over the past 30 years, real GDP has grown an average of 2.1% p.a., just short of doubling over the full period. But because population increased at a similar pace, per capita real GDP has remained unchanged. Per head of the population South Africa produces today as much as it produced (and earned and spent) in 1971. On average, this translates into nil real change over 30 years. In reality, formally employed labour increased by half in number and increased their real per capita income by nearly a quarter. Informally employed labour changed mostly in composition (less labour employed in agriculture, and a much greater presence and diversification in urban activities), modestly growing its share in national income to nearly 10%. By far the larger part of the incremental doubling in population over the period ended up unemployed and poverty-stricken (unemployment rising from an estimated 0.5 million in 1970 to nearly 7 million today), sustained mostly by government services and close family support.

The next 30 years should shape up quite differently. South Africa has since 1994 averaged 2.8% real GDP growth, but the 1990s was a decade marked by much change that prevented an even more robust performance. For the next 30 years, we may expect better returns from the economic reforms already implemented (and still to follow). This suggests an average growth of at least 3.5% p.a. to be achievable. Instead of nearly doubling real GDP, we will nearly triple real GDP over this period.

The bigger change by far will come in per capita terms. On present projections, population from domestic sources will grow by very little over the next three decades if the HIV/Aids pandemic continues unchecked. However, even if the impact of the pandemic were to lessen, population growth may not easily reassert itself. This would be directly due to any behavioural changes (which by themselves might also lead to reduced fertility). Indirectly it might be for more traditional reasons (that is, the features of advancing modernity such as higher levels of education, urbanisation, income and wealth, and female emancipation), which would get a boost from accelerated economic development.

Either route could assure a similar population outcome, and reality is likely to turn out to be a complex mix of these tendencies. It will not, however, prevent us from slightly upping our average economic growth performance compared to our 1990s performance to date, seeing that we have relatively underperformed during this past decade. To the extent that we enjoy increased levels of immigration, especially skilled and semi-educated immigration from the rest of Africa, our actual GDP growth rate could turn out even slightly higher than we have suggested. However, as such immigration can for now only remain conjecture, it is better to note a nil balance at this stage. What we are left with is a near tripling of annual real GDP in 30 years' time, on a population not much bigger than today's. Thus, South Africa's real per capita income should triple, too, compared to remaining unchanged these past three decades.

It would, however, only be a tripling on average. As to how this expected rise in real incomes would be shared out among the larger population, more people than ever before are likely to benefit through increased participation in the economy, and thus share in the increased national income. The formally employed would be likely to increase by half in number (to 10 million), and their real per capita income should increase by up to two-thirds (becoming the biggest group in society enjoying the biggest income gain by far). The informally employed may increase by around a fifth in number (to over 6 million), and their real per capita income may also improve moderately. The unemployed, though halving in number over the period (to between 3 and 4 million), are likely to largely remain poverty-stricken, though sustained by government services and family support.

Income inequality in South Africa in coming years should not worsen. On the contrary, it should lessen overall, though perhaps less dramatically than we would wish. There will be important redistributive forces at work—in terms of government taxation and spending—and, most importantly, through employment generation. To generate average real GDP growth of 3.5% p.a. may require 100 000 additional new workers annually to be absorbed into the formally employed labour force. On an unchanging population, this would mean the unemployment rate should about halve over the period (to below 20% of the total labour force on the extended definition, taking into account demoralised work seekers, too). At present, our labour force is split in roughly three equal parts: formally employed (36%), informally employed (28%), and unemployed (36%). In 30 years' time, the formally employed should constitute about half of the total, a third would still be informally employed and about a sixth would be unemployed. As employment is likely to be the biggest redistributive agent, in addition to government taxation and spending policies, it is expected that South African society will experience a quantum leap in earned real income and other benefits over the period.

As to whether the skilled labour will be there to fulfil this expectation, education may appear to be failing at present, but we can expect the number of years in school to increase, along with some increase in the numbers going on to tertiary education. To this picture we must add the likely contribution from better-educated and skilled (African) immigrants.

Employers may be the biggest contributors in making future staff additions more 'employable' through increased training. We have had comparatively little effort on this score over the past three decades, mainly because there were no people shortages of note (except among the highly specialised). In a faster growing economy at near full skill potential, this reality will change radically, and employers will be forced through sheer necessity to make a much bigger effort to train people.

Our cities will also change and there should be greater visible evidence of prosperity. We can expect the housing stock to increase annually by 100 000 units or better. Over three decades, this would make a real difference to the physical appearance of our cities. Where over the past three decades we may have gained the impression that squatter settlement expansion would eventually overwhelm all modernity, it may well happen that the squatter element could stabilise, increasingly acting as a revolving door (for some) through to the modern sector. More people would move from the rural areas to the cities as urbanisation proceeds, but it would probably be the formal housing stock that would expand most noticeably. Adding roads, water supply and electricity connections to this picture allows a major, viable expansion of city life and consumer markets. The actual size of our main urban concentrations would probably increase by not more than 30% to 60% over the period, compared to a tripling or worse that typical Third World population pressures would create. Thus, our cities should remain manageable and viable—a significant thing in a world that will count a rapidly increasing number of metropolises of over 10 million inhabitants (but too often without the necessary infrastructure to keep living conditions attractive).

Over the period, we may expect the country's car park to more than double to 10 million passenger vehicles. The railways are unlikely to win back lost market share, with ever more goods moved by road by commercial trucking. Consequently, the physical road network would need to be expanded. Only the Durban to Gauteng route is presently a dual carriage way the whole way. We would expect all national road arteries to become similarly equipped (or better) over the period, mostly by way of tollroads.

We could examine every consumer market for its expansion potential. Obviously, non-durables have the least income elasticity, so it is durables, semi-durables and especially services that will benefit most from the increase in real per capita incomes that is imminent. Nevertheless, what will count most for non-durable consumer goods will be the 50% increase in the number of formal paypackets and the one-fifth increase in informal sector ones.

Transitional Mistakes and Costs

What have been the more costly policy mistakes of the post-1994 period? The manner in which the SARB became converted in stages to a genuine floating of the rand (anchored by inflation targeting), compared to the managed floating that preceded it in the 1970s, 1980s and 1990s, had a major effect on the real economy.

The exchange rate and interest rate shocks of 1996 and 1998 encountered as part of this conversion, were probably more stormy than would otherwise have been incurred. For this we paid with economic growth foregone, and dented local and foreign confidence. Growth was dampened and development momentum was lost, at a time of deep demoralisation due to political and social changes. A sense of hopelessness prevailed, with a general refusal to see the structural reforms as viable. It was entirely the wrong moment to have to dampen growth in the domestic economy, for few people saw this as a temporary phenomenon. Instead it was seen as part of a broader malaise that confirmed the political and social trends and was steadily deteriorating the economy and society.

In the SARB's favour, this experience was part of a wider global learning curve. Many countries over a period of years had to decide on the kind of exchange rate policy best suited to their needs after the international arrangements dating from Bretton Woods had started to break down in the early 1970s. This led to Europe's many nations ultimately deciding on a monetary union, and the euro in the late 1990s, and, for example, Argentina adopting a currency board with the dollar in 1991. Other countries' currencies became free-floating to a greater or lesser degree over a period of years. It is, however, a process in which we appear as late learners and adopters.

It is perhaps disconcerting to note that the implied conclusion from the so-called 'Impossible Trinity' analysis in Chapter 4 suggests that more costs may still be incurred going forward. Countries with free-floating currencies tend to find that financial markets create currency misalignments over time, and these invariably tend to be costly in terms of the imbalances they bring in their wake.

On the up side, any appreciation potential of the rand will for a long time still be neutralised by the need to build up the foreign reserves and abolish exchange controls. This is apart from being able to afford a bigger structural current account deficit, as Australia has done so notably these past few years. Consequently, there seems to be little reason to fear rand overvaluation any time soon.

If, however, we were to argue that the too gradual privatisation of state assets should carry co-responsibility for the excessive depreciation of the rand and its associated costs (its consequences for inflation, interest rates and foreign capital inflows generally, and the way this led to a dampening of economic growth, so-called 'growth sacrifice'), these costs may be mostly laid at the government's door. This may already have been so during the second half of the 1990s, and is certainly true today. The nature of the cost is that fragile external finances—a political legacy from the past—keep the rand chronically weak, worsening any misalignment. This, in turn, forces inflation and interest rates higher than necessary in terms of the inflation-targeting objective, which interferes with our economic growth as well as with foreign perceptions of the country, thus inhibiting other capital inflows.

In the case of government culpability, the SARB could be absolved of the responsibility for keeping interest rates too high relative to what is theoretically possible, for the foreign capital that has been discouraged, and for the economic growth that has been lost. After all, the final word has not been spoken on the combination of free-floating and inflation targeting either, a policy choice over which the government has a pivotal influence.

In the sense that it allowed labour 'insiders' to acquire undue influence during the 1990s (even if this was largely an inherited dispensation), the government can also be blamed for a pervasive deepening of unemployment among less-skilled labour, and the associated social decay such as crime. This contributed heavily to marginal labour, that otherwise could have remained employed, being priced (frozen) out.

In the government's favour is the process of empowerment and affirmative action, which includes the encouragement of a better deal for (organised) labour. This general policy stance favouring Black advancement has allowed enough scope for a political consensus in favour of a more orthodox economic policy (Gear) to evolve and to stay its course, even when (bitterly) criticised by those favouring a more interventionist social policy.

The inclination to favour Black advancement in this way reflected deeply felt anger about the unfair dispensation inherited from the past. Simultaneously, it also partially absorbed criticism over the manner in which economic restructuring, especially the rationalisation of labour, eventually proceeded.

Despite the gradualist approach taken to the implementation of Gear, the forcefulness of its effect on employment rationalisation was ultimately very real. This is not an argument for not restructuring, and also not an argument for not striving for a better social dispensation quickly in order to meet legitimate political expectations. If, however, such trade-offs, between necessary structural reform, social gains, political acceptance and financial rectitude were as inescapable as they appeared to be, more compassion could have been shown for those who became 'outsiders' to the labour process. Their grinding poverty in turn reverberated on society via crime, rural as much as urban, and constituted a major burden on us all. The state cannot seriously claim that it was so short of resources that it was unable to do more. It could have tried harder to address this issue, for example, by creating some kind of minimal safety net for those who became unemployed and were willing to take on work of any kind, yet found themselves cut off from any sustenance. Admittedly, there would have been political demands (and costs) attached to such compassion, for organised labour was at all times sensitive to the development of a dual labour market.

If there was unfavourable fall-out for some Blacks, there was also unfavourable fall-out for those displaced Whites who were given packages or who decided it was better to look out for alternatives as their future was being foreclosed on them by the changes taking place. In this way, the structural costs of the political change rested where they fell.

The decision to allow the new labour 'insiders' undue advantage, further distorting the labour market at the expense of 'outsiders' who were already being marginalised in terms of the need to restructure the economy, was not an efficient one. Indeed, it was a dubious policy in the light of the government's strong political backing throughout. Nevertheless, given South Africa's apartheid past, symbolically the immediate evidence of Black advancement was a non-negotiable need. That it came at the expense of a relatively defenceless few, such as those who became unemployed and those who fell victim to crime, was apparently one of those things that tend to happen during great social dislocations.

Did these stumbles matter much? They certainly mattered a great deal to those whose real incomes declined, whose jobs were lost, or who were victims of crime. However, 50 years and certainly 100 years from now, who will remember and who will care? If history is any guide, the inheritance of future generations will shape their verdict. That there were costs, incurred in the course of a distant decade or two, is likely to be lost on distant generations. That there was a price to be paid for making this transition possible undoubtedly mattered to those who paid it, but this applies to every victim of conflict.

Strategic Imperatives Going Forward

The crucial short-term policy decisions shaping the road still to be travelled seem to revolve around ensuring that economic and social change in South Africa will be very much market-driven. With government's blessing, trade reform, labour reform, tax reform, fiscal reform, a floating rand and inflation targeting are duly transforming our performance.

In the field of macro-economic policy, the idea is to achieve less interruption from currency and interest rate shocks. Taxes and interest rates are not supposed to impose excessive burdens, freeing up space for more funding towards social delivery. Trade competition and technological change are driving economic restructuring, micro-economically achieving a more efficient allocation of scarce talent, capital and employable labour. The results are better economic returns—also known as productivity—and longer growth runs, inducing a steadily growing (and higher level of) capital formation, foreign direct investment, and eventually an increase in net formal job creation.

Strategically, there are three critical choices that will determine whether this vision of improved performance will materialise over time. It is vital that government stays the course with its chosen market-driven change processes. To evaluate whether this is happening, we should not so much pay attention to what government 'says' (for much of this is intended to keep diverse and conflicting political groupings on board the Rainbow Express), as to what it actually 'does'. The speed of implemented change may be slow, but it is incremental and cumulative, making the eventual impact over time the thing to watch.

In the short-term, but with crucial long-term consequences for the economy, is the need for privatisation in order for the country to raise more 'free' unencumbered capital. The alternative option internally is to raise taxation to fund greater social delivery. The option externally is to increase foreign borrowing to stabilise the finances. Neither option is to be recommended, as these both create burdens, disincentives and headwinds. Instead, the country should sell its proverbial family silver to wipe out two critical legacies which amount to a fundamental financial weakness. These legacies from a disinherited past are:

- a high interest burden on the budget, preventing greater social

delivery with available means; and
- weak external finances, responsible for a chronically weak rand, keeping interest rates unduly high, and foreign capital remaining offshore.

Achieving a breakthrough in these respects would finally transform the country's finances fully and greatly strengthen our chances of being able to achieve and sustain a higher economic growth rate, crucial to attracting foreign direct investment, allowing more extensive job creation and social delivery.

In the long-term, the key constraint on our performance is likely to be our labour force, specifically its quality. Education is the key to upgrading our human capital to a level where it can sustain a high rate of economic growth and effect the social transformation that remains the central tenet of all the government's many actions. Only individual empowerment and opportunity will do so effectively, in stark contrast to the artificial and limiting constraints of a discredited past.

If this favourable outcome were to be achieved over time, it would finally lay to rest De Kiewiet's (1941) famous dictum with which we opened the Introduction to this book: 'South Africa advances through political disasters and economic windfalls' (89). We have certainly experienced a stumble or two, but South Africa's latest progressions at the end of the twentieth century and the beginning of the twenty-first century have been achieved through peacefully negotiated political reform and an economic breakthrough won through self-discipline and hard work.

Policy Advice for 2003–2050

Further to all that we have discussed in the pages of this book, here are a few key (and potentially controversial) ideas and suggestions regarding the way forward to ensure that South Africa's economy continues to take shape in ways that will cement our future as a leader in Africa. We need to continue with the following policy themes:
- fiscal conservatism (small budget deficits through ongoing discipline on government current spending);
- efficient tax collection and general tax relief;
- complete privatisation early;
- abolish exchange control eventually;

- target inflation rate (flexibly);
- do not use the rand exchange rate as an anchor for monetary policy;
- maintain a presence in the currency market;
- increase infrastructure spending (roads, cities);
- continue opening up the economy (gradually);
- increase the foreign reserves (significantly);
- reduce the national debt (using privatisation proceeds);
- improve social delivery (housing, water); and
- set a public example in terms of public sector wages; administered prices; and corruption.

Policy areas that require special attention include:
- quality public education;
- the government's delivery capacity; and
- an open immigration policy for qualified skilled candidates (points scheme).

Social issues that deserve compassionate consideration include:
- creating effective HIV/Aids mass-awareness;
- providing affordable HIV medication and counselling;
- reducing non wage cost-enhancing labour legislation; and
- forming public work schemes (for those wanting work).

If we were to target South Africa's average real GDP growth at 3.5% p.a. (as envisaged by Gear), this would:
- double the national income every twenty years; and
- bring about a six-fold increase in real GDP by 2050.

This would be equivalent to Spain's living standard today. However, if we were to target South Africa's average real GDP growth at 6% p.a. (superGear), this would:
- double the national income every twelve years; and
- bring about a sixteen-fold increase in real GDP by 2050.

This would be 50% higher than America's living standard today.

Which one of these GDP growth rates we set ourselves, and the efforts we bring to bear to achieve this objective, is mostly up to us as the transition generation. It is on the outcome of our endeavours that we will be largely remembered by future generations of South Africans.

EPILOGUE

Why Pragmatic Confidence is Warranted about South Africa

If all that you have read so far has failed to convince you of South Africa's positive future prospects, it is time to take a different approach. All that we have discussed can be supported fundamentally in another way. Economics is about people, and a country like South Africa, even with its history of human oppression, has an excellent chance of making good.

In the Huntington (1998) analysis, South Africa is a 'torn' country, neither fish nor fowl, and is destined to perform only modestly, even poorly, for that reason alone. The country lacks social homogeneity, populated as it is by diverse cultures, each pulling in different directions. Such diversity may look admirable, but it can be terribly confusing as it creates cross-currents in social behaviour and mental condition. Such a country can fatally lack direction as the various cultural elements engage in an unending battle for a supremacy that fails to shape decisively.

Fortunately, the elements coming together in South African society appear to have more promise than this.

In our South African society there are five underlying cultural heritages: the Afrikaans and English traditions (which are fundamentally different to each other); the ubuntu tradition; and the Muslim and Hindu faiths.

It would be easy to get the wrong impression about the relative importance of these various parts. Of a total population of 45 million today, Muslim and Hindu adherents (mainly Coloureds and Indians) number about 1 million each; there are over 2 million Whites and Coloureds whose mother tongue is English; about 6 million Whites and Coloureds whose mother tongue is Afrikaans; and there are over 30 million Blacks who can identify with some form of ubuntu. The Afrikaans and English influences are much greater than these numbers would suggest, particularly in terms of the Christian faith. However, what matters for the purpose of this analysis is in each instance the core group and its values.

Since they subdued the land through conquest, White views prevailed at first, fundamentally clashing with the social heritage of the Black population. Colonial values favoured social stratification, and specifically excluded partnerships of any kind.

In order to remain on top, Whites exercised oppression in various forms. Slavery may have been abolished early in the nineteenth century, but political control became increasingly authoritarian in the course of the twentieth century. This took place through a mix of:

- pass laws (limiting movement);
- physical planning Acts and influx control (limiting geographical spread);
- job reservation (limiting skills and employment opportunities);
- property exclusivity (limiting land ownership); and
- a clear differentiation in access to public resources (ensuring, for example, crucial differences among racial groups in the quality of education and health care).

The outcome was a severely skewed distribution of income, wealth and human capital along racial lines, favouring Whites over all other population groups. The stark discrimination in the treatment of various population groups was such that a larger world evolving along humanitarian lines could only shake its head in disbelief. A terrible vengeance was surely building in Southern Africa, one that could ultimately break over the land and destroy all vestiges of White presence. However, events did not play themselves out in this way. Why? And what will happen next?

What follows is factual improvisation, but then truth never allows itself to be captured easily. Colonial values predominated in the nineteenth century, but on the Afrikaans side there was a dual personality, especially in the countryside. A deep paternalism came to prevail. On the one hand, Whites wished to keep their distance (a preference in which Calvinist religion and perceived social superiority dominated), but on the other hand, a deep caring was also widely evident, giving rise to sometimes imperceptible bonding relationships across cultures and colour lines. Such relationships were nurtured by deep traditional characteristics on all sides. Without this feature of South African society, racial harmony and tolerance would not have developed as naturally as it has, in a manner that has often greatly surprised foreign visitors.

The Black population had been mostly shaped in the tradition of ubuntu—a community-based credo, in which group solidarity, conformity, compassion, respect, human dignity and collective unity prevailed as leading norms. According to Mbigi and Maree (1995), ubuntu is a metaphor that describes the significance of group solidarity that is so central to the survival of African communities, who as a result of poverty and deprivation have to survive through group care and not individual self-reliance.

Sparks (1991) mentions that traditionally there was not much room in Black culture for individualism in the Western sense, for the emphasis was on the group and the individual was assigned his or her role within it. Yet the result was not oppressive or even stifling. Traditional African societies placed a high value on human worth, but it was a humanism that found its expression in a communal context rather than in the individualism of the West. The word 'ubuntu' captures the essence of this particular kind of participatory humanism, which has survived industrialisation and urbanisation. It is a subtle concept that is not easy to translate, meaning broadly that each individual's humanity is ideally expressed through his or her relationship with others and theirs in turn through a recognition of his or her humanity: 'People are people through other people' (Sparks 1991, 14).

According to Lessem and Nussbaum (1996), who talk about lessons for modern management, ubuntu means:

- to be more giving than taking;
- a need to become concerned with emotional issues rather than taking a rational perspective;
- the need to be co-operative as well as competitive;
- the need to start recognising the importance of making decisions with the participation of large groups; and
- to understand and accept the cultural value and meaning attributed to music and dance in the workplace.

For many Blacks over the centuries, the clash with White values was a bewildering experience. There was caring, in a patriarchal way, but there was also systematic oppression of the most cruel kind. These contrasts clashed fundamentally with Black values. Nevertheless, White oppression did not succeed in destroying the spirit of ubuntu. If anything, it was enhanced.

When democracy finally came to South Africa in 1994, many of the White Afrikaans-speakers carried the brunt of losing their dominance, just as they had pushed out the English-speakers a generation previously. They also went into mourning, for a lost world in which—even if they had been mostly unquestioning followers—they had been organised and strong. It was the shock, for them, of new freedoms, the requirement to start thinking as an individual and only secondly of the group, that led to a general loss of orientation.

Many emigrated within a decade to foreign shores, especially Anglo-Saxon ones, and this must have deepened their shock experience. For on those distant shores it would not be possible to rediscover their lost institutions and the certainty that they used to offer. Instead, they would mostly become supplicants, strangers in strange lands, and more than ever in need of each other.

At home in South Africa, the White Afrikaans mourning went deep, lost certainties were yearned for, and they now found themselves at the tender mercy of a once-vanquished foe. It was a condition that did not naturally make for optimism, or a sense of future possibilities. And yet what most White Afrikaans-speakers also encountered, was the spirit of ubuntu: let us together make something of the situation we find ourselves in. This was an echo of their own paternalism of previous centuries, but this time without the insistence on separateness.

Most English-speaking Whites enjoy an emotional reinforcement from the knowledge of belonging, however distantly, to a strong global civilisation whose values will mostly prevail. In a previous age this was known as a physical empire on which the sun would never set, and this remains true today in terms of values and cultural strength (Friedman 1999). Consequently, many White English-speakers did not experience South Africa's transition to an integrated political reality in anywhere near the same terms as their Afrikaans counterparts. Instead of mourning deeply, there was an eagerness to offer world-class institutions and to follow international rules of engagement, in order to ensure an effective anchoring of the general order. Unfortunately, this perspective may not always have registered what ubuntu was offering in return: communal democracy and partnership, under Black tutelage.

It will take time, possibly much time, for many Whites—Afrikaans-speakers as much as English-speakers—to come to terms with what has transpired, for ubuntu to take them completely into its embrace, and to inspire a more sympathetic response. Difference will probably never be eradicated from South African society, but as the various groups find their feet and niches, and discover that power has irreversibly passed on, they might co-operate more fruitfully than a 'torn country' condition might suggest.

The most intriguing group of all will be the Black population in all its diversity. Its numbers have won out and its values will prevail in this corner of a still Westernising world. But will ubuntu remain true to its roots?

It was especially under the leadership of President Nelson Mandela during 1994–1999 that the concept of the Rainbow Nation offered inclusivity on such generous terms to all South Africans. Since then, there has been a somewhat more exclusive tendency, but the main inclination remains one of ubuntu.

Even so, the spirit of ubuntu could easily disappear or be overwhelmed by the day-to-day hardships and demanding costs of the transformation of our society. There are also global forces at play that could easily blur the boundaries of ubuntu's philosophical substance. Consequently, we should remain careful about presuming too much about ubuntu. In this regard, Van Zyl Slabbert (2000) makes a succinct qualification about the adherence to and pervasiveness of ubuntu:

> These days, ubuntu is properly ascribed—almost as a generic characteristic—to black people. Compassion and love for others are seen as natural characteristics of black people in spite of brutal mass murders in Rwanda, faction fighting in Richmond, KwaZulu-Natal, and senseless taxi murders in various parts of South Africa. Here, there is a clear discrepancy between reality and values. Ubuntu is a collective noun for a set of values that are undoubtedly worthy of emulation, but whether these values are indeed embodied by a specific set of people is an empirical question which will be established through investigation and not through a priori reasoning (77).

Ubuntu should never be allowed to serve as a veil behind which any number of shortcomings and injustices can hide away without being called to account. That would be a travesty, just as much as any injustice perpetuated in the name of any religion.

Nevertheless, it is the very magnanimity of the ubuntu spirit after long centuries of painful struggle, as much as the key policy choices highlighted in this book, that has centrally contributed to gradually reforming the country, in a social as well as an economic sense. Such reform has today progressed to a point where we have every right to expect an even bigger payback by way of improved performance than we have so far seen. That is the promise to be harvested in the coming generation.

The Bigger Civilisational Dimension

Unlike the modern Muslim world of the Middle and Far East (see Naipaul 2002), South Africa's population does not appear to be resisting modernisation or its main proselytising force, the West. Indeed, unless appearances deceive, our population welcomes the modernity that Westernisation promises, though enriching it with deep indigenous roots (politically, socially, culturally and economically). As much as its formalisation is a Western import, democracy has strong traditional roots in South Africa. Social values are also being modernised, with traditional ways gradually weakening. The consumerism driving tastes and needs may have an indigenous component, but Western imports and brand name preferences shine through strongly with rising income and education levels. The preferred language of commerce, politics and instruction is English, though large footprints are claimed by Afrikaans as well as the Nguni and Sotho languages. The fastest-growing religions are mostly Christian in nature.

Economically, South Africa appears engaged in a straightforward development struggle, one we have in common with many ascending emerging countries in Latin America, Central Europe and Asia. It is a conversion (labour surplus) model, in terms of which a largely agrarian population is rapidly transformed into an industrial labour force, and then into a post-industrial condition. The process by which this happens has been operational for nearly two centuries now. By breaking free from the climatic cycle that governs agriculture, by investing capital in imported foreign technology, a backward country can greatly improve its national productivity by relatively cheaply catching up with more developed countries through embracing the existing stock of human knowledge and technology. It may take decades once underway, but if pursued with diligence, a nation that was initially 90% dependent on low-productivity agriculture can relatively quickly transform its labour force into the high-productivity industrial age (goods production-dominated) and thereafter into the post-industrial age (services-based).

For well over a century already, South Africa's population has been migrating from a simple rural existence to an urban industrialised complexity. There does not appear to have been widespread rebellion against this forced pace towards modernity. In most instances, though, it was a process full of coercion, for all population groups were marked by trauma of some kind or another.

The national experience suggests a striving by all population groups to make modernity their own: uprooting, urbanisation, often initially a deplorable squatter existence, only gradually improving to something better, and, of course, education and the difficult acquisition of better skills formalising the productive transformation in time.

In South Africa, this process was marked and interrupted by severe forms of social discrimination, eventual civil war, and subsequent restructuring. Indeed, given the scale of these interruptions, we can marvel that the South African economy has developed as far as it has, and that those people most affected, without too much apparent rancour, continue to opt for the hard road to modernity. But then there is probably a demonstration effect, especially in modern times, in terms of improving living standards, if still only very selectively. Thus, modernity is seen to be paying off, and for that reason alone it is willingly embraced.

Some 80% of South Africa's White, Indian and Coloured population (about a sixth of the total labour force) has in this manner achieved modernisation in the post-industrial sense. Only a quarter of the Black population has achieved comparable modernity, though qualitatively lagging behind on this development ladder because of a historic skill deficit due to past discrimination and also due to the widespread sacrifice of education during the struggle years.

In addition, at least another quarter of the Black population is struggling with its entry into modernity, finding themselves engaged in informal economic activity, a borderland to modernity where 10% of the other population groups are also engaged. This informal sector existence is no longer primarily agrarian-based, but a lack of education, skills and capital limits this part of the labour force to simple tasks, low productivity and, consequently, relatively low incomes. Even so, these people tend to be found within hailing distance of the bright city lights. Thus, about 60% of South Africa's varied population is already urbanised and either highly integrated into modernity, or at least finds itself somewhere on its development ladder in the informal sector of the economy.

Huntington (1998) suggests that Africa appears to be engaged in a broad process of de-Westernisation. The continent has certainly left colonial domination well behind it, with indigenous peoples and cultures increasingly shaping events. This has meant in many instances a resurgence in languages, values, customs and practices that had been long suppressed, a way of doing things differently from the way of Westerners.

Such indigenisation—known in our case as Africanisation—does not need to imply a receding of modernity, especially not in the one African country with the most complex Western heritage (South Africa). Languages, values, customs, practices and tastes may have been experiencing a recalibration following the arrival of inclusive democracy and Black political governance, but this does not necessarily mean the wholesale rejection of Western heritage. In 1942, according to Naipaul (2002), when the Japanese took over what is now called Indonesia, one of their first acts was to remove all public signage of the Dutch language and influence. Overnight, 300 years of history was wiped away. More importantly, the foreign influence disappeared along with it as its human stock was forcefully removed before long. This is not the experience of modern South Africa, though some place names have changed, and some 5% of those people who are not Black have emigrated in a decade.

More importantly, the Black population retains a deep eagerness to achieve progress, by way of economic and social upliftment, now that political power has been won. Central to this process are Western concepts, ideas, values, indeed languages, customs and practices. An outstanding example of this is the attempt at institutional renewal at continental level. During 2002 leading African politicians tried very hard to do a deal with the leading industrial nations through Nepad (the New Partnership for Africa's Development), the idea being in essence to create a modern-day Marshall Plan for Africa. A further major political change concerned the replacement of the Organisation for Africa Unity (OAU) with a new African Union (AU), its creation apparently very much shaped with the political governance needs of its economic policy arm (Nepad) in mind.

Though Johnson (2002) warns us not to set our expectations too high, given the OAU's record over 40 years, the very nature of what is being attempted is encouraging, in that it embraces modern institutional thinking rather than rejecting it out of hand.

In the more progressive core regions of Africa, modernity is advancing either assisted by major resource endowments (such as oil in Nigeria, Algeria, Gabon, and now Angola) or because countries have achieved a modern foundation on which they can build further. This is true of Egypt and Tunisia, and especially of South Africa.

Our country's history has been a rich one, making it potentially a stronger candidate for ongoing modernisation in which indigenous and

Western heritages continue to co-exist. South Africa's make-up is a crucial aspect in this regard. The country's history has laid down a very solid modern foundation. The new Black political leadership appears committed to deepen this modernity. The real test will come with the second-generation political leadership as the country progresses towards a more balanced development. Will indigenous features start to be given far greater preferences in shaping modernity, in contrast to Western influences remaining strongly in evidence?

In the case of South Africa, it is clear that Africanisation is well underway. At the same time, it appears as though Western influence is going to remain important in shaping South Africa's evolving modernity, if from a subordinated position.

When examining our development condition, bearing in mind similar attempts underway elsewhere in the emerging world, what stands out primarily in South Africa is the freedom of action, and only secondarily the political activism aiming to change structures by decree. The rigidity of the past is gone. There may still be friction about ways and means, but this does not interfere unduly with day-to-day economic and social expression.

There will always be pockets of resistance—either conservative rearguard actions or inclinations to different values. But what is primary and what is secondary in South Africa? Openness and market forcefulness (that is, social and economic freedom) appear to be the prime levers in the modern South African experience, instead of the limiting religious and ideological preoccupations that characterised the past or burden other societies.

Consequently, if South Africa's development process continues to be given its head and (mostly) free reins, we are likely over time to observe a further deepening of modernity. This should especially be so, if unemployment can be reduced and the general standard of living can be more visibly and decisively uplifted.

Black input will be crucial to this process, shaping its cultural appearance, just as there will continue to be participation from White, Indian and Coloured South Africans. The formal sector of the economy, which generates 90% of GDP, today has a composition of 45% White, Indian and Coloured and 55% Black. In the next three decades, these shares will change to 35% and 65% respectively as formal employment increases to some 10 million. Some 85% of the additional 3.3 million workers joining the formal sector will be Black (some of them skilled

African immigrants), in the process halving Black unemployment. This structural shift will not necessarily undo the cultural ways of doing things that are now in place, though far more deeply enriched by the African heritage than it is today.

Overall, there should be little doubt as to the fundamental nature of the development process that still succeeds in preserving our common heritage. It can be observed in the strength of the cultures already in place; the eagerness to complete modernisation; the strength of international thinking shaping the twenty-first century being taken as the main example (see Gilpin 2000); and the primary features of openness, freedom and market forcefulness to complete the job of development in hand. Mbigi and Maree (1995) comment that South Africans need 'to find out who they are so that they can find out what they can become' (60).

If we wish to prosper in the modern South Africa, peoples of very different backgrounds will have to accommodate each other in a common house. To make a success of this, there will need to be acceptance of differing cultures and religions and absorption in a common polity. There will be Africanisation, but it is being grafted on a Western model of modernity. What is crucial for the long-term, is that this modernisation attempt is not being resented or resisted from within. These features are highly promising for the future. Unless they are laid low by a major global interruption, they all but guarantee eventual development success.

SELECT BIBLIOGRAPHY

Articles and Books

Armstrong, H.C. *Grey Steel (J.C. Smuts)*. Penguin Books, 1939.

Baily, M.N. 'The New Economy: Post Mortem or Second Wind?'. *Journal of Economic Perspectives*, vol.16, no.2, Spring 2002.

Baker, P., Boraine, A., and Krafchik, W., eds. *South Africa and the World Economy in the 1990s*. The Brookings Institution, 1993.

Balcerowicz, L. *Socialism, Capitalism, Transformation*. Central European Press, 1995.

Barzun, J. *From Dawn to Decadence: 500 Years of Western Cultural Life*. Perennial, 2001.

Benson, M. *The Struggle for a Birthright*. Penguin Books, 1966.

Bhorat, H. 'Growth: Not Jobless, But Skewed'. *Business Day*, 25 April 2001.

———. 'The Impact of Trade and Structural Change on Sectoral Employment in South Africa'. *Development Southern Africa*, vol.17, no.3, September 2000.

Bhorat, H., and Hodge, J. 'Decomposing Shifts in Labour Demand in South Africa'. *The South African Journal of Economics*, vol.67, no.3, September 1999.

Boonzaier, E., Malherbe, C., Berens, P., and Smith, A. *The Cape Herders: A History of the Khoikhoi of Southern Africa*. David Philip, 1996.

Brookes, M. 'Is the Internet Better Than Electricity?'. Global Economics Paper no.49, Goldman Sachs, 20 July 2000.

Bruggemans, C.W. 'Prospects for international trade and some implications for South Africa'. Unpublished D.Com dissertation, University of Stellenbosch, June 1984.

Bureau for Economic Research (BER), Inflation Expectations Survey, March 2001, University of Stellenbosch (also as reported by the SARB in releasing its Monetary Policy Meeting Deliberations, March 2001).

———. 'The Macro-Economic Impact of HIV/AIDS in South Africa'. *BER*, no.10, 2001.

———. Quarterly Business Opinion Surveys for the Manufacturing and Building and Construction Sectors, Fourth Quarter 2000.

———. Quarterly Surveys of Business Conditions in Manufacturing; the Retail, Wholesale and Motor Trades; and Building and Construction.

Business Day, 'Africa's Grand Vision Needs Early Successes', 1 July 2002.

———. 'Coup for Mbeki', 1 July 2002.

———. 'Law Planned for "Aggressive Recruitment" of Foreign Skills', 24 April 2001.

———. 'SA's competitiveness ranking rises', 25 April 2001.

Carr, E.H. *The Bolshevik Revolution 1917–1923*. Volume 2. Penguin Books, 1966.

CIPRO. 'Registration Statistics'. www.cipro.gov.za , accessed on 9 April 2003.

Crisp, R. *The Outlanders: The Story of the Men who Made Johannesburg*. Mayflower Books, 1974.

Cross, J. 'Managing Foreign Debt and Liquidity Risks in Emerging Markets: Selected Issues from a South African Perspective'. In *Managing Foreign Debt and Liquidity Risks,* Bank for International Settlements, BIS Policy Papers, no.8, September 2000.

Dallmeyer, J., and Graf, B. 'Productivity Miracle in the US: Just an IT Phenomenon?'. *Frankfurt Voice,* Deutsche Bank Research, 15 February 2000.

Davies, G. 'Technology, the Internet and the New Global Economy'. Global Economics Paper no.39, Goldman Sachs, 17 March 2000.

De Hen, P. 'Leve kapitalisme'. *Elsevier,* 13 July 2002.

De Kiewiet, C.W. *A History of South Africa. Social and Economic.* Oxford University Press, 1941.

De Kock, G. 'New Developments in Monetary Policy in South Africa'. Presidential Address to the Economic Society of South Africa, 17 September 1981.

———. 'The New South African Business Cycle and its Implications for Monetary Policy'. Presidential Address to the Economic Society of South Africa, 13 October 1980.

De Soto, H. *The Mystery of Capital: Why Capitalism Triumphs in the West and Fails Everywhere Else.* Basic Books, 2000.

———. *The Other Path: The Invisible Revolution in the Third World.* Harper Row, 1989.

Du Plessis, T.A. 'The Industrial Growth Pattern and the Real Forces of Economic Expansion in South Africa, 1916/1917–1956/1957'. Unpublished D.Com dissertation, University of South Africa, 1965.

The *Economist.* 'Currency dilemmas', 18 November 2000.

———. 'The Heart of the Matter', 13 May 2000.

———. 'Letter of credit', 24 June 2000.

———. 'Migration: The Uses of Strangers', 31 March 2001.

———. 'Performing miracles', 17 June 2000.

———. 'Productivity on stilts', 10 June 2000.

———. 'Will Western Europe Receive the Great Unwashed: One Day?', 21 April 2001.

The European Commission, Business and Consumer Survey, May 2001.

The Euro-Zone Consumer Confidence Survey, May 2001.

The *Financial Times.* 'UK Investors See Poor South Africa Growth', 28 June 2001.

Friedman, T.L. *The Lexus and the Olive Tree: Understanding Globalization.* Farrar Straus Giroux, 1999.

Gilpin, R. *The Challenge of Global Capitalism: The World Economy in the Twenty-First Century.* Princeton University Press, 2000.

Gordon, R. 'Not Much of a New Economy'. *Financial Times,* 26 July 2000.

Greenspan, A. 'Monetary Policy Report to the Congress'. Federal Reserve, 11 February 2003.

———. Various Speeches: 1987 to the Present, Federal Reserve Board, Washington DC.

Growth, Employment and Redistribution (Gear): A Macro Economic Strategy. Pretoria, 1996.

Haldenwang, B.B. 'High, Medium and Low Projections of the South African Population, 1996–2031'. Institute for Futures Research, University of Stellenbosch, August 1999.

Hiemstra, V.G. *Job Reservation, Standard Encyclopaedia of Southern Africa*. Volume 6. Nasou Limited, 1972.

Hodge, D. 'A Tale of Two Governors: Monetary Policy and the South African Economy 1981–1999'. *The South African Journal of Economic History,* vol.16, September 2001.

Hooper, E.H. *The River: A Journey Back to the Source of HIV and Aids.* Penguin Books, 2000.

Huntington, S.P. *The Clash of Civilizations and the Remaking of World Order.* Touchstone Books, 1998.

International Labour Office (ILO), World Employment Report 2001. *Life at Work in the Information Economy.* ILO, 2001.

Johnson, R.W. 'Reality Inspectors Sorely Needed at Launch of AU'. *Business Day,* 17 July 2002.

Jones, S. 'Transformation in the External Trade of South Africa 1925–2000'. *The South African Journal of Economic History,* vol.16, September 2001.

Jones, S., and Inggs, J. 'The South African Economy in the 1970s'. *The South African Journal of Economic History,* vol.14, September 1999.

Jorgenson, D.W. 'Information Technology and the US Economy'. Presidential Address, American Economic Association, January 2001.

Joseph, H. *If This be Treason.* Contra Press, 1998.

Katz, H.C., and Darbishire, O. *Converging Divergences: Worldwide Changes in Employment Systems.* Cornell University Press, 2000.

Keppel-Jones, A. *When Smuts Goes: A History of South Africa from 1952–2010.* Shuter & Shooter, 1947.

Kissinger, H.A. *The White House Years.* Weidenfeld and Nicolson, 1979.

———. *Years of Upheaval.* Little, Brown, 1982.

Lawrence, S.V. 'China-US Ties: War By Other Means'. *Far Eastern Economic Review,* 5 April 2001.

Lessem, R., and Nussbaum, B. *Sawubona Africa: Embracing Four Worlds in South African Management.* Zebra Press, 1996.

Levy, A. 'The Annual Labour Relations Report, p.e.o.p.l.e.', April 2001.

Lewis, B. *The Middle East: 2000 Years of History from the Rise of Christianity to the Present Day.* Phoenix Press, 2001.

Lewis, J.D. 'Policies to Promote Growth and Employment in South Africa'. Discussion Paper 16, World Bank, July 2001.

———. 'Reform and Opportunity: The Changing Role and Patterns of Trade in South Africa and SADC'. Africa Region Working Paper Series 14, World Bank, March 2001.

Lewis, R. 'Nothing to Celebrate on Bastille Day'. *Wall Street Journal,* 12 July 2002.

Lipton, M. *Capitalism and Apartheid: South Africa 1910–1984.* Gower/Maurice Temple Smith, 1985.

Loots, E. 'Job Creation and Economic Growth'. *South African Journal of Economics,* vol.66, no.3, September 1998.

Luce, E., and Kehoe, L. 'A Dip in Silicon Valley'. *The Financial Times,* London, 19 April 2001.

Mandela, N. *Long Walk to Freedom: The Autobiography of Nelson Mandela.* Back Bay Books, Little Brown and Company, 1994.

Marais, H. *South Africa: Limits to Change: The Political Economy of Transformation.* UCT Press, 1998.

Mbeki, T. 'State of the Nation Address'. The Opening of the South African Parliament, February 2001.

Mbigi, L., and Maree, J. *Ubuntu: The Spirit of African Transformation Management.* Knowledge Resources, 1995.

Meiring, P. *Smuts The Patriot.* Tafelberg, 1975.

The Michigan Consumer Confidence Survey. University of Michigan, May 2001.

Mostert, N. *Frontiers. The Epic of South Africa's Creation and the Tragedy of the Xhosa People.* Pimlico, 1993.

Naipaul, V.S. *Onder de Gelovigen.* Pandora Pockets, 2002.

Paton, A. *South African Tragedy: The Life and Times of Jan Hofmeyr.* Charles Scribner's Sons, 1965.

Plaatje, S.T. *Native Life in South Africa.* Longman African Classics, 1987.

Ritter, E.A. *Shaka Zulu: The Biography of the Founder of the Zulu Nation.* Penguin Books, 1978 (first published by Longman in 1955).

Roberts, J.M. *The Penguin History of Europe.* Penguin Books, 1996.

———. *The Penguin History of the Twentieth Century.* Penguin Books, 2000.

Roche, D. 'South Africa's Capital Crisis'. *Wall Street Journal,* 9 September 1998.

Rostow, W.W. 'The Fifth Upswing and the Fourth Industrial Revolution'. *Economic Impact,* no.44, 1983 (reprinted from Challenge, 1983).

Sadie, J.L. 'The Performance of Labour in South Africa During the Sixties and Seventies'. Research Unit for Economic Demography, University of Stellenbosch, 1983.

———. Personal Communication, 2002.

Sampson, A. *Macmillan: A Study in Ambiguity.* Penguin Books, 1968.

Sampson, A. *Nelson Mandela: The Authorised Biography.* HarperCollins Publishers, 1999.

Scheepers, C.F. 'The International Trade Strategy of South Africa'. *South African Journal of Economics,* vol.50, no.1, March 1982.

Schlemmer, L. 'Better news on unemployment'. South African Institute of Race Relations, September 1996.

———. 'Unemployment: How bad is it?'. South African Institute of Race Relations, April 1996.

Schlemmer, L., and Levitz, C. 'Unemployment in South Africa: The Facts, Prospects and Exploration of Solutions'. South African Institute of Race Relations, 1998.

Schlender, B. 'The Odd Couple'. *Fortune,* 1 May 2000.

Smuts, J.C. *Jan Christian Smuts.* Cassell & Company Ltd, 1952.

South African Reserve Bank (SARB) Quarterly Bulletin, June 2001.

Sparks, A. *The Mind of South Africa.* Ballantine Books, 1991.

Statistics South Africa (StatsSA). The Labour Force Survey, February 2000, September 2002.

———. The October Household Survey, 1996, 1997, 1998, 1999.

———. South Africa in Transition, 2001.

Stiroh, K.J. 'What Drives Productivity Growth?'. *Federal Reserve Bank of New York,* vol.7, no.1, March 2001.

Strydom, P.D.F. 'Economic Growth in Open Economies'. Research Paper no.6, RAU, September 2000.

Suzman, H. *In No Uncertain Terms: Memoirs.* Jonathan Ball Publishers, 1994.

———. 'Eight Years of ANC Rule'. *The Star,* 25 July 2002.

Tilley, J.S. 'More to Fighting Aids Than Bunch of Pills'. *The Star,* 25 April 2001.

Tolstoy, L. *War & Peace.* Pan Books Ltd, 1972.

Trengove Jones, T. 'What Did Africa Really Get at G8 Summit?'. *Business Day,* 5 July 2002.

Von Clausewitz, C. *On War.* Penguin Classics, 1982.

Van der Berg, S. 'The Budget and Delivery'. The 2001 Post-Budget Conference, Stellenbosch, 22 February 2001.

Van der Merwe, J. 'Editorial on New Economy Uninformed'. *Business Day,* 2 May 2001.

Van Onselen, C. *The Seed is Mine: The Life of Kas Maine, a South African Sharecropper 1894–1985.* James Currey, 1997.

Van Zyl Slabbert, F. *Tough Choices: Reflections of an Afrikaner African.* Tafelberg, 2000.

Vulliez, E. 'South Africa's Model under Review'. *Conjoncture.* BNP PARIBAS, no.1, January 2002.

Whiteford, A., and Van Seventer, D. 'Winners and Losers: South Africa's Changing Income Distribution'. *Journal for Studies in Economics and Econometrics,* vol.24, no.3, November 2000.

Whiteside, A., and Sunter, C. *Aids: The Challenge for South Africa.* Human & Rousseau Tafelberg, 2000.

Willan, B. *Sol Plaatje: Selected Writings.* Witwatersrand University Press, 1996.

Wilson, D. 'Australian Productivity: Catching a "New Economy" Wave'. Global Economics Paper no.50, Goldman Sachs, July 2000.

Woodall, P. 'A Survey of the New Economy'. *The Economist,* 23 September 2000.

Woodward, B. *Maestro: Greenspan's Fed and the American Boom.* Touchstone, 2001.

Woodward, L. *The Age of Reform: England 1815–1870.* Oxford University Press, 1992.

Yergin, D., and Stanislaw, J. *The Commanding Heights: The Battle for the World Economy.* Touchstone Books, 2002.

Internet

The following sources, listed by chapter, can be found on the Economics website of First National Bank, http://www.fnb.co.za/economics

Introduction

Bruggemans, C.W. 'Inflaming Rhetoric Embellishes Technical Reality'. Opinion (archives), 10 October 1998.

———. 'Investing in South Africa: A Story in Relativity'. Opinion (archives), 25 January 1999.

Chapter 1

Bruggemans, C.W. 'Changing Income Distribution'. Weekly Comment (archives), 23 July 2001.

———. 'Changing the South African Economy'. Opinion (archives), 10 August 2000.

———. 'Confidence in South Africa'. Opinion (archives), 3 July 2001.

———. 'FNB/BER Consumer Confidence Index'. Weekly Comment (archives), 29 June 2001.

———. 'Mixed Messages from FNB/BER Consumer Survey'. Weekly Comment (archives), 6 July 2001.

Chapter 3

Bruggemans, C.W. 'Breaking Free from the Growth Trap'. Weekly Comment (archives), 29 September 2000.

———. 'Don't Lose Track of What Matters Most'. Weekly Comment (archives), 28 August 2001.

———. 'Economic Policy ("Gear") on Track'. Weekly Comment (archives), 7 April 2000.
———. 'The End of "Gradualism"'. Opinion (archives), 1 December 1999.
———. 'Long-Term Economic Growth'. Weekly Comment (archives), 25 August 2000.
———. 'Long-Term Hurdles for Business Expansion'. Weekly Comment (archives), 19 July 2000.
———. 'Macro-Economic Policy Objectives'. Opinion (archives), 15 February 2000.
———. 'The Many Fortunes of Gear'. Weekly Comment (archives), 30 July 2001.
———. 'Our Global Dependency'. Weekly Comment (archives), 31 August 2001.
———. 'Policy Dilemmas As Yet Unresolved'. Weekly Comment (archives), 3 April 2001.
———. 'Recasting Gear (Growth, Employment and Redistribution)'. Opinion (archives), 4 May 1999.
———. 'Turning Policy's Flank'. Weekly Comment (archives), 4 September 2001.
Strydom, P.D.F. 'South African Economic Policy'. Ruiterbosch Themes (By Invitation), 12 December 2000.
———. 'South African Unemployment: A Pressing Problem'. Ruiterbosch Themes (By Invitation), 6 March 2000.

Chapter 4

Bruggemans, C.W. 'Budget Carries Clear Fiscal Message'. Business Brief (archives), 24 February 1999.
———. 'Challenges Facing Monetary Policy'. Weekly Comment (archives), 19 July 1999.
———. 'A Disciplined Election Budget'. Weekly Comment (archives), 17 February 1999.
———. 'Don't Blame It All on Bob'. Weekly Comment (archives), 23 November 2001.
———. 'Economic Policy Choices for the Early Millennium'. Opinion (archives), 1 March 1999.
———. 'Fated to Succeed (Inflation Targeting)'. Weekly Comment (archives), 21 February 2000.
———. 'Financial Reform: The Magic Cocktail'. Weekly Comment (archives), 27 February 2001.
———. 'A Fine Art Called Targeting'. Weekly Comment (archives), 23 December 1999.
———. 'The Impossible Trinity'. Opinion (archives), 1 December 2000.
———. 'Inaugural Address of Dr Chris Stals'. Weekly Comment (archives), 29 August 2000.
———. 'Inflation Targeting as Conditioning Tool'. Weekly Comment (archives), 20 December 1999.
———. 'A Kabullish Rand'. Weekly Comment (archives), 16 November 2001.

———. 'The Limits to Financial Engineering". Opinion (archives), 30 July 2001.
———. 'A Modern Monetary Policy'. Opinion (archives), 10 January 2000.
———. 'Monetary Hiccup'. Weekly Comment (archives), 5 February 2002.
———. 'On Monetary Policy'. Weekly Comment (archives), 15 December 2000.
———. 'The Outlook for Wages and Inflation'. Opinion (archives), 4 October 2000.
———. 'Post-Budget Questions'. Weekly Comment (archives), 28 February 2000.
———. 'Rand Misalignment to Worsen'. Weekly Comment (archives), 7 September 2001.
———. 'Rand Disorderliness'. Weekly Comment (archives), 1 December 2001.
———. 'Rand Prospects'. Weekly Comment (archives), 15 January 2002.
———. 'Rand Weakness Gathers Momentum'. Weekly Comment (archives), 5 October 2001.
———. 'Rapid Adjustment to Contain Interest Rates'. Weekly Comment (archives), 7 February 2002.
———. 'Rushing Towards Inflation Targeting'. Weekly Comment (archives), 25 October 1999
———. 'SARB's Navigation of Many Icebergs'. Weekly Comment (archives), 24 March 2001.
———. 'The SARB's Steady Course'. Opinion (archives), 2 April 2001.
———. 'A Strategic Budget 2001'. Business Brief (archives), 27 February 2001.
———. 'A Tax-Reform Budget'. Weekly Comment (archives), 23 February 2000.
———. 'Transforming Our Central Weakness'. Weekly Comment (archives), 23 January 2001.
———. 'A Transforming Reality'. Opinion (archives), 10 October 1999.
———. 'Why We Are Different'. Weekly Comment (archives), 9 September 2000.
Strydom, P.D.F. 'The Effectiveness of South African Fiscal Policy'. Ruiterbosch Themes (By Invitation), 12 December 2000.
———. 'Inflation Targeting: Some Critical Observations'. Ruiterbosch Themes (By Invitation), 14 March 2000.
———. 'South African Monetary Policy: Towards the End of the Twentieth Century'. Ruiterbosch Themes (By Invitation), 12 December 2000.
———. 'Speculative Attack on the Rand'. Ruiterbosch Themes (By Invitation), 29 January 2002.

Chapter 5

Bruggemans, C.W. 'Social Blight and its Prospects'. Weekly Comment (archives), 7 August 2000.
Strydom, P.D.F. 'South African Unemployment: A Pressing Problem'. Ruiterbosch Themes (By Invitation), 6 March 2000.

Chapter 6

Bruggemans, C.W. 'HIV/Aids: The Pandemic and its Impact'. Weekly Comment (archives), 14 August 2000.

———. 'Turbulent Decades Without End'. Weekly Comment (archives), 24 July 2002.

Chapter 7

Bruggemans, C.W. 'The Promise of Social Delivery'. Weekly Comment (archives), 9 March 2001.

Chapter 9

Bruggemans, C.W. 'Breaking Free from the Growth Trap'. Weekly Comment (archives), 29 September 2000.

———. 'Changes in Income Distribution'. Weekly Comment (archives), 27 July 2001.

———. 'Entrepreneurs Do Matter'. Weekly Comment (archives), 15 December 1999.

———. 'Hello, Australia!'. Weekly Comment (archives), 4 September 2001.

———. 'The Impact of Emigration and AIDS'. Weekly Comment (archives), 1 February 2001.

———. 'Infrastructure Prospects'. Weekly Comment (archives), 13 February 2001.

———. 'Our Latin American Option'. Weekly Comment (archives), 22 August 2002.

———. 'The Prospects for Skilled Labour'. Weekly Comment (archives), 10 April 2001.

———. 'Regional Growth Inequality To Sharpen'. Weekly Comment (archives), 30 March 2001.

———. 'South Africa's Growth Story'. Weekly Comment (archives), 13 March 2001.

Chapter 10

———. 'Growth: Who Are We?'. Weekly Comment (archives), 16 July 2001.

———. 'The Next 30 Years'. Weekly Comment (archives), 21 June 2002.

———. 'South Africa's Debut'. Opinion (archives), 24 July 2002.

———. 'The Tale of Mnr Grootboom'. Weekly Comment (archives), 17 October 2000.

———. 'Three Revolutions'. Opinion (archives), 6 November 1999.

Epilogue

Bruggemans, C.W. 'South Africa's Debut'. Opinion (archives), 24 July 2002.

Lamprecht, J. 'Nepad: Could this Really be the Beginning of Bigger Things to Come?'. Emerging Markets (archives), 19 July 2002.

INDEX

A
Acquired Immune Deficiency Syndrome
 see HIV/Aids
Actuarial Society of South Africa (ASSA) 137, 165–166, 226
affirmative action 127, 147, 229, 261
Africa 33, 51, 130-131, 179, 215
 credit-risk rating in 74
 HIV/Aids in 158, 168, 171–172
 immigration 145, 165, 229
 modernisation of 8-9
 skilled labour immigration 223
Africanisation 274–277
African National Congress (ANC) 81, 84–85, 147
 achievements of government 176, 210
 Freedom Charter 2
African Union (AU) 275
Afrikaans
 language 273
 nomadic trekboers 38
 speakers 270
 traditions 268
 Whites 270–271
Afrikaner nationalism 39, 41
agriculture/al 16, 144, 214, 273
 boards 150
 composition of labour force, 1996–1999 140
 exports, 1925–2001 129
 labour growth, 1970–1999 134
Algeria 39, 229, 275
ANC
 see African National Congress
Anglo-American 122
Anglo-Boer War, 1899-1902 17, 37, 40–41
Angola 275
apartheid 21, 23, 40
Argentina 101–102, 104–105, 227, 242-243, 260
Asia 48, 64, 67, 76, 105, 113, 192, 219, 223, 229, 273
ASSA
 see Actuarial Society of South Africa
AU
 see African Union
Australia 74–76, 105, 144, 148, 153, 191, 210–211, 229-230

B
balance of payments 25, 49–50, 213
 1996–2000 66
 constraints 75, 210
Balcerowicz, Leszek 7
Base Scenario assumptions, 1996–2000 59
Base Scenario Projections 2000 59
basic health care 182
behaviour change
 and HIV/Aids 170
 impact of HIV medication, effecting 172–174
 impact of HIV medication, in absence of 171–172
Black
 consumer confidence in contrast with White 30–32
 consumers 30, 31
 convergence of confidence, post-1997 33
 homelands 20
 middle class 82
 nationalism 41
Blacks 244–245, 262
 culture 270
 income distribution 235
 income quintile, 1990 26, 240
 input 276–277
 matriculation 221
 modernity 274
 population growth 161–163
 population structure 236
 real disposable income, 1995–2000 176
 skilled labour 221
 total income 236–237
 unemployment 142
 with professional jobs 224
Botha, President 92
Botswana 74, 223
Brazil 105, 227, 242–243
Bretton Woods arrangements 90, 95
British Imperialism 37, 40, 41
budget deficits 117, 213
budgets 86, 176, 180
business confidence
 see also confidence
 in South Africa 26–30
 RMB/BER Business Confidence Index 26, 28
 surveys 26–30
business ranking
 of main constraints, fourth quarter 2000 220

C
Cameroon 223
Canada 211, 229
capital
 account 50-52, 213
 account constraints 73, 210
 inflow 99, 112
 spending 178, 214
Chile 227, 243
China 8, 10, 40, 42, 114, 144
cities 167, 258–259
clinics 176
Colombia 242
Colonial values 268–269
Coloureds 268, 276
 history 36

HIV-prevalence among 230
income distribution 235
income quintile, 1990 26, 240
income quintile, 1995 240
modernisation 274
population growth 161–163
population structure 236
real disposable income, 1995–2000 176
total income 236
unemployment 142
with professional jobs 224–225
commercial rand 96
confidence
see also business confidence
convergence of Black and White, post-1997 33
in South Africa 27–30
surveys 26–30
Congo 223
consumer confidence
contrasting Black and White 30–32
FNB/BER Consumer Confidence Index 26, 29
FNB/BER Consumer Confidence: White versus Black 29
surveys 26–30, 39
Consumer Price Index (CPI) 93
Cosatu 81
country credit rating 122, 213
CPI
see Consumer Price Index
credit-risk rating 74
crime 5, 13, 179, 229, 261–262
at democracy, 1994 44–15
and social transformation 163
Cuba 223, 229
currency 12, 57, 100
see also rand
boards 101
floating of 98, 100–102, 260
current account 51, 210
deficit 25, 49, 50

D
debt servicing 213
De Klerk, President 92, 94
De Kock, Gerhard 43, 90, 92
democracy 2, 44–45
challenges facing 45-48
crime at, 1994 44-45
economic growth at, 1994 44–45
demographic changes
before HIV/Aids 160-163
related to HIV/Aids 158–159
demographic interruption 11, 158–159
demographics
technology and 250–252
deregulation 10, 149–152
development constraints 252–255
disability grants 178
discrimination 18–21

E
Eastern Europe 8, 223, 229
economic
impact of HIV/AIDS 168
performance 53
reforms 4, 6
reforms and resulting achievements 204–211
restructuring 12
revival 56–82
struggles, 1970–1993 21–25
transformation 51
economic growth 51-53, 146, 182, 205, 245
used for growth
at democracy, 1994 44–45
constraints on 48–53
drivers for the future 218–219
during 1960–2002 22
forecasting 211–216
GDP growth, 1960–2002 22
going forward 211–216
in regions 216–218
rate 48, 163
social limits to 180–183
technology as source of 186–187
economic policy/ies 56
advice for 2003–2050 264–265
according to Gear 60-61
criticism of government's 78–79
mistakes, post-1994 4–5, 49, 63
role of 248–250
with and without Gear, 1996–2000 59
education and training 53, 182, 254
according to Gear 77
age distribution of those holding matric 228
disturbing tendencies 178, 252
revolution 11
tertiary 227
education profile
and skilled labour, 1970–1999 222
electricity provision 176–177
emerging countries 112, 124, 226, 273
emigration 229
employers 258
employment 62–63, 257–258
changes in formal 'core' employment, 1990–2000 135, 139
changes in levels of 126–127
during 1996–1999 176
expected changes in 146–147
formal versus informal 131–135
growth 163
rationalisation 76, 127–131, 139

English
culture 38
liberalism 41
speakers 270
language 273
traditions 268
Whites speaking 270–271
Erhard, Ludwig 7
Eskom 120–121
EU
see European Union
Europe 7–8, 10, 64, 67, 81, 188, 196, 201, 219, 260, 273
European Union (EU) 146, 197
Euro-zone Consumer Confidence Survey 31
exchange control/s 88–89, 260
abolition 10
liberalisation 5, 12, 52, 95–99, 124
privatisation 124
protection 204
reforms 88
relaxation 10
exchange rate/s 76, 260
expected outcomes
with and without Gear, 1996–2000 61
export/s
changing composition of, 1995–2001 129
growth 62
performance, 1996–2000 64–65

F
financial
conservatism 85
less disruptive monetary policy 113–116
rand 96–97, 99
reforms 89–91
restructuring 52, 84–124
First World War 17–18, 40, 49
fiscal
discipline 85
policy/ies 248–249
fixed investment demand 210
floating 263
of rand since October 1998 102–104
FNB/BER Consumer Confidence Index 26, 29
FNB/BER Consumer Confidence: White versus Black 29
foreign
indebtedness 213
reserves 116–118, 213, 260
trade 56, 66–68
foreign capital 47, 113, 261
disengagement of 16–33
inflow of 97, 213
formal employment
versus informal 131–135
freelancing
see self-employment
future
projections for unemployment 141–142, 257–258
prospects 204–246

G
GDP
see Gross Domestic Product
Gear
see Growth, Employment and Reconstruction
Germany 149–150
Ghana 223
global inflation 94
globalisation 149
impact of, 1990s 69
gold
exports, 1925–2001 129
mining 214
production 50
government
budget deficit, 1993–2006 87
capital expenditure 209
consumption spending 78
reduction in consumption 62
role in correcting market failure 3
spending 177
Gradualism 7
and the future 79–80
cost of 80–82
Great Britain 8, 10, 40, 77, 144, 148, 188, 229
used for United Kingdom
Gross Domestic Product (GDP) 21, 47–48, 143, 146-147, 168, 181, 211, 253, 256–257, 265, 276
average annual growth, 1960–2002 22
growth in 1990s 69
HIV/Aids impact on growth 174
investment-to-: private sector, 1960–2002 206
investment-to-: public sector, 1960–2002 207
growth
see economic growth
Growth, Employment and Reconstruction (Gear) 12, 56–82, 85, 209, 250, 261
economic policy: with and without, 1996–2000 59
expected outcomes: with and without, 1996–2000 61
objectives: prior, targeted and actual, 1996–2000 63
origins of 57–59
process steps 62–63
policy objectives of 71–78

H
Hertzog, General 38–39
high technology
see technology

history 48–53
political 36-53
HIV/Aids 11, 144–145, 251, 257, 265
adventuresome worst-case of 170
demographic changes before 160–163
demographic interruption 158–159
impact of 142, 167-170, 251, 254
impact of HIV medication 171–174
implications for business 169
migration and 229–230
mortality among skilled labour 231
orphans by 2010 165
population projection 164
skills drain 230–233
standard worst-case of 164–167
HIV medication
impact of, effecting behavioural change 172–174
impact of, in absence of behavioural change 171–172
housing provision 176, 177
human capital 183, 269
Human Immunodeficiency Virus (HIV)
see HIV/Aids

I
ILO
see International Labour Office
IMF
see International Monetary Fund
immigration 233-235, 251
Impossible Trinity analysis 100–102, 104, 112, 260
income
total, share per population group 236
income category/ies
population distribution by 237–239
racial composition of, 1975 238
racial composition of, 1991 238
racial composition of, 1996 239
income distribution 27, 236–242, 269
1990s 69-70
by population group 238–242
changing 235–237
income quintiles 25
composition by race 240
composition by race, 1990 25–26
India 114, 229
Indians 268, 276
history 36
HIV-prevalence among 230
income distribution 235
income quintile, 1990 26, 240
income quintile, 1995 240
modernisation 274
population growth 161–163
population structure 236
real disposable income, 1995–2000 176
total income 236–237
unemployment 142
with professional jobs 224
Industrial Conciliation Act of 1957 19
Industrial Revolution 10
inequality
an inheritance of 25–26
income 258
in distribution of income and wealth 16
inflation 72, 93–95
1996-2000 66–68
targeting 12, 108–113, 261, 263
influx control 269
informal employment 137
versus formal 131–135
information communication technology 77
information technology
in South Africa 202
in United States 189–191, 196
interest rate 12, 72, 213, 260–261
policy 91–93
International Labour Office (ILO 2001) 77, 133
International Monetary Fund (IMF) 101–102, 107, 194
investment-to-GDP 48
investment-to-GDP: private sector, 1960–2002 206
investment-to-GDP: public sector, 1960–2002 207

J
Japan 149, 174, 201
jobless growth, 1996–2000 68–69
see also unemployment
job reservation 18–19, 269
judicial and correctional system 179

K
Korea 7, 154, 226–227

L
labour
growth and composition 134
higher-skilled labour 127
improved surveys 135–141
less-skilled labour 82, 127, 147, 149, 261
policy/ies 5
productivity 94
rationalisation 10, 126–131
reform 263
regulations 151
semi-skilled labour 224–225
skills 254
labour force 252
composition of, 1996–1999 140

growth 132
Labour Force Survey (LFS) 139, 235
land
ownership 20, 176, 243, 269
redistribution 176
Latin America 7, 41, 75–76, 105, 144, 219, 242–246, 273
less-skilled labour 82, 127, 147, 149, 261
LFS
see Labour Force Survey
life expectancy
of HIV/Aids-infected 168
literacy 179

M
macro-economic policy/ies 52, 263
see also Gear
dilemmas 100
Mandela, President Nelson 272
Manhattan atrocity (9/11) 105
manufacturing sector 144, 215, 219, 220
change in employment, 1990–2000 135
during transition 214
exports, 1925–2001 129
market failure 3
Marshall Plan for Africa 275
matric 178–179, 182
age distribution of those holding 228
pass rates 179
Mbeki, President Thabo 106, 176
Mboweni, Tito 90, 103, 106
Mexico 8, 105, 227, 229, 243
micro-economic developments 56–82
micro-economic restructuring 52, 126–155, 205
middle class 244
Middle East 42
migration
and HIV/Aids 11, 165, 229–230
future prospects 204–246
Mines and Works Act of 1911 19
mining activities/operations 22, 129, 215, 219
change in employment, 1990-2000 135, 144
exports, 1925-2001 129
history 17
mobile capital 100
modernisation 273–274
of Africa 8–9
of economy 16–18
modernity 274, 277
monetary independence 100
monetary policy 12, 52, 56, 72, 92, 113–116, 204, 248–249
early reforms 89–91
Mozambique 223, 233
Myburgh, Justice 107
N
Namibia 223
NASDAQ 198
national debt 213
nationalism 36–44
Afrikaner 39
national savings rate 47, 117
Native Building Workers Act of 1951 19
Natives' Land Act of 1913 20
Nedlac 79
Nepad
see New Partnership for Africa's Development
net capacity addition 208
Netherlands 77
New Partnership for Africa's Development (Nepad) 275
new technology
see technology
New Zealand 144, 211, 229–230
Nguni-speaking people 36-37, 273
Nigeria 223, 275
North America 219, 228, 243
numeracy 179

O
OAU
see Organisation for African Unity
October Household Survey (OHS) 135–136, 139, 147
OECD
see Organisation for Economic Co-operation and Development
OHS
see October Household Survey
old-age pensions 178
Organisation for African Unity (OAU) 275
Organisation for Economic Co-operation and Development (OECD) 105
organised labour 76

P
pass laws 18, 269
personal savings 181
Physical Planning Act 18–19
Polish reformers, 1989 7
political
activism 7, 11, 76, 248–250, 276
leadership 276
politics 10
changes in 1990s 33
changes in 1994 2
history 48–53
preconditions for change 36–53
population distribution
by income category 237–239
population groups 20
income distribution by 239–242

share of total income per 236
population growth 160–163
and HIV/Aids 173
population projections 257
according to Haldenwang (1999) 160–161, 165
incorporating likely effects of HIV/Aids 164
price controls 150
primary exports 129
private fixed investment 64–65, 208
private sector 205, 208
investment-to-GDP in, 1960-2002 206
private security 144-145
privatisation 5, 10, 52, 78, 88, 113, 117–123, 209, 213
of public assets 10–11, 118–123
of state assets 46, 260
productivity
growth in South Africa 201
growth in United States 194–198, 201
revolution 143–146
public assets
privatisation 10–11, 118–123
public fixed investment 78
public sector 208
investment-to-GDP in, 1960–2002 207
wage moderation 80, 148, 255

R
race
composition of income quintiles by 240
racial composition
of income categories, 1975 238
of income categories, 1991 238
of income categories, 1996 239
rand
see also currency
commercial 96
crisis of late 2001 104–108
depreciation of 62, 64, 67, 72, 105–107, 204
financial 96
floating of, since October 1998 102–104
stability 52
rationalisation
labour and employment 127–131
of employment 46
RDP
see Reconstruction and Development Programme
real
disposable income during 1995–2000 176
interest rates 99
private fixed investment, 1996–2000 65–66
public fixed investment, 1996–2000 65–66
wage growth 147–149
recession 194, 196, 198
Reconstruction and Development Programme (RDP) 56, 85
redistribution 181
religious strife 13
restructuring
see economic restructuring
RMB/BER Business Confidence Index 26, 28
Russia 8, 10, 40, 105, 114, 166

S
SADC
see Southern African Development Community
SARB
see South African Reserve Bank
savings rate 116–118
Second World War 17, 22, 40, 49, 166
self-employment 77, 133
used for freelancing
semi-skilled labour 224–225
separate development 21
services delivery
improvement of 179–180
physical and social 177–179
services sector 219
skilled labour 76, 127–128, 231–232, 236, 253
and social transformation 163
education profile and, 1970-1999 222
emigration of 46, 221, 223
estimated changes in composition of, 1970–1995 225
HIV/Aids 233
HIV-linked morality 231
immigration of 221, 223, 227
prospects for 219-229
skills
drain 230–233
reservoir 134
surplus 135
Smuts, General 38–40
social
delivery 5, 56, 78, 86, 147, 176–183, 213
inequality 180, 243
transformation 158–174, 176
Sotho-speaking people 36, 273
South African Reserve Bank (SARB) 43, 74, 79, 88, 108, 110–112, 114–115, 118, 260–261
South America 243
South East Asia 192
Southern African Development Community (SADC) 146
South Korea 182
Spain 31, 265
Stals, Chris 90, 92–93, 102
state
privatisation of assets 46, 260
property 121
STEE

see Survey of Total Employment and Earnings
subsistence farming 140
Survey of Total Employment and Earnings (STEE) 135-136, 143
surveys, improved labour 135-141
Swiss finances 84, 86

T
tax/taxation 181
incentives 62
reform 10, 263
relief 181
revenues 181
technology 10, 251–252, 273
and demographics 250–252
as source of growth 186–187
high 201
information communication 77
information 189–191, 196, 202
in South Africa 201–202
new economy 190–198
new wave 187–190
temporary interruption 198-200
Technology Revolution 186–202
telephone lines provision 176
Telkom 78, 120–121
tertiary education 227
tourism 77, 219
trade
liberalisation 10, 128
protection 129
reform 146, 263
sanctions 23
transitional
mistakes and costs 259–262
Transnet 120–121
Transvaal Natives' Congress 18

U
Ubuntu tradition 268, 271–272
unemployment 5, 80, 130–131, 252, 261
see also jobless growth
among Blacks 142
among Coloureds 142
among Indians 142
among Whites 142
future projections for 141–142, 257–258
United Kingdom
see Great Britain
United States (US) 8, 10, 48, 75–77, 101, 103–105, 113, 148–150, 229, 265
economy 190-196
productivity growth 191, 193–195
technology revolution in 186, 188
urbanisation 142, 145
and HIV/Aids 161, 167
and social transformation 163

V

W
water provision 176–177
wealth distribution 27, 241, 269
welfare
child support grants 178
Child Welfare 178
disability grants 178
old-age pensions 178
services 178
spending 182
Western Europe 8, 228
Western heritage 275–276
White Afrikaner colonists 37
White confidence
convergence of, post-1997 33
White consumer confidence
in contrast with Black 30–32
White consumers 30
sentiment 31
Whites 262, 268–269, 276
HIV-prevalence among 230
income distribution 235
income quintile, 1990 26, 240
income quintile, 1995 240
matriculation 221
modernisation 274
population growth 161–163
population structure 236
real disposable income, 1995–2000 176
skilled labour 221, 225
total income 236-237
unemployment 142
World Trade Centre 105, 196
World Trade Organisation (WTO) 146
WTO
see World Trade Organisation

X
xenophobia 233

Y

Z
Zambia 168–169, 223
Zimbabwe 39, 51, 223, 229, 233, 241–242